Optimise

Student's Book

A2 Key for Schools

macmillan education

LISTENING	SPEAKING	LANGUAGE IN USE	WRITING
Identifying differences 3-option multiple choice (pictures)	Talking about yourself Questions Talk2Me	Using prepositions Open cloze	Understanding the task Guided writing (an email)
Listening for words that mean the same Matching	Talking about free time activities Questions Talk2Me	Predicting the answer 3-option multiple-choice cloze	Using your own words Guided writing (a note)
Predicting what the speaker will say 3-option multiple choice (dialogue)	Explaining likes and dislikes Questions Talk2Me	Using conjunctions Open cloze	Making and replying to suggestions Guided writing (a note)
Listening for important information Gap fill	Asking someone to explain Discussion (pictures) Talk2Me	Choosing the right word 3-option multiple-choice cloze	Punctuation and spelling Guided writing (an email)
Understanding when things happen 3-option multiple choice (pictures)	Talking about preferences Discussion Talk2Me	Using determiners Open cloze	Using linking words Picture story
Listening for the main idea 3-option multiple choice (monologues and dialogues)	Describing and expressing opinions Discussion (pictures) Talk2Me	Identifying words that go together 3-option multiple-choice cloze	Using a variety of tenses Guided writing (a note)
Thinking about the missing information Gap fill	Talking about the future Questions Talk2Me	Commonly confused words 3-option multiple-choice cloze	Using adjectives Picture story
Listening for important information Matching	Giving opinions Discussion (pictures) Talk2Me	Using modal verbs Open cloze	Writing in an informal style Guided writing (an email)
Understanding the speakers' questions Multiple choice (pictures)	Talking about a topic Questions Talk2Me	Identifying conditional sentences 3-option multiple-choice cloze	Expressing preferences An email
Identifying incorrect answers 3-option multiple choice (monologues and dialogues)	Giving yourself time to think Discussion Talk2Me	Using the present perfect Open cloze	Writing a good ending Picture story
Taking notes Gap fill	Talking about jobs Questions Talk2Me	Using indefinite and relative pronouns Open cloze	Planning an article An article
Checking your answers 3-option multiple choice (dialogue)	Agreeing and disagreeing Discussion (pictures) Talk2Me	Identifying words that show the order of events 3-option multiple-choice cloze	Writing a story A story

▶ LISTENING p 140–141 ▶ SPEAKING / SPEAKING TEST VIDEO p 142–143

Student's Resource Centre

- *Talk2Me* videos (flipped classroom)
- Speaking test video
- *Optimise your grammar* worksheets
- *Optimise your vocabulary* worksheets
- *Say it right* pronunciation worksheets
- Culture and CLIL worksheets
- Class and Workbook audio

1 Time out

READING | 3-option multiple matching | Online article

1 In pairs or as a group, answer the questions.

1 What are the most popular hobbies in your country at the moment?
2 Which of these hobbies do you do or would you like to do?
3 How do you usually choose your hobbies?

2 Read the online article on page 5 quickly. Which teenagers give advice about how to choose a hobby?

____

3 1.01 **Read the article again and decide if the statements are T (True) or F (False).**

1 Kareem spends all his free time playing video games online. **T / F**
2 People have opinions about Kareem's blog. **T / F**
3 Jake thinks you can find the perfect hobby straight away. **T / F**
4 Jake doesn't go skateboarding alone. **T / F**
5 Amaya decided to join a group that shares her interests. **T / F**
6 Amaya's photography club meets once a month on Thursdays. **T / F**

4 In pairs, write a highlighted word from the article to match each definition.

1 a machine for taking pictures ____________
2 easy ____________
3 an online diary ____________
4 the best thing for you ____________
5 not the same ____________
6 something you enjoy doing in your free time ____________
7 a person who belongs to a club ____________
8 to talk about ____________

EXAM SKILL

Scanning

- Scanning means reading a text quickly to find specific information.
- Look for dates, numbers or names, etc. in the text(s) and underline them.
- You don't need to understand every word, only the important information.

The right HOBBY for you

I often play video games, but I don't spend all my free time playing online. I also write a blog about new video games every month. I enjoy blogging because I love writing and the blog gives me the chance to share what I write. It's also great to read the comments that people leave on my blog. They say they are better players after they read it. It's nice to know that they're learning something from my hobby.

Kareem

I like adventure and I love trying new activities. It's a good idea to look at websites for ideas about different clubs and activities in your area. People don't usually find the perfect hobby immediately, but it's fun trying out new things. My favourite hobby is skateboarding. I found out a lot about it on the internet after watching a TV show. My friends and I always go skateboarding in the park after school even when it rains. It's really exciting!

Jake

Hobbies help you to make friends. Just think about what you usually like doing. Do you prefer big or small groups? Outdoor or indoor activities? I like being outdoors with other people and I enjoy taking photos inside interesting buildings or outdoors of nature. This year, I wanted to meet new people, so when I got a new camera I became a member of a photography club. We meet every Thursday evening to discuss new ideas and post our photos online. It's simple to choose the right hobby.

Amaya

5 **Read the article quickly and list the hobbies that are mentioned.**

____

____

____

____

OPTIMISE YOUR EXAM

3-option multiple matching

- Read the three texts quickly once to get their general meaning.
- Then read the question and underline the information you are looking for.
- Read the texts again. This time, scan the texts to find the words that are related to the underlined words.

6 **Read the article again. For each question, choose the correct answer.**

	Kareem	Jake	Amaya
1 Who suggests finding information about hobbies online?	A	B	C
2 Who helps people to improve at their hobby?	A	B	C
3 Who takes part in a group once a week?	A	B	C
4 Who writes about their hobby?	A	B	C
5 Who has two hobbies?	A	B	C
6 Who does their hobby outdoors only?	A	B	C
7 Who says it isn't difficult to choose a hobby?	A	B	C

THINK | RESEARCH | CULTURE | LEARN | ME

In pairs or groups, say which activity from the article you would like to do and why.

▶ **Workbook Unit 1:** Reading, pages 4–5, exercises 1, 2, 3

GRAMMAR 1 | Present simple, adverbs of frequency, imperatives

Grammar in context

Find and read these sentences in the texts on page 5 and answer the questions.

1 *I often **play** video games, ...* (Kareem)

2 *Hobbies **help** you to make friends.* (Amaya)

Which sentence uses the present simple for the following?

a) a habit ____

b) something that is usually true ____

Which word in sentence 1 is the adverb of frequency ____________

REMEMBER

- We use the present simple for:
  - habits or things we do often: ***Do** you **walk** to school? I **ride** my bike to school every day.*
  - things that are usually or always true: *We **live** in a small house. We **don't live** in a city.*
- We use adverbs of frequency with the present simple to say how often something happens:

  never sometimes often usually always

  0% ———————————— 100%

  They go before the main verb, (*I **never eat** cheese.*) or after the verb *to be* (*He is **often** late.*).
- We use time expressions to show when something happens:

  all/every day/week/month, once/twice a day/week/month / three times a day, etc.

▶ **See Grammar reference, Unit 1,** page 144

1 **Complete the sentences with the verbs in the box.**

go	goes	~~has~~	have	play	plays

1 She likes music. She ___has___ a guitar and a piano.

2 He usually ____________ to the park on his bike after school.

3 They ____________ English lessons on Mondays and Fridays.

4 She ____________ tennis and likes to go swimming.

5 I ____________ football in the park after school.

6 We ____________ swimming every Wednesday.

2 **Choose the correct word or phrase to complete each question.**

a) When **do / does** you go swimming? ____

b) Where **do / does** you play football? ____

c) What **do / does** she like? ____

d) When do they **have / has** English lessons? ____

e) What does he do when he **get / gets** home? ____

f) What sports does she **play / plays**? ____

3 **Work in pairs. Match the answers in Exercise 1 to the questions in Exercise 2.**

4 **Rewrite the sentences including the words in bold.**

1 It's very cold in the winter. **often**

____

2 I watch TV with my sister. **usually**

____

3 He goes to bed at 9 o'clock. **always**

____

4 I drink cola for breakfast. **never**

____

Grammar in context

Look at these sentences from different notices.

Turn off *mobile phones in swimming pool area.*

Please use *other door.*

REMEMBER

- We use imperative forms to give instructions or orders.
- We can use *please* with orders to be polite.

▶ **See Grammar reference, Unit 1,** page 144

5 **Choose the correct words to complete the imperative sentences.**

1 **Remember / Remembers** to do your homework.

2 **Don't / No** forget to bring your camera.

3 **Please open / Open please** the door.

6 **Complete the text with the correct form of the verbs in the box.**

be	have	hit	live
love	put	ride	watch

TWO HOBBIES IN ONE

Every weekend I go to the mountains with my bicycle. I go with my cousin. He (**1**) ____________ in a town near here. When we (**2**) ____________ our mountain bikes, we usually film the action. We have small cameras which we (**3**) ____________ on our helmets. It is really exciting. Mum always says, '(**4**) ____________ careful!' But sometimes one of us (**5**) ____________ an accident. My cousin often (**6**) ____________ something and falls off his bike. When we get home we (**7**) ____________ our video on the laptop. We (**8**) ____________ it.

▶ **Workbook Unit 1:** Grammar 1, page 6, exercises 1, 2, 3

Words connected with *hobbies*

1 1.02 **Write the correct word for each picture. Use the words in the box. Listen and check.**

cycling | horse-riding
painting | playing computer games
reading | rock climbing
skateboarding | swimming

1 ______________

2 ______________

3 ______________

4 ______________

5 ______________

6 ______________

7 ______________

8 ______________

2 1.03 **Match the words in the box to the correct description. Listen and check.**

barbecue | beach | collect
magazine | photograph | tent

1 You can take one of these with a camera. ______________
2 People who like swimming in the sea often go here. ______________
3 A thin paper book with photographs, articles, stories, etc. ______________
4 When you buy and keep books or magazines, for example, you do this. ______________
5 A meal where you cook and eat food outdoors. ______________
6 You stay in this when you go camping. ______________

Nouns/verbs

3 1.04 **Complete the table. Listen and check.**

object	person	verb
painting	(1) ______________	to paint
photograph	(2) ______________	to photograph / take photographs
music	(3) ______________	to make/play music
guitar	guitarist	to (4) ______________ the guitar
(5) ______________	video (6) ______________	to play video games

4 **Complete the sentences with words from the table in Exercise 3.**

1 Anja loves ______________ and uses really bright colours.
2 I sometimes listen to ______________ in bed before I go to sleep.
3 He's a good guitarist. He ______________ every day.
4 The ______________ took lots of pictures of us climbing.
5 I want to be a ______________ one day and play the piano.
6 I like video games, but I'm not really a big ______________ .

SAY IT RIGHT

Resource centre: Unit 1
Word stress

Phrasal verbs

5 1.05 **Match the meanings (a–g) to the phrasal verbs (1–7). Listen and check.**

1 come in ____
2 come round ____
3 get back ____
4 get off ____
5 look after ____
6 turn off ____
7 turn on ____

a) to return after going somewhere
b) to start a machine
c) to stop a machine
d) to leave a bus or train
e) to enter
f) to take care of someone or something
g) to visit

6 **Choose the correct word to complete each sentence.**

1 Please turn **off** / **on** that loud music!
2 Welcome to 'Games Night'! Come **round** / **in** and join us.
3 Let's watch a film. Please turn **on** / **off** the TV.
4 Quick, we need to get **back** / **off** the bus here. The park's just over the road.
5 Alex is going to come **round** / **in** this afternoon. I want to play my new video game with him.
6 Can you look **under** / **after** my bag, please?
7 We won't get **back** / **off** until quite late after the football match.

▶ Vocabulary reference, page 156 ▶ Workbook Unit 1: Vocabulary, page 7, exercises 1, 2, 3

1 LISTENING | 3-option multiple choice (pictures)

1 **In pairs or as a group, look at the pictures in Exercise 4.**

1 What is the same about the pictures in each set?
2 What are the differences between the pictures?

EXAM SKILL

Identifying differences

- When you are asked to look at pictures while you listen, first look at the pictures and note down the differences between them. Then listen to the recording. For example, if someone is doing different activities, write down the different activities you can see. This will help you answer the question.
- When listening, you often hear about places and where they are, for example, *the shop next to the hotel*. Note down any prepositions such as *next to* that give important information.

2 **Look at the set of pictures below (A–C) and match them to the notes (1–3).**

A

B

C

1 *camping, busy campsite, tents together* ____

2 *camping, campsite, tent on grass* ____

3 *camping, campsite, tent under tree* ____

3 1.06 **Listen to the conversation. Write a word or phrase in each gap.**

Girl: So, where is your cousin's tent?
Boy: It's in a good place. There aren't any other tents (**1**) ______________ it.
Girl: Is it (**2**) ______________ of that field?
Boy: No, it's (**3**) ______________ that big tree.

OPTIMISE YOUR EXAM

3-option multiple choice (pictures)

- Read the questions carefully and underline the important words you need to listen for.
- Be careful. When you listen, you will hear words that are about all three pictures, but only one picture will fully answer the question.

4 1.07 **Listen to the five conversations. There is one question for each conversation. For each question, choose the correct picture.**

1 What game do they play?

A

B

C

2 What does Helen like to read?

A

B

C

3 What time does football practice usually start?

A

B

C

4 What do they have for dinner?

A

B

C

5 When does the girl have art lessons?

A

B

C

5 1.07 **Listen again and check your answers.**

▶ **Workbook Unit 1:** Listening, page 8, exercises 1, 2

GRAMMAR 2 | Possessive 's, prepositions of time and place

Grammar in context

Look at these sentences from the audio in the listening lesson and answer the question.

1 *My brother's new video game is good.*
2 *I sometimes look at my sister's pop magazine.*
3 *Ryan's dad brings us home in the car.*

Which statement is true, a or b? ____

a) one of the sentences uses 's to replace *is*.
b) all of the sentences use 's to show possession.

REMEMBER

- We use **'s** to show possession: *It is the bag that Amy owns.* ➔ *It is Amy's bag.*
- We can use **'s** to show possession with plurals: *The children's books are on their desks.*
- For plurals ending in **s**, we just add an apostrophe: *My parents' house is near here.*

Note: Apostrophes are also used in contractions to indicate missing letters, e.g. ***She's** my sister.* = ***She is** my sister. **He's** got a book.* = ***He has** got a book.*

▶ **See Grammar reference, Unit 1,** page 145

1 **Complete the second sentences using possessive 's.**

1 This book belongs to Anna.
This is __________ .
2 The bags that belong to the boys are all here.
The __________ are all here.
3 My parents own that red car.
That is __________ red car.
4 The desks for the children aren't very big.
The __________ aren't very big.

2 **Decide the use of 's in each sentence – possession (P) or the verb *to be* (B).**

1 Your mother's brother is your uncle. ____
2 That woman's married to Jim. ____
3 Your aunt's son is your cousin. ____
4 My sister's very good at English. ____

Grammar in context

Look at these sentences from the audio in the listening lesson. Match the words in bold to a function (a or b).

1 *It's **in** a good place. There aren't any other tents **near** it.*
2 *No, it's **under** that big tree.*
3 *It always begins **at** 9.30.*
4 *We had pizza **on** Monday.*

a) describing place __________ , __________ , __________
b) describing time __________ , __________

REMEMBER

- We use a variety of prepositions in time expressions:

at	in
6pm, midnight, New Year, the weekend, the moment	the morning/afternoon/ evening, June, summer, 2022, two weeks' time
on	**no preposition**
Saturday, Monday morning, New Year's Day, 22 June, holiday, my/your/ her, etc. birthday	today, yesterday, tomorrow, last night, two weeks ago, yesterday evening, tonight

- We use prepositions of place to show where things are:
*The book is **on** the table. My school is **next to** the library. There is a park **in front of** my house. We usually meet **at** the park.*

▶ **See Grammar reference, Unit 1,** page 145

3 **Choose the correct word or phrase to complete each sentence.**

1 We went to the cinema **in last week** / **last week**.
2 Our team plays football in the park next **to** / **of** the museum. We play **at** / **on** Saturday morning.
3 We usually go on holiday **in** / **at** August.
4 **In** / **On** two weeks' time I'm going to England.
5 We usually go to the pool every day **in** / **on** summer, but it's closed **today** / **at today**.
6 Do you usually have a party **at** / **on** your birthday?

4 **Complete the text with the words in the box.**

at	in	in front	near	next	on

Last year when we were **(1)** __________ holiday **(2)** __________ Greece. We stayed with my mum's best friend, Alexandra. She's Greek and she lives **(3)** __________ the sea. She's really good at painting and has a studio **(4)** __________ to the house with amazing sea views. **(5)** __________ the weekend, she paints beautiful pictures of the sea and of birds flying **(6)** __________ of her studio. This is one of her pictures.

1 SPEAKING | Questions

Flipped classroom

1 **Watch the *Talk2Me* video and answer the questions.**

1 Who are Jojo and Max? Who is Evie?
2 Which two days of the week are they all free to practise their dance?
3 When is the competition?

2 **Watch the video again. Underline the words and phrases in the *Phrase expert* box that you hear on the video.**

PHRASE EXPERT

My (sur)name is … | That's R-I-C-H-A-R-D-S-O-N. | In my free time, I usually …
At lunchtime / After school / In the evenings / At the weekend / In the holidays …
I/We always/usually/often/sometimes/never …

3 1.08 **Listen and repeat the alphabet. Then in pairs, ask and answer the questions.**

Aa Bb Cc Dd Ee Ff Gg
Hh Ii Jj Kk Ll Mm Nn Oo Pp
Qq Rr Ss Tt Uu Vv
Ww Xx Yy Zz

What's your name?
What's your surname?
How do you spell it?

EXAM SKILL

Talking about yourself

- Learn to give basic information about yourself such as your name, age and where you are from.
- Also learn to talk about things in your regular daily life such as school, home, hobbies and interests. Use phrases such as *I go to … school. I like … because …, In my free time, I …*
- Learn to talk about specific events in your life, such as *What did you have for lunch yesterday?*
- Check that you can describe your hobbies and interests by learning vocabulary related to them.

Talk2Me
In my free time …

4 1.09 **Listen to two students talking to an examiner. Complete the notes below.**

Student A

Name:	*Victor*
Hobbies:	
Evenings:	
Last weekend:	

Student B

Name:	
Weekends:	
People:	

5 1.09 **Listen again. Write down the questions the examiner asks.**

1 ____________________
2 ____________________
3 ____________________
4 ____________________
5 ____________________
6 ____________________
7 ____________________

6 **Write down the phrase the student used to ask for the question to be repeated.**

____

____

OPTIMISE YOUR EXAM

Questions

- If you don't understand the examiner, ask him/her to repeat the question. Use phrases like *(Sorry,) could/can you repeat the question, please?*
- You can give a short answer for your name and your age. You should give a longer answer to other questions.
- For longer answers, think about the types of topics you may have to talk about and what you could say about them.

7 **Work in pairs. Take turns asking and answering the questions.**

- What's your name?
- How old are you?
- Where do you live?
- What activities do you do at the weekend?
- Who do you spend time with at the weekend?
- Tell me what you did last weekend.

▶ **Workbook Unit 1:** Speaking, pages 8–9, exercises 1, 2, 3

LANGUAGE IN USE | Open cloze

1 **Work in pairs. Read the text below and answer the questions.**

1 What can you do at the club?
2 Can anyone use it?
3 How much is it to use the club?
4 Would you like to join the club? Why / Why not?

JOIN OUR CLUB!

Come and make new friends or try a new activity!

These are some of the fun things you can do at Eight-Mile Wood adventure club:

climb trees, ride your bike, build dens, join an art class, learn nature photography or cook wild food!

On Fridays we organise a barbecue. Every month there is a mini music festival. Bring your tent and camp between the trees.

It's free to join the club, but you pay £10 for special classes.

Children 11 years and over are welcome. You just need to fill in a form with your parents' contact details.

EXAM SKILL

Using prepositions

- Remember that prepositions are used to talk about time (***at*** *three o'clock*), place (***in*** *Greece*), and can be used with verbs (*turn* ***off***).
- Prepositions often come before a noun (*Max is* ***at*** *home.*), before a pronoun (*Come* ***with*** *us.*) or after a verb to form a phrasal verb (*Let's find* ***out***.).
- Some adjectives go with certain prepositions (*I'm good* ***at*** *English. The town is famous* ***for*** *its history.*).

2 **Look at the advert in Exercise 1 and underline the prepositions. Decide whether they are used to talk about time or place, before a noun/pronoun or as part of a phrasal verb.**

3 **Complete the sentences with the prepositions in the box.**

at	of	on	out	up	with

1 Come and have an adventure __________ us!
2 We meet every Friday __________ 8pm.
3 Meet us in front __________ the bank and then we can go to the cinema together.
4 You need to get __________ early tomorrow.
5 Find __________ more on our website.
6 We'll give you more information when we are __________ the bus.

OPTIMISE YOUR EXAM

Open cloze

- Read each sentence carefully and look for clues before and after the gap.
- If the missing word is before a noun or pronoun or after a verb, it could be a preposition. Some prepositions have more than one word, for example, *over to*, *on top of*.
- Decide what kind of preposition you need for the gap (time, place, etc.).

4 **For each question, write the correct answer. Write ONE word for each gap.**

Hi, I'm writing to you about ___*a*___ new club near my house. It's great because they do so many things there. 'Gaming Club' is (**1**) __________ Mondays and you can play video games (**2**) __________ other members. It starts at 7pm in the clubhouse. Every Wednesday members can (**3**) __________ skateboarding together. I want to try skateboarding (**4**) __________ the problem is you need to have your own skateboard. They meet at 6pm in the park next (**5**) __________ the school. (**6**) __________ you want to come with me on Monday? Let me know!

Anna

THINK | RESEARCH | **CULTURE** | LEARN | ME

Work in groups and answer the question.

- Do you think there are enough places for young people to do activities outdoors in your country? Why / Why not?

WRITING | Guided writing (an email)

1 In pairs or as a group, answer the questions.

1 Do you go to any clubs or sports activities? Where? When?

2 Are after-school clubs popular with teenagers where you live? Why / Why not?

3 What kind of club would you like to go to? Why?

2 Read the email below. How many pieces of information are given in the email? Underline them.

From: Sam

To: Alex

Hi Alex,

Let's meet at the sports club. We can meet on Saturday. I want to play basketball.

Bye,

Sam

3 Tick the questions that Sam answers in his email.

1 Who does he want to meet? ☐

2 Where does he want to meet? ☐

3 Which sport does he want to play? ☐

4 When does he want to meet? ☐

5 Where is the sports club? ☐

6 Why does he want to play basketball? ☐

EXAM SKILL

Understanding the task

- Read the task carefully. It will tell you what type of text you need to write (note, email, etc.), who it is for and what kind of information you must include.
- Plan what you are going to write. Think about the things you could write about and make notes. Then choose your best ideas.
- Make sure you include everything the task asks you to write about.

4 Look at this task and Sam's email in Exercise 2. Then answer the questions.

You are going to a sports club with your English friend, Alex, tomorrow. Write an email to Alex.
In your email:

- tell Alex where you want to meet
- say what date you want to meet
- say which sport you want to play.

Write **25 words** or more.

1 Does Sam answer all the questions in the email? ____________

2 How many sentences does Sam write in the email? ____________

3 Does each sentence in the email answer a different question? ____________

5 Complete the sentences with the information in the box.

near the school. | because it's so much fun! | at 3 o'clock.

1 Let's meet at the sports club ____________

2 We can meet on Saturday ____________

3 I want to play basketball ____________

OPTIMISE YOUR **EXAM**

Guided writing (an email)

- The task asks for three pieces of information in bullet points. Make sure you supply the information for each bullet.
- Don't write less than 25 words or you will get a lower mark. Don't write many more than 25 words – the more you write, the more likely you are to make a mistake.
- **To:** *(Name)* and **From:** *(Name)* are not included in the total number of words. However, greetings and endings, for example *Hi*, *See you soon*, etc. are included.

6 Read the exam task and the email. Then answer the questions.

You are going to an activity club with your English friend, Pat, next week. Write an email to Pat.
In your email:
- tell Pat which day you want to go
- say how you can travel there
- say which activity you want to try.

Write **25 words** or more.

From: Jo
To: Pat

Hi Pat,

Let's go to the club on Wednesday afternoon. We can meet at my house and take a bus. I'd like to try the art class because it sounds interesting.

See you soon,

Jo

1 How many words does Jo write in her email to Pat? ______
2 What sentences does Jo use to start and end the email? ______
3 Does Jo complete the task successfully? Why / Why not? ______

______

7 Plan **Now plan your email to Pat. Complete the table with your notes.**

	Detail	My notes
Point 1	*say which day to go*	
Point 2	*say how to travel*	
Point 3	*say which activity*	

8 Write **Write your email to Pat in an appropriate style. Write 25 words or more.**

9 Check **Before you hand in your email, complete this checklist.**

Checklist ✓

- ◯ I've followed my writing plan.
- ◯ I've included information for the three bullet points.
- ◯ I've used most of my own words.
- ◯ I've written 25+ words.

▶ **Writing reference,** page 163 ▶ **Workbook Unit 1:** Writing, page 10, exercises 1, 2, 3, 4 and Progress check 1, page 11

2 That's entertainment!

READING | 3-option multiple choice (long text) | A magazine article

1 In pairs or as a group, answer the questions.

1 What do you like doing for entertainment on school days and at the weekend?

2 What do you like doing for entertainment with your friends and what do you like doing with your family?

3 What entertainment is popular with young people in your area?

EXAM SKILL

Skimming

- Skimming means reading a text quickly to find out the topic and understand the general idea.
- You don't need to read and understand every word when you skim a text.
- Skimming can help you understand where the text is from, for example, a newspaper, a blog or a magazine, and who it is for, for example, teens, parents, business people, etc.

2 Read the first and second paragraphs of the article and answer the question.

Who is the article for?

A young people who play video games

B fans of video games who play alone

C people who think playing video games is popular

OPTIMISE YOUR EXAM

3-option multiple choice (long text)

- After skimming, read the text again more carefully.
- Underline the important words and phrases in the questions and answer options. Then find and underline the words and phrases in the text that mean the same.
- Compare each answer option with the words underlined in the text and choose the answer that is closest in meaning to the text.

GAMING IS BIG BUSINESS

1 **These days, more young people are playing video games. The world of video gaming entertainment is growing quickly. If you're a gaming fan, read this.**

2 Video gaming is now a very popular form of entertainment in the world (not quite as popular as listening to music and watching TV, though). Both girls and boys play video games regularly, mostly for fun. Some people play alone and others play in big competitions. There are places like the e-sports Gfinity Arena in London, where hundreds of people go to play online games with other fans around the world.

3 However, a small number of people make money from gaming. One person who does exactly that is teenager Brandon Relph. Brandon knows a lot about computer games. He started playing them when he was 10. He designed and built fantastic digital worlds using *Minecraft*. Now Brandon works on his business for a few hours every night, when he isn't doing his homework. Brandon still designs attractive worlds, but now people buy them and use them in adverts.

4 Brandon earned £10,000 from his business before he was 16! And he lives with his parents, so he doesn't need to spend money on an office.

5 Brandon works with a German teenager called Florian and they have friends in 13 different countries to help. At the moment, they are making ads for YouTube, gaming channels and films.

6 Brandon and Florian are a good example of people who have made gaming a business. If you're a gamer, who knows – the next person to do this could be you!

3 1.10 **Read the article and the questions. For each question, choose the correct answer.**

1 Which activities does the writer say are most popular with young people?
- **A** listening to music and video gaming
- **B** watching TV and listening to music
- **C** video gaming and watching TV

2 What can people do at the Gfinity Arena?
- **A** play sports for fun
- **B** play sports only for boys
- **C** play against other people

3 What happened when Brandon Relph was 10 years old?
- **A** He first became interested in gaming.
- **B** He learnt how to build computers.
- **C** He made his own computer games.

4 How did Brandon learn about computer games?
- **A** He studied them at school.
- **B** He went to Gfinity.
- **C** He created his own world in *Minecraft*.

5 How does Brandon earn money?
- **A** He works for *Minecraft*.
- **B** He sells his digital worlds.
- **C** He plays computer games.

6 How do Brandon's friends help?
- **A** They create advertisements.
- **B** They start channels on YouTube.
- **C** They make films.

4 **Write a highlighted word from the text to match each definition.**

1 on your own ____________
2 someone who likes a sport, game, etc. very much ____________
3 beautiful or pretty to look at ____________
4 another word for 'adverts' ____________
5 people can win prizes in these ____________
6 on the internet ____________

GRAMMAR 1 | Present simple and present continuous

Grammar in context

Find the sentences in the text on page 15 and then answer the questions.

1 *These days, more young people* ***are playing*** *video games.* (paragraph 1)
2 *Both girls and boys* ***play*** *video games regularly, …* (paragraph 2)
3 *Brandon* ***knows*** *a lot about computer games.* (paragraph 3)

Which sentence:

a) talks about a habit or routine? ____
b) uses a stative verb? ____
c) talks about something happening around now? ____

REMEMBER

- We use the present simple to talk about habits, routines, facts and permanent situations.
- We use the present continuous to talk about things that are happening at this moment. We use it to describe what is happening in pictures or photos, actions happening around now and temporary or changing situations.
- There are some verbs called stative verbs, e.g. *like, agree, know, understand* that are usually only used in the present simple to express states, not actions.

▶ **See Grammar reference, Unit 2,** page 145

1 Choose the correct form of the verb to complete each sentence.

1 I**'m learning** / **learn** to play the piano at the moment.
2 She **goes** / **'s going** to the art gallery almost every weekend.
3 Sam **plays** / **is playing** video games every weekend.
4 We**'re doing** / **do** our homework now, so we can't go out.
5 I**'m usually spending** / **usually spend** my money on clothes.
6 He**'s wearing** / **wears** his new trainers today.
7 They**'re never reading** / **never read** fashion magazines.
8 Amy**'s not liking** / **doesn't like** loud music.

2 Use the prompts to write sentences using the present simple or the present continuous.

1 every week / Dad / read / an online newspaper
____
2 at moment / I / play / a video game
____
3 Mum / not work / this week
____
4 Chris / come from / Slovenia / and / speak / three languages
____
5 I / usually / like / his books / but / I / not enjoy / this one
____
6 I / like / fruit / but / I / not eat / it / every day
____

SAY IT RIGHT

Resource centre: Unit 2
Pronunciation of *-ing*

3 Complete the paragraph using the correct present simple or present continuous form of the verbs in brackets.

Karl (**1**) _______ (**love**) being with his family and he (**2**) _______ (**spend**) a lot of his free time watching his children do their hobbies. His son, Marc, (**3**) _______ (**play**) the violin in a youth orchestra and Karl (**4**) _______ (**go**) to see Marc play whenever he can. But today is a special day for Megan, Karl's daughter. Her hobby is hip-hop dance and today she (**5**) _______ (**dance**) in a musical show. Karl (**6**) _______ (**prefer**) rock to hip-hop, but he (**7**) _______ (**enjoy**) the show and Megan (**8**) _______ (**do**) really well. Karl feels happy and he (**9**) _______ (**smile**). Karl's father is at the show too, but he (**10**) _______ (**not watch**) the dancing. In fact, he (**11**) _______ (**sleep**)!

THINK | RESEARCH | CULTURE | LEARN | **ME**

Work in pairs. What's your favourite type of entertainment? Tell your partner about it.

▶ **Workbook Unit 2:** Grammar 1, page 14, exercises 1, 2

Words connected with *entertainment*

1 1.11 **Match the places (A–F) to the entertainment (1–6). Listen and check.**

A museum

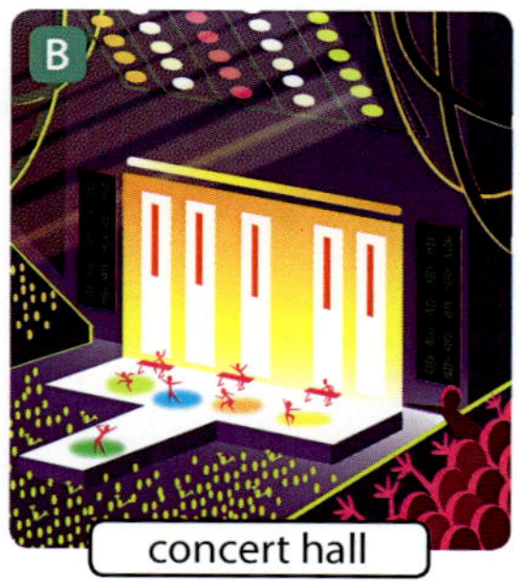
B concert hall

C art gallery

D theatre

E gaming café

F opera house

1 see an exhibition of famous paintings ____
2 see a play ____
3 learn about a period in history ____
4 listen to a famous classical singer ____
5 download a game ____
6 see a well-known band ____

2 **Complete the sentences using words from Exercise 1.**

1 We saw a really cool exhibition of fashion photography at the ______________ .
2 His brother's playing the violin at a ______________ in London. They are showing it on TV!
3 My parents are going to the ______________ to listen to some world-famous singers.
4 Joe's playing a game online at the ______________ . He's playing with people from all over the world.
5 You can see lots of interesting things from hundreds of years ago at the ______________ .
6 We saw a great play at the ______________ last Saturday.

Words + prepositions

3 1.12 **Read the descriptions of what different people do for entertainment. Choose the correct preposition to complete each sentence. Listen and check.**

1 On Friday nights I stay **in** / **out** and listen **at** / **to** music. Every Saturday evening I go **in** / **out** with my friends.

2 We like looking **at** / **with** the new fashions. Sometimes we try **on** / **out** different clothes.

3 I really like the theatre. I go to an after-school drama club. I want to act **in** / **out** a play.

4 I love street dancing. Most kids I know prefer to play video games, but they thought it was cool when I danced **on** / **with** my club in a competition. And we won!

Collocations with nouns

4 1.13 **Complete the phrases in bold with the words in the box. Listen and check.**

article | game | player
programme | screen

1 Chess is a well-known **board** ____________ . I love playing it.
2 Did you read the **newspaper** ____________ ? There are some good photographs in it.
3 I'm watching a great **TV** ____________ about the history of rock music.
4 I'm getting a new **MP3** ____________ soon – I want one I can record films on, too.
5 I'm going to watch a film on the big new 3-D **cinema** ____________ in town.

2 LISTENING | Matching

1 **In pairs or as a group, look at the photo and answer the questions.**

1 How much television do you watch each day?
2 How do you prefer to watch programmes – on TV or online?
3 What do you prefer to do – play video games or watch films?

EXAM SKILL

Listening for words that mean the same

- In matching tasks, the speakers sometimes use different words to say the same thing.
- It's important to read all the answer options carefully and think of different words the speakers might use to say the same thing.

2 **Read the sentences below. Think of different ways to say the underlined words.**

1 I don't want to play this game anymore. It's not very interesting and it's too hard. ____
2 I'm listening to a new song by Jane's favourite band. It's really nice but a bit slow. ____
3 He told me the book was excellent, but it's not. The story is too unusual. ____

3 **Read the sentences (a–c) then match them to the sentences (1–3) in Exercise 2 which have the same meaning.**

a) It's pleasant but not very fast.
b) It's really terrible and quite strange.
c) It's a bit boring and really difficult.

4 **Work in pairs. Discuss which words helped you to match the sentences in exercises 2 and 3.**

5 **Look at the 'opinion/feeling' words (A–H) in Exercise 6. For each one, think of another word that has the same meaning. Compare your ideas with a partner.**

OPTIMISE YOUR EXAM

Matching

- Before you listen, make notes on the different ways you can say the words (A–H).
- When you listen the first time, check your notes before you choose the answers.
- The second time you listen, check your answers carefully.

6 1.14 **You will hear Paul talking to his cousin Kacey about what he watches on TV. What opinion/feeling is associated with each programme/channel?**

TV programme/channel	opinion/feeling
Example: sport _H_	
1 cartoons ____	A clever
2 action films ____	B excellent
3 the news ____	C exciting
4 video gaming ____	D funny
5 music videos ____	E terrible
	F noisy
	G unhappy
	~~H interesting~~

7 1.14 **Listen again and check your answers.**

THINK | RESEARCH | CULTURE | LEARN | ME

In pairs or groups, discuss the questions.

- How is the internet changing the entertainment industry? Are these changes good or bad?

▶ **Workbook Unit 2:** Listening, page 16, exercises 1, 2, 3

GRAMMAR 2 | Present continuous for future use

Grammar in context

Match these sentences from the audio in the listening lesson to the descriptions.

1 ***I'm doing*** *a school project on entertainment.*
2 ***We're watching*** *a new one tonight.*

a) describe an action happening around now. ____
b) talk about future plans and arrangements. ____

REMEMBER

- When we use the present continuous to talk about future plans and arrangements, we usually give a future time (e.g. *tomorrow*):

  *He'**s taking** me to watch a football game **on Saturday**.*
  *They **aren't coming** to the theatre with us **tonight**.*
  ***Are** you **seeing** your friends **this weekend**?*
- We can also use the present simple to talk about the future when we're talking about timetables or programmed events:

  *The train **leaves** at 11:15.*

▶ **See Grammar reference, Unit 2,** page 146

1 **Complete the questions with the correct form of the verbs in the box. Use one verb in each set of questions (1–6).**

cook	do	~~go~~	meet	study	play

1 ___Are___ you ___going___ anywhere this weekend?
Where ___are you going___ ? Who ___are you going___ with?
2 ________ you ________ anyone after this lesson?
Who ______________________________ ?
3 What video games ________ at the weekend?
Who ______________________ them with?
4 ________ you ________ anything special for dinner tonight?
What ______________________________ ?
5 ________ you ________ anything exciting next week?
What ______________________________ ?
6 ________ you ________ this evening?
What subjects ______________________ ?

2 **In pairs or groups, take turns asking and answering the questions from Exercise 1.**

Example:

A: Are you going anywhere this weekend?
B: Yes, I am.
A: Really? Where are you going?

3 **Complete the texts with the correct present simple or continuous form of the verbs in brackets.**

ENTERTAINMENT!

We continue our series about entertainment by talking to three teenagers from around the world. We asked them about their favourite forms of entertainment.

A I'm really into fashion and I (**1**) ____________ (**follow**) a few different fashion vloggers online. At the moment I (**2**) ____________ (**learn**) all about different ways to dress, and what the latest styles are. Next week I (**3**) ____________ (**start**) a course on clothes design. For the first few weeks of the course, the students (**4**) ____________ (**have**) lessons in college. But in March we (**5**) ____________ (**go**) on a trip to Paris! I can't wait. The only problem is that the plane (**6**) ____________ (**leave**) at 6 in the morning, so it's a very early start!

Alexandra, Moscow

B This week I (**1**) ____________ (**listen**) to a lot of new hip hop music. It's a useful way to learn new English words. Next weekend, I (**2**) ____________ (**make**) playlists for my friends to listen to. Our exams (**3**) ____________ (**start**) soon so next week we (**4**) ____________ (**go**) to the library every day to study. I (**5**) ____________ (**spend**) my evenings studying at home, too. If I do well in my exams, I (**6**) ____________ (**get**) a new smartphone. Then I can download more music.

Piotr, Krakow

C Later this evening my brother and I (**1**) ____________ (**play**) a game called *Carcassonne*. In this game, you (**2**) ____________ (**live**) in the past, and (**3**) ____________ (**build**) a city. It's lots of fun, and makes you think a lot. A few of my friends also play board games. They usually (**4**) ____________ (**play**) online, but next week they (**5**) ____________ (**meet**) at my house so we can all play face to face. Next month my brother Josh and I (**6**) ____________ (**design**) a board game about the music business. I'll let you know what happens!

Johnny, Manchester

Flipped classroom

1 Watch the *Talk2Me* video and answer the questions.

1 Who has piano lessons on Mondays?
2 When do they decide to go to the cinema?
3 What are they doing after the cinema?

2 Watch the video again. Underline the phrases in the *Phrase expert* box that you hear on the video.

PHRASE EXPERT
It starts at (6) o'clock and finishes at (8) o'clock. |
It's every (Thursday) from (8) until (10) pm. |
They meet on (Fridays) at (7) in the evening. |
What time does it start?

3 In pairs, look at the poster and answer the questions.

1 What day is the activity on?
2 What time does the activity start?
3 How long does the activity last?

EXAM SKILL

Talking about free time activities

- Learn to talk about your free time activities. Think about the places you go to and the activities you enjoy doing. For example, think about your answers to questions such as *Where do you go at the weekend? What do you do in your free time?*
- Learn the vocabulary you need to talk about the topic. For example, activities: *watch a movie, listen to music,* when you do them (*at 4 o'clock, in the mornings,* etc.) and how often you do them: *once a week, every Saturday,* etc.
- Learn the correct prepositions to use with time phrases: *from 9 to 12, on Sunday morning,* etc.

4 1.15 Work in pairs. Look at the prompts and pictures then take turns to ask and answer questions. Listen and check.

1 what time / concert / start

Example:
What time does the concert start?
It starts at 8:00 pm.

2 what / be / opening hours / museum

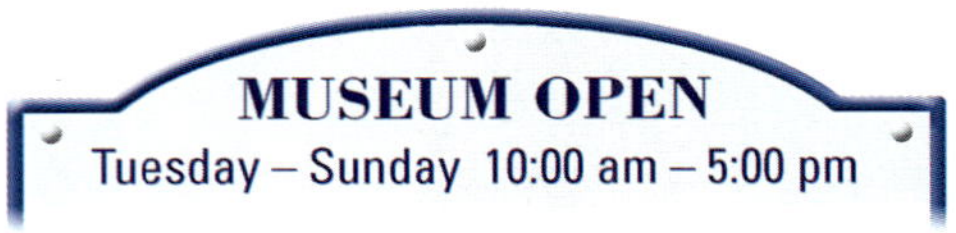

3 how long / film / last

4 when / be / football training

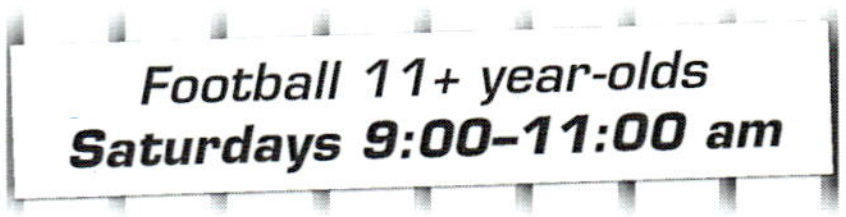

5 what time / concert / finish

OPTIMISE YOUR EXAM

Questions

- Remember to give longer answers in this part of the test. For example, if you are asked *Did you do anything last weekend?* don't reply *Yes, I did.* Say something like *Yes, I went to the cinema with my friends on Saturday.*
- Give a detailed answer if the examiner says *Tell me about ...* e.g. *Tell me about activities you do with friends.* You can answer *We often go to the cinema on Saturdays because we love watching films. We also play basketball because it's fun.*

5 Take it in turns to ask and answer these questions.

Student A: Do you prefer watching movies at home or at the cinema?
What's your favourite TV programme?
What time is your favourite TV programme on?
Tell me about the last TV programme you saw.

Student B: What do you do in your free time?
Do you prefer spending your free time alone or with friends?
What activity would you like to learn?
Tell me about what you did in your free time last week.

▶ **Workbook Unit 2:** Speaking, pages 16–17, exercises 1, 2

1 Work in pairs or groups. Read the text and answer the questions below.

There are lots of ways to find out what is happening in the world. A lot of people read the news by looking at online newspaper websites and social media. These are now more popular than TV. A study showed that over 60% of young people read news online. Fewer young people are listening to the radio or reading a newspaper to find out about the news. Only 6% buy or read a newspaper every day.

The problem is that anyone can put news online so we don't always know if it is correct or not. But it does mean that more free information is available. In the future probably more and more people will read news online.

1 Where do most people get their news from in your country, the TV, newspapers, the internet or somewhere else?
2 Which is best? Why?

EXAM SKILL

Predicting the answer

- You can read a text which has some gaps in it and still understand what it is about.
- Read the text first to get the general idea.
- Read through all the options before reading the text for a second time. As you read the text again, try to think of the meaning of the gapped sentence with each of the options.

2 Choose the correct word to fill each gap.

1 Theeveningnews.com gives you ___________ from around the world.
   a) stories   **b)** sights
2 People read ___________ to get information quickly.
   a) radio   **b)** websites
3 Today, fewer people get their information from ___________.
   a) the internet   **b)** TV
4 Not everyone believes the information they read ___________.
   a) in newspapers   **b)** online
5 The art gallery had a lot of ___________ next to each painting.
   a) information   **b)** news
6 The best way to get ___________ for the theatre is to use the online booking system.
   a) places   **b)** tickets

OPTIMISE YOUR EXAM

3-option multiple-choice cloze

- Think of your own ideas before you look at the possible answers. This will help you to identify the correct words.
- Then look at options A–C. If an option is similar to your ideas, it may be correct.
- Before you choose your answer, try each option in the gap to be sure.

3 For each question, choose the correct answer.

How to make a school newspaper

Many schools have a school newspaper. School newspapers are a good **(1)** ____ for students and teachers to know what's going on. They're also very useful for students who want to practise their writing. First, find a **(2)** ____ of students who want to make a newspaper. Then tell a teacher what you are planning and find somewhere to work. Next, decide who does what, such as writing or **(3)** ____ photographs. Also **(4)** ____ about when you want people to read the newspaper, and the type of stories to **(5)** ____ . Try to have something for all interests. It is a good idea to ask students at school what they like reading so you can make sure that your newspaper will be **(6)** ____ with students.

	A	B	C
1	**A** practice	**B** way	**C** road
2	**A** group	**B** kind	**C** type
3	**A** looking	**B** deciding	**C** finding
4	**A** agree	**B** discuss	**C** think
5	**A** include	**B** show	**C** enter
6	**A** popular	**B** famous	**C** well-known

THINK | RESEARCH | **CULTURE** | LEARN | ME

Work in groups and answer the questions.

- Do schools in your country have school newspapers or websites? What types of stories do they include?
- Do you think the stories and news are interesting? Why / Why not?

2 WRITING | Guided writing (a note)

1 **In pairs or groups, answer the questions.**

1 Who writes notes to you? Why?
2 When did you last write a note? What was it about?

EXAM SKILL

Using your own words

- When you answer a question, it is important to use your own words.
- Underline the key words and phrases in the question, then think of different ways to say the same thing before you start writing. For example, to answer the question *Do you enjoy looking at art?* don't say, *Yes, I enjoy looking at art.* Say something like *Of course! I love art.*

2 **Read the note below. Underline the questions in the note.**

> What are you doing this afternoon? Can you come to the art gallery? There's a fantastic photography exhibition on. I'm meeting Jessica there at 4pm. Are you free then?
>
> Andy

3 **Work in pairs. Look at the two answers to Andy's note. Which answer is better? Why?**

A

Hi Andy,

I'm visiting the art gallery. I really like photographs. Tell Jessica I'm meeting you later today too.

See you later.

B

Hi Andy,

Sorry, I'm busy this afternoon because I'm practising for a concert. So, I'm not free to go to the art gallery with you and Jessica.

Have fun!

The Art Gallery of South Australia

4 **Work in pairs. Discuss different ways to say the underlined words and phrases in the students' answers in Exercise 3.**

OPTIMISE YOUR EXAM

Guided writing (a note)

When you write a note, read the instructions carefully and think about:

- who you are writing the note to.
- why you are writing the note.
- what information is required.
- what order to put the information in.

5 **Look at this writing task and answer the questions.**

You are going to the cinema tonight with your friend, Kris. Write a note to Kris.

> *What are you doing tonight?*
> *Do you want to see a new comedy at the cinema at 6.30? We can go for a pizza afterwards. Do you want to come?*
> *Kris*

Write **25 words** or more.

1 What does Kris ask? Underline the questions.
2 What does Kris suggest you do first?

___

3 What does Kris suggest you do next?

___

6 **Look at the plans and decide which one (A or B) you will follow for your note to Kris.**

A *You're busy and can't go out with Kris*

1 Apologise
↓
2 Explain
↓
3 Suggest another time

B *You're free and can go out with Kris*

1 Where and when to meet
↓
2 Ask about the film
↓
3 What to do after the film

7 Plan

Now plan your note. Use the table to help you.

	Detail	My notes
Point 1		
Point 2		
Point 3		

8 Write

Write your note in an appropriate style. Write 25 words or more.

9 Check

Before you hand in your note, complete this checklist.

Checklist

- ◯ I've followed my writing plan.
- ◯ I've started and ended the note in the right way.
- ◯ I've answered the three questions.
- ◯ I've used some of my own words.
- ◯ I've written 25+ words.
- ◯ I've checked my spelling, grammar and punctuation

▶ **Workbook Unit 2:** Writing, page 18, exercises 1, 2, 3, 4 and Progress check 2, page 19

PROGRESS CHECK UNITS 1–2

GRAMMAR AND VOCABULARY

1 Choose the correct word to complete each sentence.

1 Do you stay in a **tent** / **beach** when you go camping?
2 I really love that **painting** / **painter**, the colours in it are beautiful.
3 He's really famous. I read a newspaper **article** / **programme** about him.
4 I like going **swimming** / **cycling** in the sea when I'm on holiday.
5 William goes **in** / **out** with his friends on Saturdays.
6 She's a very good **music** / **musician**. She plays the violin and piano.
7 What's your favourite board **game** / **player**?
8 Mum and Dad are at an **museum** / **art gallery** this evening.
9 My sister is a **gamer** / **game** and she plays on her computer most days.
10 Adam usually meets his friends at the gaming **house** / **café** at the weekend.

__/10

2 Complete the sentences using the correct form of the verbs in brackets.

1 Let's go and see my cousin. He usually ______________ (**play**) football in the park on a Saturday morning.
2 I ______________ (**look**) for a book about rock music. Have you got one?
3 Let's hurry. The film ______________ (**start**) in ten minutes.
4 Don't be late for class! We ______________ (**practise**) a new dance this afternoon.
5 Oliver is at home this evening. He ______________ (**watch**) something on TV.
6 The boys are upstairs. They ______________ (**do**) their homework at the moment.
7 Does your grandmother ______________ (**live**) near you?
8 Amy always ______________ (**try**) to climb higher than anyone else.

__/8

3 Choose the correct word to fill each gap.

I love using my digital camera and I (**1**) ____ make short films with it. My brother, Samuel, likes writing stories, and sometimes we act (**2**) ____ one of (**3**) ____ stories in a film. We design our own costumes, too! Some of our films are terrible, but (**4**) ____ learning a lot (**5**) ____ how to make good films. There's a film club at our school and Samuel and I go there (**6**) ____ Wednesday. It's a great place to share ideas. Mr Watson, our teacher, gives us tips on how to use our digital cameras. I always listen (**7**) ____ him very carefully because he knows a lot about cameras! Sometimes my classmates come (**8**) ____ to my house and we all make a film together. That's usually a lot of fun!

1 **A** often **B** am **C** never
2 **A** at **B** out **C** in
3 **A** their **B** its **C** his
4 **A** it's **B** he's **C** we're
5 **A** about **B** from **C** for
6 **A** a **B** the **C** every
7 **A** at **B** to **C** for
8 **A** round **B** off **C** after

__/8

4 **Complete the sentences with the verbs in the box.**

come	get	go	look	stay	turn

1 The bus goes past the park, and then into town. We __________ off at the museum.
2 Hello, nice to see you. Please __________ in.
3 I like to __________ out with my friends at the weekend.
4 My grandparents are going to __________ after me and my brother during the school holiday.
5 Please can you __________ off the television and come and speak to your auntie?
6 I have to __________ in and do my homework this evening. Tomorrow I'm going to the cinema.

__/6

5 **Complete the text with one word in each gap.**

My name is Pablo Riva. I'm 14 and I live **(1)** __________ Turin. I **(2)** __________ two sisters, Laura and Anna. Both of **(3)** __________ are younger than me. **(4)** __________ live with our parents and grandmother in a big house. Next **(5)** __________ the house is a park. I always **(6)** __________ skateboarding there with my friends. We like to go in **(7)** __________ afternoon, when school is over. My sisters don't like skateboarding at all, so they **(8)** __________ come with me. They like riding their bikes. At the moment, I **(9)** __________ studying English. **(10)** __________ is my favourite subject.

__/10

6 **Read the descriptions. What is the word for each one? The first letter is given.**

1 When people stay in a tent on holiday they are doing this. c_ _ _ _ _ _ _
2 If you are in this you could win a prize. c_ _ _ _ _ _ _ _ _ _ _ _
3 People use this to take photographs. c_ _ _ _ _ _
4 This is what we call a person who plays the guitar. g_ _ _ _ _ _ _ _ _ _
5 This describes something beautiful or pretty to look at. a_ _ _ _ _ _ _ _ _ _ _
6 This word describes a person who is part of a group or club. m_ _ _ _ _ _
7 Something that is shown on television to make people buy things. a_ _ _ _ _ _
8 This describes something that is liked by many people. p_ _ _ _ _ _ _ _

__/8

Total score __/50

EXAM SKILLS

Tick the statements that are true for you. Review the skills in the unit if you need more help.

I can ...	Unit/page
☐ scan a text to find information	Unit 1 p4
☐ identify differences to answer picture multiple-choice questions	Unit 1 p8
☐ answer questions about myself	Unit 1 p10
☐ use prepositions in an open-cloze task	Unit 1 p11
☐ understand a guided writing task	Unit 1 p12
☐ skim a text for information	Unit 2 p14
☐ listen for words that mean the same	Unit 2 p18
☐ answer questions about free time activities	Unit 2 p20
☐ predict the answer in multiple-choice cloze activities	Unit 2 p21
☐ use my own words in a note	Unit 2 p22

3 What's for dinner?

READING | Gapped text | A magazine article

1 In pairs or as a group, answer the questions.

1 Describe the food in your country. What's your favourite national dish?

2 What type of food do you like cooking?

EXAM SKILL

Understanding *who* or *what*

- Pronouns are words like *he*, *she*, *it*, *me*, *his*, *one*, etc.
- They are used to talk about someone (the *who*) or something (the *what*) that has already been mentioned in the text.
- Read the sentences before the pronoun to find the *who* or the *what* that the pronoun is referring to.

2 Read the sentences. Match the people in the box to the words in bold.

busy people | people who don't eat fish | everybody | the person reading the article

1 **We** all know it's important to eat healthy food. ____________

2 Some people don't cook because **they** don't have free time. ____________

3 Some people don't eat fish because **they** don't like it. ____________

4 So, how can **you** learn how to cook? ____________

3 Read the sentences (1–3) and decide *who* or *what* the underlined words refer to.

1 Many people prefer eating in restaurants to eating at home. They think <u>it</u>'s a nice experience.

2 Matt worked as a waiter in the UK over ten years ago. He was good at <u>it</u>, but he decided to become a chef.

3 Sue is planning to be the head chef of a famous hotel one day. <u>It's</u> her dream job.

4 Read the sentences in Exercise 3 again and decide if they refer to the past, the present or the future.

5 Read the magazine article on page 27 quickly. Which purpose (A, B or C) best explains why the article was written?

A to advertise a new cookery show

B to make teenagers want to learn to cook

C to share different recipes

Kids in the kitchen

In the UK, 60% of 18-year-olds can't cook five easy meals. There are, however, many different ways young people can learn to cook.

1 Some people learn by watching TV cooking competitions like *Junior MasterChef*. **(1)** ____ The idea for it was simple – to help people think about the food they eat. In the show, young people prepare different delicious dishes every week. **(2)** ____ And some of the food is amazing. Everyone remembers the famous alligator chilli one junior chef made!

2 *Junior MasterChef* winners can help people learn to cook by sharing their recipes online. **(3)** ____ However, many winners learnt to cook when they helped their parents at home.

3 There are also cooking courses and schools for teenagers in the UK. At one school, the teacher, Ben Coyle-Larner, isn't a chef. **(4)** ____ . Thanks to his music he is now teaching kids to cook. When Ben was a teenager, he found it difficult to study. Ben says, 'My brain is always busy, but with cooking there is no time to think about other things.' In 2016, Ben opened his cooking school to help teenagers like him.

4 So, next time you're online, why not look up the recipe of your favourite dish or watch a video about how to cook it? **(5)** ____ Then start cooking!

OPTIMISE YOUR EXAM

Gapped text

- Read the text first to understand the general idea and meaning. As you read, try to guess what the missing sentences will say.
- Pay attention to the sentences before and after the gap. Tenses and pronouns can help you to decide which sentence goes in the gap.
- Choose the answer which fits both the grammar and the meaning.

6 **Read the magazine article about a TV cooking competition. Five sentences have been removed from the text. For each question, choose the correct answer. There are three extra sentences which you do not need to use.**

A He's a successful rapper called Loyle Carner.
B Their favourite meals were lunch and dinner.
C The one who cooks the best food is the winner.
D The programme started in the UK 20 years ago.
E Or watch the latest cookery show to get some great ideas.
F But he enjoys teaching them how to create recipes.
G One winner said she actually learnt to cook by watching YouTube videos.
H They often went to the library to look at cookbooks.

7 1.16 **Now listen and check.**

8 **Write a highlighted word from the text to match each definition.**

1. a cook in a restaurant ____________
2. to make food ready for eating ____________
3. something or someone a lot of people know about ____________
4. suggestion or plan ____________
5. to learn by reading or doing homework ____________
6. lunch is an example of one of these ____________
7. instructions on how to make different dishes ____________
8. another word for 'programme' ____________

THINK | RESEARCH | **CULTURE** | LEARN | ME

In pairs or groups, choose a dish from your country and write the recipe. Compare your ideas with other students.

3 GRAMMAR 1 | Past simple: regular verbs, *Wh-* words

Grammar in context

Choose the correct word or phrase to complete each sentence. Then find them in the text and exercise 6 on page 27 and check your answers.

1. *The programme **starts / started** in the UK 20 years ago.* (paragraph 1)
2. *However, many winners learnt to cook when they **help / helped** their parents at home.* (paragraph 2)
3. *In 2016, Ben **opened / opens** his cooking school to help teenagers like him.* (paragraph 3)

REMEMBER

- We use the past simple to talk about:
  - something that happened once in the past.
  - something that happened again and again in the past.
  - something that was true for a period of time in the past.
- We often use time expressions with the past simple, e.g. *in 2014, last year, last month, yesterday, this morning.*

▶ **See Grammar reference, Unit 3,** page 146

Grammar in context

Read this question: *When did you learn to cook?*

a) Is the question about the present or the past? ______

b) Is the question asking about a time or a place? ______

REMEMBER

- We use *wh-* words at the beginning of questions that are asking for information. You can't answer a *wh-* question with *yes* or *no*: ***Where** did you live? **Who** did you live with?*

▶ **See Grammar reference, Unit 3,** page 146

1 **Complete the text with the past simple of the verbs in the box.**

ask	bake	practise	prefer
start	use	want	watch

Sweet dreams

Amy-Beth Ellice (**1**) __________ baking at the age of three. As a child she (**2**) __________ her mother carefully while she prepared their meals. That's how she learnt to cook.

Amy-Beth quickly became very good at cooking because she worked hard and (**3**) __________ baking skills every day. Many of her friends (**4**) __________ spending their time chatting on social media, but Amy-Beth (**5**) __________ her free time to bake.

Amy-Beth (**6**) __________ cakes for friends and family, and put pictures of them online. People saw the pictures and (**7**) __________ her to make cakes for them too. Now Amy-Beth bakes cakes for celebrity parties and weddings.

Amy-Beth always (**8**) __________ to be a good chef, but now she is a famous one too!

SAY IT RIGHT

Resource centre: Unit 3
Pronunciation of *-ed*

2 **Match the things we ask about (a–f) to the *Wh-* words (1–6).**

	We use	To ask about
1	What/Which f	**a)** a person
2	Where ____	**b)** a possession
3	Why ____	**c)** a place
4	Who ____	**d)** a reason
5	When ____	**e)** a time
6	Whose ____	~~**f)** a thing~~

3 **Choose the correct words to complete the interview.**

Young start-ups

article rating ★★☆

Today we're (**1**) **talking** / **talked** to Leo and Izzy, two teenagers who started an ice-cream business in London.

Q: (**2**) **When** / **Who** did you decide that ice cream was a good idea for a food business?

A: A few years ago we (**3**) **travelling** / **travelled** to Ireland. We saw lots of young people eating ice cream although it wasn't hot. We (**4**) **decided** / **decide** it was one of the most popular snacks available.

Q: (**5**) **Who** / **Why** did you talk to to find out more?

A: We (**6**) **talk** / **talked** to other young people and we learnt that teens want ice cream to be fun, fashionable and healthy.

Q: (**7**) **When** / **Where** do you make your ice cream?

A: We make it in the kitchen of a café and our customers test our new flavours.

Q: (**8**) **What** / **Which** do you make it with?

A: We use coconut milk because it's sweet but healthy.

Q: (**9**) **Why** / **Which** ice cream do you sell the most?

A: Chocolate is the most popular.

Q: (**10**) **What** / **When** can you tell other young people who want to start a food business, Leo?

A: Find a food people like, and make it in a new or exciting way!

Words connected with *food*

1 1.17 **Complete the food lists with the words in the box. Listen and check.**

~~apple~~ | banana | ~~beans~~ | ~~beef~~ | ~~bread~~
carrots | cereal | ~~cheese~~ | chicken | ~~honey~~
lettuce | milk | oil | onions | oranges
pasta | potatoes | rice | salt | steak
strawberries | tomatoes | vinegar | yoghurt

Vegetables	Fruit	Carbohydrates
beans	*apple*	*bread*
______	______	______
______	______	______
______	______	______
______		
______		

Meat	Dairy	Other
beef	*cheese*	*honey*
______	______	______
______	______	______
		______

2 **Complete the text using words from Exercise 1.**

MY FAVOURITE SNACK

What's my favourite breakfast snack? Well, if I'm feeling lazy, I have a bowl of (**1**) ______ – usually with milk, but sometimes (**2**) ______. Or a slice of (**3**) ______ with some (**4**) ______ on it. But if I'm feeling hungry, I often go into the kitchen and make something a bit more interesting. Sometimes I make a burger – not like the ones you get at fast-food places, but a really good one. It's quite easy. You take some good meat, like (**5**) ______ and make it into flat circles. You put a little (**6**) ______ on it, then you cook it under the grill for about eight minutes on each side. I always add a slice of (**7**) ______, too, to make it a cheeseburger, and some fried (**8**) ______. I usually have a salad with tomatoes and (**9**) ______ as well, and then some fruit – a bowl of lovely red (**10**) ______ or a banana.

Verbs/adjectives

3 1.18 **Complete the table. Listen and check.**

verb	adjective
bake	(1) ______
boil	(2) ______
(3) ______	fried
grill	(4) ______
roast	(5) ______

4 1.19 **Choose the correct word to complete each sentence. Listen and check.**

1 I ate some delicious **fried** / **fry** fish at the new Thai restaurant.
2 He **boiled** / **boil** the pasta for a long time. It tasted terrible.
3 We need to **grilled** / **grill** this chicken for 20 minutes.
4 I like **baked** / **bake** potatoes with cheese and beans.

5 **Look at the meal review. Underline the adjectives.**

I ate some delicious fried fish at the new Thai restaurant. Then I had some cold coconut ice cream with fresh green grapes.

REMEMBER

- In English, we usually put adjectives of opinion before adjectives describing qualities.
- The usual order for adjectives is: opinion, size, shape, age, colour, nationality, material. We don't often use all the types of adjective in one sentence.

6 **Tick the correct sentence, A or B.**

1 **A** I love eating big red apples. ____
B I love eating red big apples. ____
2 **A** That's a lovely mountain bike. ____
B That's a mountain lovely bike. ____
3 **A** Mum bought a round, big French cheese. ____
B Mum bought a big, round French cheese. ____

Collocations with verbs

7 1.20 **Complete the phrases with the words in the box. Listen and check.**

bake | do | have | make | take

1 ______ lunch / a drink / a good time
2 ______ an exam / a train / a photo
3 ______ homework / the washing-up / sports
4 ______ breakfast / a picnic / a mistake
5 ______ bread / a cake / a potato

8 **Tick the correct sentences. Underline the mistake in the incorrect sentences and write the correct word.**

1 Make sure you <u>have</u> the washing-up. *do*
2 We bake lunch at 12. ______
3 Ask Mia to take a photo of us. ______
4 I'm going to bake Mum a cake for her birthday. ______
5 Let's do sandwiches and go to the park. ______

▶ Vocabulary reference, page 157 ▶ Workbook Unit 3: Vocabulary, pages 22–23, exercises 1, 2, 3

3 LISTENING | 3-option multiple choice (dialogue)

1 **In pairs or as a group, answer the questions.**

1 How often do you go to cafés and restaurants?
2 What kind of café is popular where you live? Why?

EXAM SKILL

Predicting what the speaker will say

- You can often use the questions and options to predict what the speaker is going to say.
- Read the instructions, questions and options carefully to help you understand what you will hear.

2 **Read the exam question below and underline any important words.**

> **You will hear Kay telling a friend about a new café.**
>
> 1 The reason Kay likes the café is
> **A** the cheap cake.
> **B** the good coffee.
> **C** the friendly staff.

3 **Read the students' notes, A and B. Which do you think are better? Why?**

A

Lion Street café
1. Kay likes the café because ________
A cake is free
B coffee is good
C staff are friendly

B

Lion Street café
1. Like because
A not expensive / doesn't cost much
B coffee great / amazing / fantastic, etc.
C helpful / friendly / waiter / waitress

4 1.21 **Listen to part of a conversation and choose the correct answer in Exercise 2. You can use the notes in Exercise 3 to help you.**

1 ____

5 **Read the questions and the options in Exercise 6. Underline key words. Write short notes predicting what you will hear.**

OPTIMISE YOUR EXAM

3-option multiple choice (dialogue)

- In this part of the exam you will hear a conversation between two speakers. Look at the questions and underline key words to help you predict what the speakers might discuss.
- Listen carefully to both speakers because the answers to the questions can come from either of the speakers.

6 1.22 **You will hear Clare talking to her friend Simon about a trip to a café. For each question, choose the correct answer.**

1 Clare went to the music café on
A Friday evening.
B Saturday afternoon.
C Saturday evening.

2 The café had
A three tables.
B four tables.
C five tables.

3 Simon thought the food was
A enjoyable.
B not fresh.
C fantastic.

4 Clare decided to eat
A an omelette.
B fish.
C a vegetable curry.

5 Clare finished her meal with
A a cold drink.
B some fruit.
C a dessert.

7 1.22 **Listen again and check your answers.**

THINK | **RESEARCH** | CULTURE | LEARN | ME

Work in pairs or groups and answer the questions.

- Find out about interesting cafés or places to eat near you.
- Choose your favourite, and tell the class.

▶ **Workbook Unit 3:** Listening, page 24, exercises 1, 2, 3, 4

GRAMMAR 2 | Past simple: irregular verbs

Grammar in context

Look at these sentences from the audio in the listening lesson. Choose the correct word to complete each sentence.

1 *Did you **go** / **went** to the new music café ...?*
2 *It was a bit smaller than I **think** / **thought**.*
3 *I **have** / **had** grilled fish for my main, ...*
4 *But the best thing was that I didn't **paid** / **pay**.*
5 *... they **say** / **said** it was my birthday present!*

Note: Irregular verbs (*get, have, say, teach, go*, etc.) don't follow a pattern. You need to learn the past simple of these verbs. See the *Irregular verbs reference* on page 167.

REMEMBER

- To make negatives, you put *didn't* before both regular and irregular verbs:
  *She **didn't order** a drink.*
  *I **didn't eat** anything.*
- In questions, you use *Did/Didn't* + the infinitive of regular and irregular verbs:
  ***Did** you **like** the café?*
  *What **did** they **have** to eat?*

▶ **See Grammar reference, Unit 3,** page 147

1 Write the sentences in the past simple. Use the words in brackets.

1 Alana eats lunch in the café next door. (**yesterday**)
Alana ate lunch in the café next door yesterday.
2 Helen doesn't go to the restaurant. (**last week**)
____
3 Paul gets up early. (**this morning**)
____
4 He sees his friends after school. (**last night**)
____
5 Rob can't come for dinner. (**last Monday**)
____
6 She buys a sandwich at the local shop. (**this morning**)
____
7 We meet in the park. (**in 2018**)
____
8 I have a lot of comics. (**as a child**)
____

2 Use the prompts to write past simple sentences that are true for you.

1 you / eat / for breakfast / this morning
I ate cereal and milk for breakfast this morning.
2 the teacher / teach / you / English / last year
____
3 the best programme / you / see / on TV / yesterday
____
4 you / go / with your friends / at the weekend
____
5 you / do / before bed / last night
____
6 the best meal / you / have / last week
____

3 Work in pairs. Ask and answer the questions from Exercise 2.

What did you eat for breakfast this morning?

I ate cereal and milk for breakfast this morning. How about you?

4 Complete the text using the correct past simple form of the verbs in brackets.

The emoji menu

On Monday I (**1**) ________ (go) to an interesting café with my grandparents. When they (**2**) ________ (see) the menu they (**3**) ________ (get) a bit of a surprise – it (**4**) ________ (not have) any words on it! When I first (**5**) ________ (hear) about the way the Little Yellow Door café was using emojis on menus, I (**6**) ________ (think) it sounded difficult to understand. But actually it worked well. Customers (**7**) ________ (say) that they (**8**) ________ (understand) exactly what all the pictures were. I ordered a big salad with potatoes and fish. It was delicious and I (**9**) ________ (eat) it all. My grandma was pleased because I (**10**) ________ (not leave) anything on my plate.

THINK | RESEARCH | CULTURE | LEARN | **ME**

Work in pairs and take turns to tell your partner about an interesting restaurant you visited with your family.

▶ **Workbook Unit 3:** Grammar 2, page 23, exercises 1, 2, 3

3 SPEAKING | Questions

Talk 2 Me
It's my favourite because ...

Flipped classroom

1 **Watch the *Talk2Me* video and answer the questions.**

1 What did the twins make for their mum last week?
2 What type of cake did Evie make?
3 What did Evie's dad buy in the supermarket?

2 **Watch the video again. Underline the phrases in the *Phrase expert* box that you hear on the video.**

> **PHRASE EXPERT**
> I love/hate … because it's (delicious) …
> I prefer … | It's my (least) favourite because …
> The reason I (prefer) … is …

EXAM SKILL

Explaining likes and dislikes

- Listen very carefully to the examiner. Listen for key words. Answer exactly the question he or she asks. For example, Q: *What is your **favourite** food?*
A: *My **favourite** food is … because …*
- When you talk about what you like and/or dislike, remember to give a reason for your opinion.

3 **In pairs or as a group, answer the questions. Use phrases from the *Phrase expert* box.**

1 Which is your favourite meal of the day? Why?
2 Do you prefer healthy food or fast food? Why?

4 1.23 **Listen to a student answering these questions. Write the foods.**

1 What's your favourite type of food? ____________
2 What type of food don't you like? ____________
3 Tell me about the food you eat at festivals and parties. ____________

5 1.23 **Listen again and note down the reasons the student gives for his answers.**

1 ____________
2 ____________
3 ____________

6 **Complete the mind map with your own answers to the questions in Exercise 4. Write the food and the reason.**

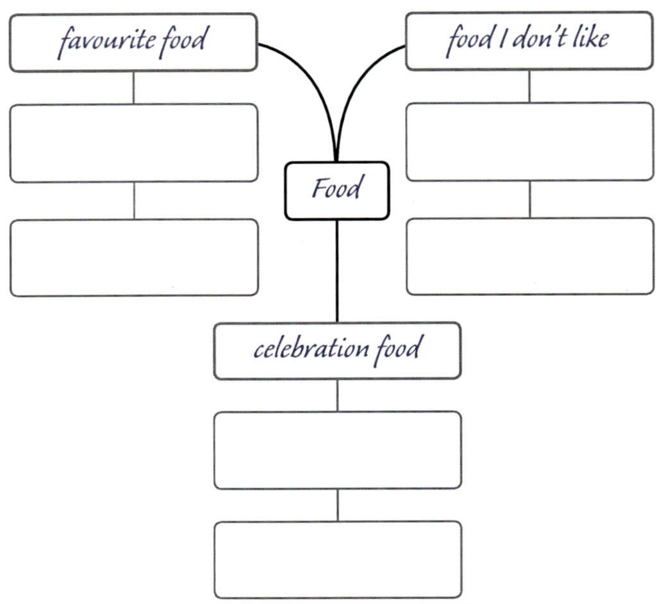

OPTIMISE YOUR EXAM

Questions

- In this part of the test, the examiner may ask about your likes and/or dislikes. You can prepare and practise for this, but don't learn long sections because your answer won't sound natural.
- The examiner won't always ask the same questions, so you need to think of different possible questions and answers that you might be asked.
- Make notes of possible questions, useful vocabulary and ideas for your answers.

7 **Work in pairs. Take turns asking and answering the questions in Exercise 4. Use your notes in the mind map in Exercise 6 to give examples and reasons.**

▶ **Workbook Unit 3:** Speaking, page 24, exercises 1, 2, 3, 4

1 **What is the most important thing about where you choose to eat? Order the points from 1 (most important) to 6 (least important).**

- The food is good. ____
- The food is cheap. ____
- The waiters and waitresses are friendly. ____
- It's clean. ____
- It's a cool place to go. ____
- There's a lot to choose from on the menu. ____

2 **Work in pairs or groups. Compare your ideas in Exercise 1 and give reasons for your choices.**

3 **In your pairs or groups, agree on a final order for the points in Exercise 1. Tell the class. Think of examples of places you know.**

EXAM SKILL

Using conjunctions

- Conjunctions are also known as linking words because they 'link' two ideas. For example, *Do you want a pizza* ***or*** *a burger?, He had some popcorn* ***and*** *a drink., The ice cream is really tasty,* ***but*** *it isn't my favourite food., Mum didn't go shopping* ***because*** *she worked late.*
- The conjunction ***and*** can join two phrases or ideas; ***or*** can be used to talk about choices; ***but*** can show two ideas that are different or opposite; ***because*** gives a reason.

4 **Work in pairs. Decide which word completes each sentence. Say why.**

and	but	because	or

1 Would you prefer fruit for dessert ________ would you like some ice cream?
2 I've got an old recipe book ________ I always use it when I make cakes.
3 Mum cooked steak ________ chips for lunch.
4 I love sweets ________ I know they aren't good for my teeth!
5 I didn't bake you a cake ________ the oven doesn't work.
6 She's very interested in food, ________ she isn't a very good cook.

OPTIMISE YOUR EXAM

Open cloze

- Think about the meaning of the sentence. If you think there is a conjunction in the gap, decide what the conjunction needs to do. For example, is it joining two ideas (*and, also*), is it talking about choices (*or*) or is it talking about two ideas that are different (*but*)?
- Complete the easy gaps first, then go back and look at the more difficult ones.
- Make sure you only write one word in each gap, and always write an answer for every gap.

5 **For each question, write the correct answer. Write ONE word for each gap.**

Hi, my name is Samuel. I come __*from*__ the Netherlands. Last year my family went (**1**) ________ holiday to Italy and the food was amazing! We visited two cities: Florence and Bologna. One evening in Florence we went to (**2**) ________ old restaurant near the train station. It looked strange (**3**) ________ the food was fantastic. We could have either pasta or steak. They also baked bread and made homemade ice cream. After dinner we walked back (**4**) ________ our hotel (**5**) ________ we all needed to get (**6**) ________ exercise before going to bed.

THINK | RESEARCH | CULTURE | LEARN | ME

Write down at least three sentences to describe a favourite food. Do not name the food you're describing.

Work in groups. Say your sentences to your group. Ask them to guess the food.

WRITING | Guided writing (a note)

1 **In pairs or groups, answer the questions.**

1 How often do you eat out with your friends?

2 What fast food do young people in your country eat?

2 **Read the exam task below. How many questions does Toni ask? Underline the important word(s) in each question.**

Read the note from your friend, Toni.

Hi. I'm not busy today. Maybe we could go for lunch. What do you like eating? Where would you like to go? What time can we meet?

Toni

Write a note to Toni. Answer his questions. Write **25 words** or more.

EXAM SKILL

Making and replying to suggestions

- Revise expressions for making suggestions. For example, ***Would you like to*** *go to the café?* ***Let's*** *get a fruit salad.* ***How about*** *meet****ing*** *at the pizzeria?*
- Don't forget to use a question mark if your suggestion is in the form of a question.
- Make sure you understand the question you are being asked. For example, *Would you like to …?* is a suggestion, but *What ice cream do you like? (I like chocolate ice cream.)* asks your preference and *What's it like? (It's really fun!)* asks for a description.

3 **In pairs, read the two replies to Toni's note below. Then complete the table by ticking the statements that are true.**

A Hi Toni,

Do you like fish and chips? Let's eat some today. I'll meet you at one o'clock. OK?

Zoltan

B Hi Toni,

I love pizza! There's a great pizzeria on Bond Street. How about going there? The pizzas are fantastic and they're cheap. Would you like to meet at one o'clock?

Dan

	Note A	Note B
1 There are fewer than 25 words.		
2 All the questions in Toni's note are answered.		
3 The writer makes suggestions.		
4 The writer includes some extra information.		

4 **Read another reply to Toni's note. Then rewrite the sentences in your own words.**

Hi Toni,

I'm also not busy today. I like eating pizza! There's a new pizzeria in town. I would like to go there. We can meet at one o'clock.

Jane

1 I'm also not busy today.

____

2 I like eating pizza.

____

3 I would like to go there.

____

4 We can meet at one o'clock.

____

OPTIMISE YOUR **EXAM**

Guided writing (a note)

- Remember, there are three questions in the note. Identify and underline them.
- Before writing:
  - make sure you understand what each question in the note is asking.
  - plan how you will answer each question.
  - use your own words where possible.

5 **Look at this writing task and make notes to answer questions 1–6.**

Your friend Ella wants to go to cookery classes. Read Ella's note and reply to her.

Oh wow, you went to cookery classes! I'm interested in them too. What were they like? What did you learn to cook? Why don't we meet so you can tell me more?
Ella

Write **25 words** or more.

1 Who are you writing to? ______
2 How many words do you need to write? ______
3 How many questions do you have to answer? ______
4 What do you have to explain? ______ ______
5 Which tenses should you use? ______
6 Which words or phrases from this unit could you use? ______ ______

6 **Plan** **Plan your note. Use the table to help you.**

	Detail	My notes	Useful language
Question 1			
Question 2			
Question 3			

7 **Write** **Write your note in an appropriate style. Write 25 words or more.**

8 **Check** **Before you hand in your note, complete this checklist.**

Checklist

- ◯ I've followed my writing plan.
- ◯ I've answered the three questions.
- ◯ I've used the correct tenses.
- ◯ I've used a good range of vocabulary.
- ◯ I've written 25+ words.
- ◯ I've checked my spelling, grammar and punctuation.

▶ **Workbook Unit 3:** Writing, page 26, exercises 1, 2, 3, 4 and Progress check 3, page 27

4 On your way

READING | 3-option multiple matching | Blog posts

1 In pairs or as a group, answer the questions.

1 When did you last go to these places?

- airport
- bus station
- campsite
- petrol station
- train station
- city centre

2 Why did you go there?

Example: *I went to a train station at the weekend to catch a train to Nottingham.*

2 1.24 **Read the blog posts on page 37 quickly. Match each paragraph (A–C) to the tips (1–3).**

1 **TIP**: Wear comfortable shoes for walking tours. ____

2 **TIP**: Always take a good book with you when you travel. ____

3 **TIP**: For outdoor events, go prepared for the weather. ____

3 Read the blog posts again. Write a highlighted word from the text to match each definition.

1 travelling round a place to see interesting things ____________
2 to put things in a bag to take with you ____________
3 the act of going somewhere for a time and then returning ____________
4 the acts of travelling from one place to another ____________
5 weather with lots of rain and strong wind ____________
6 the opposite of dry ____________
7 a journey through the air in a plane ____________
8 lots of films, music, etc. happening in one place ____________

EXAM SKILL

Understanding words from context

- When you read a text, you probably won't know all the words.
- To help you to understand what a word or phrase might mean, look at the words before and after it.
- If you still don't understand, read the next sentence as this may make the meaning of the word clearer.

USEFUL TRAVEL TIPS

Readers share their experiences

A I hate long journeys. Last winter I went to Mexico City with my family. When we arrived at the airport in London, our flight was delayed because there was a terrible storm. Luckily, I had my tablet with me, so I downloaded an ebook. We were waiting there for five hours but I was reading an exciting story, so the time went quickly.

Kat

B Last July, I went to a language school in the UK. I made some new friends and when I wasn't studying, we spent time together. One weekend we went to a music festival for teenagers. It was raining all day, but we had a lot of fun. Most people were wearing boots, but I didn't pack any, so my new sandals got really wet and muddy. The music was brilliant, and I kept my dirty sandals as a souvenir!

Jess

C Last summer I went on a school trip to Edinburgh. On the first day we went sightseeing – my favourite place was Edinburgh Castle but it was really busy because it's so popular. However, I was walking all day in uncomfortable shoes, so by late afternoon my feet were hurting. That evening I decided to stay in the hotel to rest. What were my friends doing while I was in the hotel? A tour guide took them on an exciting night tour of the city – by bus!

Allisa

4 **Read the sentences and choose the word or phrase, a or b, that means the same as the underlined word.**

1 The bus was <u>delayed</u> this morning. I waited an hour for it to arrive.
   a) late **b)** full of people

2 It started to rain while David was playing football and now his clothes are <u>dirty</u>. He'll wash them when he gets home.
   a) wet **b)** not clean

3 Alice's tooth <u>hurts</u> when she eats. That's why she's going to the dentist tomorrow.
   a) is sore **b)** is broken

OPTIMISE YOUR EXAM

3-option multiple matching

- Don't worry about words you don't know.
- The answer to the question will not depend on the meaning of one word.
- Try to understand the general meaning of the sentence or paragraph.

5 **Read the blog posts again. For each question, choose the correct answer.**

	Kat	Jess	Allisa
1 Who travelled to a country to learn something?	A	B	C
2 Who says they visited somewhere very crowded?	A	B	C
3 Who couldn't travel until the weather improved?	A	B	C
4 Who missed an interesting activity?	A	B	C
5 Who was outdoors when the weather was bad?	A	B	C
6 Who did an enjoyable activity when there was a problem?	A	B	C
7 Who prefers travelling for only a short time?	A	B	C

THINK | RESEARCH | CULTURE | LEARN | ME

What advice could you give to people when they travel? What can they take to make their journey easier / more fun?

▶ **Workbook Unit 4:** Reading, pages 28–29, exercises 1, 2, 3, 4, 5

Grammar in context

Choose the correct verb form to complete each sentence. Then find them in the texts on page 37 and check your answers.

1 *We were waiting there for five hours, but I* ***was reading / read*** *an exciting story, …* (paragraph A)

2 *I made some new friends and when I* ***wasn't studying / didn't study****, we spent time together.* (paragraph B)

3 *What* ***did my friends do / were my friends doing*** *while I was in the hotel?* (paragraph C)

REMEMBER

- We use the past continuous to talk about something that was happening over a period of time in the past:
  I ***was watching*** *TV all yesterday afternoon.*

▶ **See Grammar reference, Unit 4,** page 147

Grammar in context

Complete the sentences with a linking word in the box. Then find them in the texts on page 37 and check your answers.

because	but	when

1 *… our flight was delayed* ___________ *there was a terrible storm.*

2 *I made some new friends and* ___________ *I wasn't studying, we spent time together.*

3 *It was raining all day* ___________ *we had a lot of fun.*

REMEMBER

- We use linking words (*and, because, but, or, when*) to connect one phrase, clause or sentence with another.
- We can use the linking word at the beginning or in the middle of the sentence:
  When *we arrived at the airport, there was a terrible storm.*

▶ **See Grammar reference, Unit 4,** page 147

1 **Complete the conversation using the past continuous form of the verbs in brackets.**

Ben: I think I saw you yesterday when I (1) ___________ (**walk**) into town. Were you in a black car with your dad and your brother?

Joe: Yes, I was.

Ben: I'm sure there were bikes in the car, too. Where (2) ___________ (**you go**)?

Joe: Dad (3) ___________ (**drive**) to Sanders Hill. We've both got new mud bikes and Dad (4) ___________ (**take**) us out to ride them on a hill for the first time.

Ben: Great! How was it?

Joe: I (5) ___________ (**do**) well until my bike went over a stone.

Ben: Were you riding too fast?

Joe: Well, we (6) ___________ (**both cycle**) quite fast but we (7) ___________ (**be**) careful. Anyway, I (8) ___________ (**not look**) in the right place so I didn't see the stone. I hit it and fell off my bike.

Ben: So that's why you've got a bandage on your arm today, then.

Joe: Exactly!

2 **Use the prompts in brackets to answer the questions.**

1 What were you doing yesterday? (ride bike)
I was riding my bike yesterday.

2 When was she playing music? (last night)
____

3 Who was studying in London last year? (James)
____

4 Were you studying in Scotland last summer? (no / sightseeing)
____

3 **Complete the text using the past continuous of the verbs in brackets or a word from the box.**

and	because	but	when

AROUND THE WORLD IN 80 WAYS

Posts from teen travellers, telling us their experiences.

I love going to South America. Last year I went to Peru with my parents. One day, my dad (**1**) ___________ (**feel**) tired, so he stayed in the hotel, (**2**) ___________ Mum and I decided to go on a bus trip to Lake Titicaca. We left the city and we (**3**) ___________ (**travel**) through the countryside (**4**) ___________ the bus suddenly stopped. The driver told us there was a problem with the engine. Luckily, there was a café nearby where we could wait. Mum (**5**) ___________ (**speak**) to Dad on the phone when a mechanic arrived. While he (**6**) ___________ (**work**) on the engine, I talked to his son, Roberto. He's a football fan, and I am too, so we had lots to talk about!

I gave him my contact details (**7**) ___________ I really liked him. The mechanic fixed the engine, so we all got back on the bus. As we (**8**) ___________ (**leave**), I waved goodbye to Roberto. When I got home, Roberto messaged me straight away. A year later and we're still in touch.

Jordan

SAY IT RIGHT

Resource centre: Unit 4
/ə/

Words connected with *travel*

1 1.25 **Complete Jo's message about how to get to school with the words in the box. Listen and check.**

bridge | bus stop | delayed | miss railway station | roundabout | traffic traffic lights

Hi Amelie,

Here is the information about getting to school tomorrow. We can catch the bus at the (**1**) ________ outside my house at 7.40am.

We arrive at school at about 8.15, unless the bus is (**2**) ________ or we (**3**) ________ it. ☹ We don't need tickets because we have student ID cards. We cross the (**4**) ________ over the river, then Kelly gets on the bus in town. We go through three (**5**) ________ , then arrive at Jamie's stop. Then we go past the (**6**) ________ , where we pick up passengers from the train – so, Yasmin and Leo get on the bus there. Next, the bus goes round a (**7**) ________ and then after a few more stops we arrive at school. Sometimes there's a lot of (**8**) ________ and the journey's slow – but then we get more time to chat! ☺

2 **Read the travel and transport descriptions and complete the words.**

1 A big circle where roads meet and cars go around: r_ _ _ _ _ _ _ _ _
2 The cars and other vehicles that use a road: t_ _ _ _ _ _
3 A way over a river, road or railway, to help people cross: b_ _ _ _ _
4 The place to wait for a bus: b_ _ s_ _ _
5 Lights used to make cars and other vehicles stop and start: t_ _ _ _ _ _ l_ _ _ _ _

Compound nouns

3 1.26 **Match the words (a–h) to (1–8) to make compound nouns. Listen and check.**

1 car ____	**a)** ride
2 driving ____	**b)** boat
3 helicopter ____	**c)** station
4 petrol ____	**d)** park
5 sailing ____	**e)** licence
6 ticket ____	**f)** guide
7 tour ____	**g)** machine
8 traffic ____	**h)** news

4 **Complete the sentences with the compound nouns from Exercise 3.**

1 We checked the ________ online before starting our journey.
2 We looked round the city centre with a ________ and she showed us the sights.
3 When we were in New Zealand, we went on a ________ over the mountains. It was incredible!
4 We wanted to hire a car, but nobody had a ________ .
5 You can book your train journey online or use a ________ at the station.
6 When we arrived at the concert hall, the ________ was full, so we had to leave the car somewhere else.
7 Before going on a long journey, you should fill up the car at a ________ .
8 I'd love to go around the Mediterranean islands on a ________ .

Phrasal verbs

5 1.27 **Complete the definitions with the phrasal verbs in the box. Listen and check.**

come in | go in | pick up | set off take off | turn off

1 to enter a place ________
2 to leave the ground and go into the sky ________
3 to start a journey ________
4 what somebody says to invite you into a place ________
5 to collect something or somebody, often in a car ________
6 to leave a main road ________

6 **Complete the message with the phrasal verbs from Exercise 5. There is one phrasal verb you do not need.**

Posts Comments

School skiing trip – update …

Dear parents,

As you know, the weather in Geneva is very bad and the plane did not (**1**) ________ at 10:30. It will be two hours late. The bus that is going to (**2**) ________ the children will (**3**) ________ to the airport this afternoon. You are welcome to (**4**) ________ to school this evening and wait for the bus to arrive. Don't forget you must leave your car behind the school – you need to (**5**) ________ the road after the petrol station to get into the car park.

▶ Vocabulary reference, page 157 ▶ Workbook Unit 4: Vocabulary, pages 30–31, exercises 1, 2, 3

4 LISTENING | Gap fill

1 **In pairs or as a group, look at the photo and plan a holiday together. Think about:**

- what kind of holiday you will go on (beach, walking, adventure, etc.).
- how you will travel.
- what you need to take with you.

EXAM SKILL

Listening for important information

- You often need to listen for prices, numbers, times and dates.
- Listen carefully because you might hear more than one price, number, etc.
- Also listen for words that can sound like numbers: *free – three, for – four, ate – eight.*

2 1.28 **Listen to the conversations. Write the numbers. Compare your answers with a partner.**

1 Where the girl lives ______________
2 Biscuits eaten ______________
3 The phone number the caller wanted ______________
4 The birthday ______________
5 The train time ______________

3 1.28 **Listen again and decide if the statements are T (True) or F (False).**

1 The girl lives in a house. T / F
2 Maria ate three biscuits. T / F
3 The caller wanted to speak to Jon. T / F
4 It's Paul's 16th birthday on Sunday. T / F
5 The train is on platform 12. T / F

4 1.29 **Listen and write the words the speakers spell out.**

1 *Jeremiah Gayle*
2 ______________
3 ______________
4 ______________
5 ______________
6 ______________
7 ______________
8 ______________

OPTIMISE YOUR EXAM

Gap fill

- Sometimes the answer is a name. The speaker often spells this out.
- Write each letter carefully as the speaker says it.
- Remember that speakers sometimes make mistakes and change the spelling. Listen for phrases like *No, it's …*

5 1.30 **For each question, write the correct answer in the gap. Write one word or a number or a date or a time. You will hear a teacher giving information about a sailing trip.**

Day of trip: *Monday*
Bus leaves: **(1)** ______________ am
Meet: **(2)** ______________ building
Lunch: **(3)** on the ______________
Toilet: **(4)** in ______________
Bring: **(5)** ______________

6 1.30 **Listen again and check your answers.**

THINK | RESEARCH | CULTURE | **LEARN** | ME

Work in pairs. Discuss the question.

- What different ways can you think of for checking the spelling of new vocabulary?

▶ **Workbook Unit 4:** Listening, page 32, exercises 1, 2, 3

Grammar in context

Look at this sentence from the audio in the listening lesson and answer the questions.

*Last year while we **were sailing** someone **fell** into the water.*

a) What are the two action verbs in the sentence? ______ and ______

b) Which action was the longest? ______

c) Which action happened in the middle of another action? ______

REMEMBER

- We use the past simple to say what we did and when:
  *I **played** a video game **last night**.*
- We use the past continuous to describe continuous actions that were happening before and after a particular time in the past:
  *What **were** you **doing** at 8 o'clock last night?*
  *I **was watching** a film.*
- We use the past continuous to talk about what was happening when another action happened. We use the past simple for the other action:
  *I **was listening** to music **when** my mobile phone **rang**.*
- In stories, we use the past continuous to describe the situation and the past simple for the main things that happened:
  *The sun **was shining**, so we **decided** to go for a long walk.*

▶ **See Grammar reference, Unit 4,** page 148

1 Choose the correct verb form to complete each sentence.

1 When I **arrived** / **was arriving** at the barbecue, everyone **had** / **was having** a good time.

2 I **was listening** / **listened** to my favourite song when you **called** / **were calling**.

3 How **did you break** / **were you breaking** your arm? **Were you running** / **Did you run** at the time?

4 I **rode** / **was riding** my bike very fast and I **fell** / **was falling** off.

5 Last week the police **stopped** / **were stopping** a man because he **was driving** / **drove** his car at 135 kilometres an hour.

6 While I **shopped** / **was shopping** this afternoon, I **lost** / **was losing** my backpack.

2 Complete the sentences using the past simple or past continuous form of the verbs in brackets.

1 I ______ (**say**) hello to the tourists, but they didn't answer me because they ______ (**look**) at the sights.

2 When we ______ (**walk**), we ______ (**see**) Maria. She ______ (**shop**).

3 I ______ (**not want**) to get up today. It ______ (**rain**) outside.

4 They ______ (**drive**) through the countryside when the car suddenly ______ (**stop**).

5 The traffic lights ______ (**change**) when we ______ (**chat**) to each other.

3 Complete the travel blog using the past simple or past continuous of the verbs in brackets.

Sorry I (**1**) ______ (**not post**) any blogs last week while Mum, Dad and I (**2**) ______ (**stay**) on the Uyuni Salt Flats in Bolivia. There were beautiful night skies – but there wasn't any wi-fi! I (**3**) ______ (**not stream**) any videos either, so I'm posting these pictures instead.
We (**4**) ______ (**not camp**) – we stayed in an old-fashioned caravan, in the middle of the salt flats. Our guide, Arturo, (**5**) ______ (**take**) us outside when it (**6**) ______ (**begin**) to get dark, so we could see the stars. I (**7**) ______ (**look**) up at the sky when at least 20 shooting stars (**8**) ______ (**fly**) past. While we (**9**) ______ (**take**) lots of photos, Arturo (**10**) ______ (**start**) a fire. Soon there was hot chocolate for everyone, which (**11**) ______ (**keep**) us warm. We stayed up all night. I (**12**) ______ (**stand**) looking at the sky when the sun came up. It was amazing!

THINK | RESEARCH | CULTURE | LEARN | ME

Work with a partner. Take turns to tell each other about the things you and your family were doing:

- last Friday evening / Saturday morning / Sunday

▶ **Workbook Unit 4:** Grammar 2, page 31, exercise 1

Talk2Me
Did you say … ?

Flipped classroom

1 Watch the Talk2Me video and answer the questions.

1 What does Evie think about running?
2 Why does Jojo think it's a good idea to buy bikes?
3 Where did they get the bikes from?

2 Watch the video again. Underline the questions in the *Phrase expert* box that you hear on the video.

PHRASE EXPERT

Did you say …? | I'm sorry, could you repeat that? | Pardon? | Please could you say that again?

EXAM SKILL

Asking someone to explain

- When you don't understand the examiner or your partner, you may need to ask them to explain a bit more.
- Use phrases like *I'm sorry, I don't understand.*, *Could you (please) explain?* or *Did you say …?* to check what was said. Be polite. Don't say, *What?*

3 In pairs, use the prompts to talk to your partner and then change roles. Talk for one minute.

Student A: Talk about different ways you travel, and why you use this type of transport.

Student B: Use phrases from the Phrase Expert box to ask your partner to repeat and explain.

4 1.31 Listen to two students talking about different types of holidays. Which types of holidays are they discussing?

1 ______________ 4 ______________
2 ______________ 5 ______________
3 ______________

OPTIMISE YOUR EXAM

Discussion (pictures)

- When you discuss the activities in the pictures with your partner, it is important to show that you are interested in what he/she is saying.
- As well as looking at your partner and nodding your head when you agree with them, use phrases like *I see*, *Great!* and *OK* to show that you are really listening and that you understand what he/she is saying.

5 In pairs, do the exam task. Look at the question and pictures and discuss.

Here are some pictures of different **types of holidays**. Do you like these different types of holidays? Say why or why not.

Do you like these different types of holidays?

6 Take it in turns to ask and answer these questions.

Student A: Do you think cycling holidays are popular?
Which of the types of holidays in the pictures from Exercise 5 do you like best?

Student B: Do you think cruises are exciting?
Which of the types of holidays do you like best?

▶ **Workbook Unit 4:** Speaking, pages 32–33, exercises 1, 2, 3

1 Choose the best answer.

1 We were on a ____ of the city when it started to rain.
A tour B journey C explore

2 Excuse me. I think that's my ____ .
My ticket says 17B.
A engine B seat C luggage

3 While we were checking in our ____ ,
we remembered our passports were in the car!
A luggage B tickets C seat

4 Our bus stopped but a ____ came and fixed it.
A tourist B explorer C mechanic

5 The ____ from London to Paris took less than three hours by train.
A travel B sailing C journey

6 We took three ____ with us when we went on holiday last summer.
A suitcases B luggage C tickets

7 We want to see all the famous sights, so we plan to ____ the city with a tour guide.
A trip B travel C explore

8 There are lots of things for ____ to see in this city.
A tourists B journeys C transport

EXAM SKILL

Choosing the right word

- Some tasks with a gapped text give you a set of answer options to choose from. The options for each gap are always all the same part of speech, for example, nouns, verbs, adjectives, linking words, etc.
- The answer options also often have a similar meaning, for example, *trip* (n), *journey* (n), *holiday* (n) or *travel* (n), but only one is correct.
- Before choosing your answer, pay attention to the words before and after the gap. They will give you clues to help you choose the correct answer.

2 Look at the words before and after each gap. Choose the correct word to complete the sentence. Then underline the word before or after the gap which gave you the clue.

1 I feel ill when I travel by car, so I never have a ____________ meal before I go on a long car journey. **big / daily**

2 We waited at the railway ____________ until Aunt Ruby's train arrived. **stop / station**

3 Mum loves beach ____________ but Dad prefers going to the mountains. **journeys / holidays**

4 We arrived at the hotel ____________ late so we were too late for dinner. **really / especially**

5 We aren't ____________ away this year because I have a summer job. **travelling / going**

OPTIMISE YOUR EXAM

3-option multiple-choice cloze

- When answer options have similar meanings, think about how they are different. For example, *trip* (n), *journey* (n), *holiday* (n) are similar, but only one can complete the sentence *Lucy went on ____________ with her friends last year.* (Note: *holiday* is the only correct option as it collocates with *on*.)
- Read the sentences with each option before you choose your answer. If you are not completely sure which option to choose, cross out any that you think are wrong and then choose the most likely option.

3 For each question, choose the correct answer.

In 2012 Australian teenager Réka Kaponay was living in Melbourne and doing the things most students do in the holidays. She often **(1)** ____ away with her parents who enjoyed **(2)** ____ all over Australia. They wanted to show Réka a lot of famous **(3)** ____. Then one day they **(4)** ____ to sell everything and go on a long **(5)** ____. They only took two suitcases with them! They began in North America, then in the next four years they went to 32 countries and six continents. Réka posted pictures of her **(6)** ____ most days on her blog. While she travelled she studied and found out about the people and places she visited and, in 2016, she wrote a book about all the places she saw.

	A	B	C
1	came	moved	went
2	travelling	moving	hopping
3	sights	views	scenes
4	decided	discussed	planned
5	visit	journey	travel
6	tours	practices	adventures

▶ Vocabulary reference, page 157 ▶ Workbook Unit 4: Language in Use, page 33, exercises 1, 2

4 WRITING | Guided writing (an email)

1 In pairs or groups, answer the questions.

1 Are there any famous places in your town or city? Which ones?

2 Do many tourists visit these places? Why / Why not?

3 What do you think makes a place interesting for visitors?

2 Read the email below and answer the questions.

Read this email from your friend, Agnes.

From: Agnes

To:

Hello,

Heres a photo of my town.

Please send me a photo of yours.

Why do people visit your town? how do people get there? What's the best way to get round?

Write an email to Agnes and answer her questions. Write **25 words** or more.

1 What are the three questions Agnes asks?

____

____

2 What does Agnes want you to send?

____

3 Read Agnes' email again and find three mistakes in punctuation and spelling.

____

EXAM SKILL

Punctuation and spelling

- Check your spelling. Remember the spelling changes you need to make in the present simple, for example, *go* → *goes*. Be careful with the past simple too, especially with irregular verbs, for example *go* → *went*, *see* → *saw*.
- Also check your punctuation. Check your work for capital letters, commas, question marks, apostrophes and full stops.

3 Read the email below. There are five mistakes. Find them and match them to the descriptions 1–5. Then correct the mistakes.

From: Maria

To: Agnes

Dear Agnes,

My town is near the sea. most visitors come by ship. Their are lots of ships ariving every day. You can walks from the sea to your hotel. Its not far.

Maria

1 This word needs a capital letter because it begins a sentence: ______________

2 This is a word that sounds like another, but has a different spelling: ______________

3 There is a spelling mistake because the word needs double letters: ______________

4 There is a grammar mistake here because the wrong verb form is used. ______________

5 This is a contraction (two words together), but the apostrophe is missing: ______________

4 Work in pairs or groups. Decide which answer to Agnes' email is better, A or B. Use the questions below to help you.

- Are the three questions answered clearly?
- Is it easy to understand what the writer means?
- Does the answer start and end in a good way?
- Does the writer use interesting words and phrases?

A

From: Julia

To: Agnes

Hello Agnes,

We get lots of visitors to my town because it's interesting. There is a castle and a museum. People usually use the bus or the tram to get around.

Julia

B

From: Jordi

To: Agnes

Dear Agnes,

People visit my town to see the beautiful old buildings. Most people come here by plane. The airport is large and very busy. The best way to get around is by walking.

Jordi

OPTIMISE YOUR **EXAM**

Guided writing (an email)

- You will lose marks for incorrect spelling in the exam. If you don't know how to spell a word, think of a different word to use or another way to say the same thing.
- Spend about five minutes at the end of the exam to check your writing and correct any spelling, grammar and punctuation mistakes.
- Remember that a contraction such as *he's* = *he is* counts as one word.

5 **Look at this writing task and make notes to answer questions 1–6.**

You want to tell your English friend, George, about your holiday.
Write an email to George.

In your email:
- say where you are
- tell George about the place
- ask George about his last holiday.

Write **25 words** or more.

1 Who are you writing to?
____

2 How many words should you write?
____

3 What questions should you ask?
____

4 What information are you going to tell George?
____
____

5 Which tenses should you use?
____

6 Which words or phrases from this unit could you use?
____
____

6 **Plan** **Plan your email. Use the table to help you.**

	Detail	Useful language	My notes
First line			
Question 1			
Question 2			
Question 3			
Last line			

7 **Write** **Write your email in an appropriate style. Write 25 words or more.**

8 **Check** **Before you hand in your email, complete this checklist.**

Checklist

- ◯ I've followed my writing plan.
- ◯ I've answered the three questions.
- ◯ I've used the correct tenses.
- ◯ I've used a good range of vocabulary.
- ◯ I've written 25+ words.
- ◯ I've checked my spelling, grammar and punctuation.

▶ **Writing reference,** page 163 ▶ **Workbook Unit 4:** Writing, page 34, exercises 1, 2, 3, 4 and Progress check 4, page 35

PROGRESS CHECK UNITS 3–4

GRAMMAR AND VOCABULARY

1 Complete the sentences with the words in the box.

in	near	off	on	outside	ride	stop	there

1 Where's the bus ____________ for the number 22 bus?
2 Excuse me, is the station ____________ here?
3 That restaurant looks nice. Let's go ____________ and have something to eat.
4 We can sit ____________ the grass and wait for the bus.
5 Come in and get warm – but leave your wet boots ____________ , please.
6 They all went on a helicopter ____________ over the city.
7 To get to the park, turn ____________ this road at the traffic lights.
8 That Turkish restaurant is very good. Shall we go ____________ tomorrow?

__/8

2 Choose the correct word to complete each sentence.

1 Clare phoned earlier. She'll pick me **off** / **up** at 8 o'clock.
2 Don't stand outside in the cold. Come **in** / **on** and get warm.
3 We were waiting for ages before the plane took **on** / **off**.
4 This place looks nice. Shall we go **in** / **out** and order something to eat?
5 We're going the wrong way. Let's turn **over** / **off** this road, park the car and look at the map.
6 Did you **do** / **bake** this bread? It's delicious.
7 Let's ask the waiter to **make** / **take** our photo.
8 What time do you usually **have** / **take** lunch?

__/8

3 Choose the correct word to fill each gap.

Last month, Jessica **(1)** ____ everything she had because she **(2)** ____ to travel around the world. But **(3)** ____ not just a tourist. In 2016, Jessica **(4)** ____ a food blog where people can share information **(5)** ____ their favourite meals. She **(6)** ____ a lot of time in Greece, taking photos of local food, and learning family recipes. While she was **(7)** ____ there, she **(8)** ____ an article about eating in Athens.

1 **A** sell **B** sells **C** sold
2 **A** wanted **B** wants **C** 's wanting
3 **A** she's **B** she **C** her
4 **A** starts **B** started **C** starting
5 **A** about **B** of **C** in
6 **A** spend **B** spends **C** spent
7 **A** stay **B** staying **C** stayed
8 **A** was posting **B** posted **C** post

__/8

4 Complete the sentences using the correct form of the verbs in brackets.

1 I ______________ (**ask**) the waiter for some water, but he didn't hear because the chef ______________ (**shout**).
2 While I ______________ (**travel**) in Vietnam, I ______________ (**eat**) some amazing street food.
3 We ______________ (**decide**) to have a picnic because the sun ______________ (**shine**) this morning.
4 Last weekend, I ______________ (**buy**) some Chinese food from the supermarket because we ______________ (**cook**) a special meal for Mum's birthday.

__/8

5 **Complete the email with the words in the box.**

did | was | weren't | what | when | where | which | who | whose | why

Hi Lily,

How was your weekend? (**1**) ____________ did you do? (**2**) ____________ you go out at all?

I had a great time at the school disco, and do you know (**3**) ____________ was there? The boy (**4**) ____________ mother works in the school library! He's really nice. I (**5**) ____________ talking to him for a long time. He asked me (**6**) ____________ you weren't there, so I think he likes you!

(**7**) ____________ were you yesterday morning? I didn't see you at the football game. I hope you (**8**) ____________ feeling ill.

I want to ask you about homework. Do you know (**9**) ____________ maths exercises we've got to do? And, (**10**) ____________ does the teacher want us to give her our projects? Does she want them tomorrow?

Thanks.
Kirsty

__/10

6 **Read the descriptions. What is the word for each one? The first letter is given.**

1 Instructions on how to make different dishes are r_ _ _ _ _ _.
2 When food is cooked in oil or hot fat, it is f_ _ _ _.
3 To make food ready to eat, is to pr_ _ _ _ _ it.
4 A long trip somewhere is sometimes called a j_ _ _ _ _ _.
5 Cars must stop when there is a red t_ _ _ _ _ _ _ l_ _ _ _.
6 People fill up their car at the p_ _ _ _ _ s_ _ _ _ _ _.
7 The place where you get on and off trains is the r_ _ _ _ _ _ s_ _ _ _ _ _.
8 The person who gives you information about a place you visit is a t_ _ _ g_ _ _ _.

__/8

Total score __/50

EXAM SKILLS

Tick the statements that true for you. Review the skills in the unit if you need more help.

I can …	**Unit/page**
☐ identify *who* and *what* pronouns refer to	Unit 3 p26
☐ predict what the speaker will say	Unit 3 p30
☐ explain likes and dislikes	Unit 3 p32
☐ use conjunctions	Unit 3 p33
☐ make and reply to suggestions	Unit 3 p34
☐ understand words from the context	Unit 4 p36
☐ listen for important information	Unit 4 p40
☐ ask someone to explain	Unit 4 p42
☐ choose the right word in multiple-choice cloze activities	Unit 4 p43
☐ use correct punctuation and spelling	Unit 4 p44

5 Technology talks

READING | 3-option multiple choice (short texts) | Notices and short messages

1 In pairs or as a group, answer the questions.

1 How do you communicate with your friends and family?

2 Do you prefer to send a text message or call someone? Why?

3 What signs and notices do you see on your way to school?

EXAM SKILL

Understanding text type

- If you know what type of text you are reading (a notice, a message, an email, etc.), it helps you to understand what the text says.
- Look at the design of the text. Does it look like something on a noticeboard or something on a phone, etc.?
- Different types of texts have different kinds of information. For example, a notice tells you what, where or when something is happening; an email from a friend may ask you a question about something, etc.

2 Look at the texts (1–3) and match them to the text types (a–c).

1

From: Jane

To: Lucy

Do you have my maths book? It isn't in my bag and I have to do my homework!

2

Photo Show: Ages 12–15

Print your photos. Write your name and age on the back.

3

Hi Becky,

I'm going shopping with Tanya tomorrow. We're meeting at the station at two. Do you want to come?

Anna

a) a notice ____ **b)** an email ____ **c)** a text message ____

3 Read the texts (1–3) again and choose the sentence, a or b, that is correct.

1 **a)** Jane gave Lucy her book.
b) Jane thinks she has lost her book.

2 **a)** It says what to do to show your work.
b) It tells you how to take the photos.

3 **a)** Anna is telling Becky to meet Tanya tomorrow.
b) Anna is inviting Becky to go shopping.

4 Work in pairs. Say what the people in Exercise 2 should do.

SAY IT RIGHT

Resource centre: Unit 5
Missing vowel sounds in questions

OPTIMISE YOUR EXAM

3-option multiple choice (short texts)

- Read the short messages carefully and decide where they are taken from and who they are for.
- Then decide what each message is doing, for example, is it giving information, asking for help, inviting, telling someone what to do?
- Understanding the purpose of the text will help you to answer the exam question *What should (X) do?*

5 2.01 **For each question, choose the correct answer.**

1

From: Liam

To: Jenny

Call me tonight after 7 about football practice. Don't call my mobile – it's broken. My home number is 96507699.

What should Jenny do?

A Not use her mobile to call Liam.

B Call Liam on the number he has given her.

C Contact Liam before football practice at 7 o'clock.

2

Kids' Store

New video games

Lots of books for kids

Half-price computers for school

Shop here if you want to

A buy a board game.

B find a book for a young adult.

C pay less for something.

3

Hi Carly,

The new football stadium is open! Let's go and watch the match this Sunday. Let me know before Friday.

Alan

What should Carly do?

A Tell Alan if she wants to see a match.

B Decide what to do at the weekend.

C Go to the stadium before Friday.

4

From: Sofia

To: Luke

Hi from Spain! I'm spending every day at the beach. Here are a few photos I took.

See you next week!

A Sofia is inviting Luke to Spain.

B Sofia is telling Luke about the beach.

C Sofia will see Luke soon.

5

Customers can now buy tickets online but must collect them at the cinema.

www.Prices-Cinema.com

A You should only buy your film tickets at the cinema.

B You need to buy tickets online to be able to get a discount.

C You can pay for tickets on the website before getting them at the cinema.

6

Hi Tony,

I've got some ideas for our history project. Let's discuss them tonight. Do you have any free time for a video chat?

Bella

A Bella wants to talk with Tony online.

B The project needs to be done tonight.

C Bella wants to do the project online.

6 **Write a highlighted word or phrase from the text to match each definition.**

1 go to get something from somewhere ___________

2 another word for 'talk' ___________

3 a way to say 'tell me' ___________

4 the American word for a shop ___________

5 doing something for a period of time ___________

6 a number for a phone you can't take with you ___________

THINK | RESEARCH | CULTURE | LEARN | ME

Work in pairs or groups and answer the question.

- What are the good and bad things about owning a mobile phone?

▶ **Workbook Unit 5:** Reading, pages 36–37, exercises 1, 2, 3, 4, 5

GRAMMAR 1 | Quantifiers with countable and uncountable nouns

Grammar in context

Choose the correct word or phrase to complete the sentence. Then find them in the short messages on page 49 and check your answers.

1 *Lots / Lot of books for kids.*
2 *Here are **a little** / **a few** photos I took.*
3 *I've got **some** / **much** ideas for our history project.*
4 *Do you have **many** / **any** free time …?*

REMEMBER

We use quantifiers to talk about quantities and amounts.

- We use *some* with countable and uncountable nouns, in positive sentences:
  *I have **some** photos from the trip.*
- We use *any* with countable and uncountable nouns, in negative sentences and questions:
  *There is**n't any** information on this site. Are there **any** apps you use every day?*
- We use *(not) much* with uncountable nouns and *(not) many* with countable nouns, in negative sentences and questions:
  *I **don't** listen to **much** music online.*
  *Are there **many** landlines in your country?*
- We use *a lot of / lots of* to talk about a large quantity:
  *I have **a lot of** apps on my phone.*
- We also use *a few* or *a little* to talk about a small number or quantity:
  *We have **a few** computers in our classroom. (= not many)*
  *She has **a little** free time later. (= not much)*

▶ **See Grammar reference, Unit 5,** page 148

1 Choose the correct words to complete each sentence.

1 I think I need **much** / **a little** help with my IT project.
2 I downloaded **a lot of** / **many** songs. I don't have time to listen to them all!
3 A **lot** / **few** people in my class don't write emails.
4 Do you need **any** / **many** help downloading the information?
5 There are **a little** / **a lot of** people here today.
6 I don't know how to use this app, and there's not **a few** / **much** information about it online.
7 **Some** / **A little** people prefer to stream movies, I prefer to download them.
8 **A few** / **Much** people in my class are into blogging but I don't like to post personal information online.
9 I don't make **a lot** / **many** phone calls, I prefer to text my friends.
10 I can't find **any** / **some** information online for my history project!

2 Complete the text about a school project. Choose the best answer (A, B or C).

(**1**) ____ of teachers think that speaking to students in different countries is important, so (**2**) ____ young people have pen friends in other countries. It's a great way to learn about how other people live. Our teacher wanted our class to speak online to children in Ghana. (**3**) ____ of students said 'yes' to the idea. We don't know (**4**) ____ children in Africa, so it's very interesting.

Now we regularly speak to students in Ghana online. Once every two weeks, we turn on the screen in our classroom and have a video chat with a school in Accra.

At first, it was a bit difficult because (**5**) ____ students were speaking at the same time. But after (**6**) ____ conversations, we decided to write down (**7**) ____ questions in class before chatting. Now different students ask (**8**) ____ questions every week and everyone can hear them. It's interesting talking to our friends in Accra, and it's (**9**) ____ fun too.

	A	B	C
1	A Many	B Lots	C Little
2	A some	B few	C any
3	A Lot	B A lot	C A little
4	A much	B many	C few
5	A much	B few	C a lot of
6	A a little	B a lot	C a few
7	A few	B some	C much
8	A a little	B lot	C a few
9	A a lot of	B a little	C many

3 Use the words in the box to write six sentences about modern technology. Use a quantifier in every sentence.

emails | mobile phone | music | photos
social networking | video games

Example: *I don't send many emails.*

Words connected with *communication and technology*

1 2.02 **Complete the names for the things in the picture with the words in the box. Listen and check.**

camera | keyboard | laptop
mouse | printer | screen

1 _ _ _ _ _ _
2 _ _ _ _ _ _ _ _
3 _ _ _ _ _ _
4 _ _ _ _ _ _ _
5 _ _ _ _ _ _
6 _ _ _ _ _

2 2.03 **Complete the text with the words in the box. Listen and check.**

blogging | camera | download | graphics
keyboard | laptop | mouse | ~~online~~
printer | screen | software | stream

Hi everyone! Sorry I've been quiet! I've just moved house. It's good to get (**1**) *online* again – I missed (**2**) ________ ! I have a lovely big desk for my (**3**) ________ in the new house. So, I can use that when I'm at home. It's got a really big (**4**) ________ , which is perfect for watching videos. I decided to get a (**5**) ________ as well, so I can print the photos I like. The laptop is good for gaming too. The (**6**) ________ in the games look much better. The (**7**) ________ is a bit different from my last one, so sorry if I make any spelling mistakes! The wireless (**8**) ________ is great and isn't noisy when you click it. I still need to (**9**) ________ my files from the old computer. And I need some new (**10**) ________ so that I can (**11**) ________ music faster. Tomorrow, I'll use the (**12**) ________ and upload some photos of me at my new desk!

Share Like Comment

Compound nouns

3 2.04 **Write the words in the box on the correct line to make technology words. Listen and check.**

computer | phone | player | web

CD / DVD / MP3 (**1**) ________

camera / cell / mobile (**2**) ________

(**3**) ________ address / page / site

laptop / personal / (**4**) ________ /
(**4**) ________ file / software

4 **Choose the correct word to complete each sentence.**

1 Let's listen to music on the **DVD** / **MP3** player.
2 This **website** / **address** is full of adverts.
3 The new information is on their web **address** / **page**.
4 I bought some computer **files** / **software** to help me change the way photographs look.

Collocations with verbs

5 2.05 **Complete the phrases with the words in the box. Sometimes there may be more than one answer. Listen and check.**

download | make | open
send | start | take

1 ________ a phone call
2 ________ a piece of software
3 ________ a file
4 ________ a photograph
5 ________ a text message
6 ________ a conversation

6 **Complete the sentences using the correct form of the collocations from Exercise 5.**

1 I met her on the train and she ________ with me. We talked about social networking sites.
2 Lola can't come out because she's ________ to her brother in Canada. They talk every week.
3 Can I use your laptop? I need to ________ that has my school project in it.
4 You need to ________ so your computer works faster. It's getting old.
5 Would you ________ of me and my cat, please? I want to post it on Instagram.
6 If you can't come to the barbecue, ________ to Mum so she knows.

▶ Vocabulary reference, page 158 ▶ Workbook Unit 5: Vocabulary, pages 38–39, exercises 1, 2, 3

5 LISTENING | 3-option multiple choice (pictures)

1 In pairs or as a group, look at the photo and answer the questions.

1 What is happening in the picture?
2 Have you ever made anything like this? If so, where and when? If not, would you like to, and why?
3 How do you think we will use robots in the future?

EXAM SKILL

Understanding when things happen

- It is important to understand if someone is talking about the past, the present or the future.
- The tense and words like *first*, *next* and *later* can help you decide when different things happen.

2 Read the conversation. Match the underlined phrases to the tenses.

Boy: Oh, no! My new printer doesn't work.
Girl: Look at this information. There's a number to phone for help. Why not call it?
Boy: No, I looked on their website. It says to send them an email, so I'm writing one now.
Girl: It might be quicker to phone …

1 past simple ______
2 present continuous ______
3 present simple ______

3 Put the events (a–d) in the order they happened (1–4) in Exercise 2.

a) The girl read the information. ___
b) The boy wrote an email. ___
c) The boy looked at the website. ___
d) The boy tried the printer. ___

OPTIMISE YOUR EXAM

3-option multiple choice (pictures)

- In short conversations, you often hear someone asking for and giving opinions.
- Listen carefully to the questions. *What's it like?* and *Do you like it?*, don't mean the same thing.
- Listen carefully to the opinions. *I don't really like it.* and *It's not what I like.* both mean the speaker doesn't like something.

4 2.06 For each question, choose the correct picture.

1 How does Sarah contact her pen friends in other countries?

A

B

C

2 What are Kirsty and her brother doing later?

A

B

C

3 What is the man going to buy his son?

A

B

C

4 How many people were in the chat room?

A

B

C

5 Which app is Mum going to download?

A

B

C

5 2.06 Listen again and check your answers.

▶ **Workbook Unit 5:** Listening, page 40, exercises 1, 2

GRAMMAR 2 | Comparatives and superlatives

Grammar in context

Look at these sentences from the audio in the listening lesson. Choose the correct word to complete each sentence.

1 *... I hope it's* ***good / better*** *than the football game we played!*

2 *... I think the phone's* ***nicer / nicest*** *than the camera.*

3 *It's* ***most / more*** *exciting than the football game.*

REMEMBER

- We use the comparative form of adjectives + *than* to compare two people/things: *My laptop is* ***bigger than*** *yours. Maths is* ***more difficult than*** *English.*
- We use *the* + the superlative form of adjectives to compare more than two people/things: *Vicki is* ***the oldest*** *girl in the class. This is* ***the most interesting*** *website of all.*

▶ **See Grammar reference, Unit 5,** page 149

1 Write sentences using the comparative form of the adjectives in the box + *than*.

big | expensive | interesting | long
modern | ~~old~~ | popular | strange

1 I bought the football game in 2018. I bought the adventure game in 2016.
The adventure game is older than the football game.

2 The PC is £499 and the laptop is £359.
____

3 Lots of my friends like rock music, but more of my friends like rap.
____

4 Your blog has lots of good things to read. Her blog has more good things to read.
____

5 The video of the skateboarder is a bit unusual. The video of the surfer is very unusual!
____

6 There are 30 people in my computing class, and 10 in the photography class.
____

7 Her email was 150 words. His email was 250 words.
____

8 The design of the PC is not new. The design of the laptop is very new.
____

2 Choose the correct comparative or superlative form to complete each sentence.

1 My smartphone is **the newest / newer than** my laptop.

2 Her new laptop is **the biggest / bigger than** her old one.

3 Phones in this shop are **more expensive / most expensive** than ones anywhere else.

4 Ida's technology project was **the best / better than** in the class.

5 His idea is **more / the most** interesting than the one we heard yesterday.

6 This old phone is **the heaviest / heavier than** my new one.

7 Online gaming is **the most popular / more popular than** hobby for teenage boys.

3 Complete the extract from a blog using the comparative or superlative form of the adjectives in brackets.

Last month, my class did a project on technology. It was a (**1**) ______________ (**exciting**) project than the one we did last year. The teacher said it was for a competition. He told us, 'The group with (**2**) ______________ (**interesting**) idea will go to London!'

We had to think of a (**3**) ______________ (**good**) idea. One group tried to build a 3-D printer, but it didn't work. Lots of students worked quickly, but we were (**4**) ______________ (**careful**) than them. We talked about it a lot and decided to make an electronic drum machine. It was (**5**) ______________ (**difficult**) than we thought, and the others finished before us. But we didn't care because we knew our project was (**6**) ______________ (**good**) in the class!

We won a school prize for our project ... and we went to the competition in London. London is very big and it's (**7**) ______________ (**busy**) than my town, but I loved it.

The judges really liked our drum machine and said it was (**8**) ______________ (**unusual**) project. We didn't win first prize, but we had a great time in London.

THINK | RESEARCH | CULTURE | LEARN | **ME**

In your opinion, what's the most useful piece of technology? Why? Discuss your ideas with a partner.

▶ **Workbook Unit 5:** Grammar 2, page 39, exercises 1, 2

Flipped classroom

1 **Watch the *Talk2Me* video and answer the questions.**

1 Why does Evie like shopping online?
2 Name four things that they buy online.
3 What did the cat do?

2 **Watch the video again. Underline the phrases in the *Phrase expert* box that you hear on the video.**

> **PHRASE EXPERT**
> I like … more than anything else / the best.
> … is better than … | It's better to (go) …
> It's better for (shopping) … | It's my favourite way to (relax). | The best thing is …
> The most difficult thing is …

A

B

3 **In pairs or as a group, look at the photos and answer the questions.**

1 Which way of communicating is the best? Why?
2 How do you usually talk to your family and friends?

EXAM SKILL

Talking about preferences

- Often in a speaking exam, you will be asked to talk about your preferences.
- Make sure you know how to say what you prefer when you are comparing things. Use phrases like:

  I prefer + noun + *to* + noun. For example, *I prefer tennis to basketball.*

  I prefer -ing to -ing. For example, *I prefer online shopping to going to the supermarket.*

  I like + noun + *the best*. For example, *I like Mara's blog the best!*

4 2.07 **Listen to four students answering questions about their preferences. Choose the correct answer.**

1 Do you prefer to **be with your friends** or to **chat with them online**?
2 Do you prefer to **watch a film** or **to go on your computer**?
3 Do you prefer **shopping with friends** or **shopping online**?
4 Do you prefer **blogging** or **playing games online**?

5 2.07 **Listen again and number the comparison phrases (A–D) in the order that you hear them.**

A more than anything else ____
B I think it's quicker ____
C It's my favourite way to relax ____
D I like … the best. ____

OPTIMISE YOUR EXAM

Discussion

- When you say you prefer one thing to another, you should also explain why.
- Practise giving reasons for your preferences. For example, *I prefer tennis to basketball **because** …* or *Tennis is … . **That's why** I prefer it.*

6 **Work in pairs. Take turns asking and answering the questions from Exercise 4. Use phrases from the *Phrase expert* box in your answers.**

▶ **Workbook Unit 5:** Speaking, pages 40–41, exercises 1, 2, 3

1 2.08 **Listen to the teenagers talking about technology. Match the ways of communicating (A–C) to the speakers.**

A instant messaging
B video chat
C video sharing

It's good to talk

How do you keep in touch with people?

1 Peter 2 Chloe 3 Sam

___ ___ ___

2 **In pairs or as a group, answer the questions.**

1 Which ways of communicating in Exercise 1 do you use?
2 Which way do you think is best? Why?
3 Do you communicate with different people in different ways? Why? How?

EXAM SKILL

Using determiners

- Determiners are words which come before a noun. They tell us if the noun is specific or general. For example, *Have you read* ***this*** *book?* (specific); *He bought* ***a*** *new car.* (general).
- The most common determiners are **articles** (*a*, *an*, *the*), **pronouns** (*this*, *that*, *these*, *those*), **possessives** (*my*, *your*, *mine*, *yours*) and **quantifiers** (*much*, *a few*, *a lot of*).

3 **Choose the correct determiner to complete each conversation.**

1 A: Whose new laptop is that?
B: It's **my** / **mine**. I got it yesterday.
2 A: What are you reading?
B: **This** / **The** really great book by Michael Morpurgo.
3 A: I haven't got any photos from the party.
B: Don't worry, I took **a lot** / **much**. I'll send them to you.
4 A: Are you listening to Taylor Swift?
B: Yes, I really like **a** / **the** songs on her last album.

OPTIMISE YOUR EXAM

Open cloze

- Determiners are important words which help us understand which noun we are talking about, so they are often tested in this part of the exam.
- Read the sentence before the gapped sentence carefully. Try to identify the noun (sometimes the noun is the gapped word). Then decide if the noun is singular or plural and what kind of determiner you need.

4 **For each question, write the correct answer. Write ONE word for each gap.**

From: Bill@bill.com
To: Jade@jade.com
Subject: Games!

Hi Jade,

I want to tell you ___about___ a great new game I'm playing. It's (**1**) ____________ online game so you can play it with your family or friends. I really like adventure games like this. You have (**2**) ____________ go across (**3**) ____________ of different countries and find special coins. When you have ten of (**4**) ____________, you can go to the next level. It's really fun (**5**) ____________ you can learn lots about the countries you travel through. I've got an idea! (**6**) ____________ don't you come round tonight and we could play it together?

Billy

THINK | RESEARCH | CULTURE | LEARN | ME

Work in groups and answer the questions.

- Why do you think it is important to communicate with people from other countries?
- What are the best ways to communicate with people?

▶ **Vocabulary reference,** page 158 ▶ **Workbook Unit 5:** Language in Use, page 41, exercises 1, 2, 3

WRITING | Picture story

1 In pairs or groups, answer the questions.

1 How do you use technology at home?

2 How do you use technology at school?

2 Look at the three pictures that tell a story. In pairs or groups, say what you think the story is.

3 Complete the table about the story in Exercise 2. For each picture, write brief notes about who the people are, where they are and what they are doing.

	Who?	Where?	What?
Picture 1			
Picture 2			
Picture 3			

EXAM SKILL

Using linking words

- When you write a story, the order of the events must be clear to the reader. Use linking words such as *next*, *then*, *after that*, *later*, etc. to connect the different parts of your story from start to finish.
- Remember to plan your story. Your story should have a beginning, a middle and an end, and these must be in a logical order. Use linking words to help you do this.

4 Underline the linking words and phrases that we use to show the order of events.

after (that) | afterwards | again | as well | before | both | finally | first | later | nearly | next | next to | or | then | when | while

5 Circle the correct words to complete the paragraph.

Marie needed a new mobile phone. (1) **Afterwards** / **First**, she looked online to compare all the different phones and prices. Luckily, she found one that she liked and it wasn't expensive. (2) **Finally** / **Next**, she read reviews about it and they were all good. (3) **After** / **Before** that, she decided to buy it.

6 Look at the picture story in Exercise 2 and answer the questions.

1 In picture 1, which two actions are happening at the same time? ____________

2 In picture 2, which two actions are happening at the same time? ____________

3 Which tense should you use to describe these actions? ____________

4 Which word can you use to show that two actions were happening at the same time? ____________

7 Use your notes from Exercise 3 to write the story in Exercise 2. Use the correct tense and linking words.

OPTIMISE YOUR EXAM

Picture story

- Ask yourself if the characters in the story are friends, neighbours, family members, etc. and give them names. Make notes about where your characters are and what they are doing.
- Set the scene with an introductory sentence before you write about the first picture. For example, *It was Saturday afternoon and Max and Anna were at home.*
- We usually use different past tenses such as the past simple and the past continuous to tell a story.

8 **Look at this exam task and make notes to answer the questions.**

Look at the three pictures.
Write the story shown in the pictures.
Write **35 words** or more.

1 How many scenes in the story must you write about? ____________________
2 How many words do you need to write? ____________________
3 Which tenses should you use? ____________________
4 How can you set the scene? ____________________
5 Which words or phrases from this unit could you use? ____________________

9 Plan

Plan your story. Use the table to help you.

	Who?	Where?	What?
Picture 1			
Picture 2			
Picture 3			

10 Write

Write your story in an appropriate style. Write 35 words or more.

11 Check

Before you hand in your story, complete this checklist.

Checklist

- ◯ I've followed my writing plan.
- ◯ I've written an introductory sentence.
- ◯ I've written about the three pictures.
- ◯ I've used the correct tenses.
- ◯ I've used linking words.
- ◯ I've used a good range of vocabulary.
- ◯ I've written 35+ words.
- ◯ I've checked my spelling, grammar and punctuation.

▶ **Writing reference,** page 164 ▶ **Workbook Unit 5:** Writing, page 42, exercises 1, 2, 3, 4, 5, 6, 7 and Progress check 5, page 43

6 Teen fashion

READING | Gapped text | An online article

1 In pairs or as a group, answer the questions.

1 What kind of clothes do you usually wear / do you like wearing?
2 Where do you buy your clothes?
3 Do you wear different clothes on school days and at the weekend?

EXAM SKILL

Understanding linking words and phrases

- Words and phrases such as *because*, *but*, *for example*, etc. connect words, sentences and ideas and help us to understand the logic of a text.
- It's important to know what linking words and phrases mean and do. For example, *because* introduces a reason; *but* introduces an opposite idea; and *for example* introduces an example.
- Read both the sentence before the linking word and the sentence with the linking word to see if they make sense together.

2 Circle the correct linking words and phrases.

1 Buy clothes you like. **For example / Then**, look for cool shoes to wear with them.
2 You can change your style easily. **So / Because** don't be afraid to try new things.
3 Fashion isn't only about clothes. You **also / finally** need great jewellery.

3 Complete the sentences with the linking words and phrases you did not circle in Exercise 2.

1 Everyone knows Romeo Beckham. ___________ his parents are famous, he's well known.
2 First, look online for new trends. Then decide what you like. ___________ , try on the clothes at the shops.
3 Peter loves wearing comfortable, casual clothes. ___________ , jeans and T-shirts.

4 Complete the definitions with the linking words and phrases from Exercise 2.

1 We use ___________ to say 'the result of something you have talked about before'.
2 We use ___________ to add more information.
3 We use ___________ to say what happens last.
4 We use ___________ to talk about the next thing that happens.
5 We use ___________ to give the reason for something.
6 We use ___________ to say 'like this'.

fashion changes

1 Online shopping has changed the world of fashion. We can buy clothes from all over the world, compare prices and find the best places to shop. What other things have changed the fashion world?

2 (1) ____ Some of them are famous, like Romeo Beckham, but many are normal teenagers who use social media to show people how to dress well. A lot of people follow them on social media. (2) ____ These teens don't just follow fashion, they make it. To them, it doesn't matter if something is old or new. The most important thing is that it looks good.

3 Have you ever worn a T-shirt made from old plastic bottles? (3) ____ This is because many people are interested in looking after the world, and some customers think carefully about this when buying fashion. They choose clothes made of different plants, like bamboo, coconut and banana, or from recycled materials like bottles, tyres and coffee. (4) ____ They're amazing!

4 Many people buy their clothes online, but shopping centres are still very busy. There are lots of clothes shops to choose from. Some shops use unusual ideas to try and get more customers. (5) ____ And it's an experience they won't forget. The shop assistant puts your clothes in special boxes. I've never visited the store, but it must make you hungry!

OPTIMISE YOUR EXAM

Gapped text

- Look for words in the missing sentence that connect it with the sentences before and after the gap.
- If there are linking words or phrases, try to understand their purpose. Look back at Exercise 4 to see how we use some common linking words and phrases.

5 Read the online article about fashion. Five sentences have been removed from the text. For each question, choose the correct answer. There are three extra sentences which you do not need to use.

A Clothes are often made from different things these days.
B Because without online shops, it is difficult to find what you need.
C There are a lot of new people starting new trends, especially teenagers.
D For example, Johnny Cupcakes is a clothes shop that smells of cakes!
E But it doesn't cost a lot of money to buy it.
F So clothing companies now look at their ideas.
G It looks like the other shops in the street.
H And now you can even buy shoes that make electricity when you walk.

6 2.09 **Now listen and check.**

7 Write a highlighted word or phrase from the text to match each definition.

1 feeling that you want food ____________
2 not unusual or special in any way ____________
3 the cost of different things ____________
4 to be interested in someone online and regularly look at their social media sites ____________
5 full of people ____________
6 a person who works in a shop ____________
7 not normal ____________
8 people who buy things in shops ____________

THINK | RESEARCH | **CULTURE** | LEARN | ME

Work in pairs or groups and answer the questions.

- What kinds of clothes are in fashion at the moment?
- Look at the list below. Who changes fashion the most, and how?
  - newspapers and magazines
  - celebrities (actors, sports stars, etc.)
  - vloggers and bloggers

▶ **Workbook Unit 6:** Reading, pages 44–45, exercises 1, 2, 3

GRAMMAR 1 | Present perfect simple with *ever* and *never*

Grammar in context

Find these sentences in the text on page 59 and fill in the missing words.

1 *Online shopping* __________ ***changed*** *the world of fashion.* (paragraph 1)
2 *What other things **have** __________ the fashion world?* (paragraph 1)
3 __________ *you **ever worn** a T-shirt made from old plastic bottles?* (paragraph 3)
4 ***I've*** __________ ***visited*** *the store, ...* (paragraph 4)

REMEMBER

- We use the present perfect simple to talk about past actions when the time they happened isn't important or isn't known:
  *I've **bought** lots of pairs of shoes.*
- We use the present perfect to talk about experiences: *He's **been** to lots of fashion shows.*
- *Ever* and *never* are often used with the present perfect simple, in questions and negative sentences: *Have you **ever** seen one of these? I've **never** worn a tie.*

▶ **See Grammar reference, Unit 6,** page 149

1 Use the prompts to write questions using *Have you ever ...?*

1 have you / make / a meal for your family ____
Have you ever made a meal for your family?
2 you / travel / by train alone ____
____
3 you / see / the Eiffel Tower ____
____
4 you / wear / socks in bed ____
____
5 you and your friends / eat together in a restaurant ____
____
6 you and your family / move / house ____
____

2 Match the answers (a–f) to the questions in Exercise 1.

a No, we haven't. We've always lived in the same house.
b Yes, we have. We've been to all the fast-food restaurants in our city together.
c No, I haven't. But I have worn a hat!
d Yes, I have. I've made pizza and salad for my mum a few times.
e Yes, I have. I've travelled to Wales alone to visit my grandparents.
f No, I haven't. I've never been to Paris.

3 Work in pairs. Take turns asking and answering your questions from Exercise 1.

Have you ever made a meal for your family?

No, I haven't. But I help Mum make meals sometimes.

4 Complete the conversation.

A: Have you ever (**1**) __________ to France?
B: No, I (**2**) __________ , but my sister has.
A: Really? Which cities (**3**) __________ she been to?
B: Only Paris, I think. She loves fashion and art.
A: Right. Has she (**4**) __________ visited London? There are so many great shops and galleries there.
B: No, she (**5**) __________ . But she's planning to go there for a short holiday.
A: (**6**) __________ you been to the UK?
B: No, I've (**7**) __________ been there. Have you?
A: Yes, I (**8**) __________ . I've been to Cambridge. I went to a summer language school there.

5 Complete the text using the present perfect form of the verbs in brackets.

Hi guys! Well, I (**1**) __________ (**have**) a great week! We've been in the UAE – sightseeing and shopping. Today we went to the most amazing place. (**2**) __________ (**you / ever / hear**) of Mall of the Emirates? I think it's the coolest place to shop in Dubai. I (**3**) __________ (**never / see**) such a huge building! There are more than 700 different stores, and over 100 different places to eat. This week, my parents and I (**4**) __________ (**eat**) a lot of delicious food. Inside the mall is a theme park called Magic Planet. It's got a 4-D cinema and a huge roller coaster, which I (**5**) __________ (**ride**) on three times so far. It's fantastic! But the best thing is the ski slope. I (**6**) __________ (**never / try**) skiing, but Dad and I are going tomorrow!

Sorry that I (**7**) __________ (**not / write**) to some of you who sent comments and messages last month. And I (**8**) __________ (**not / forget**) that I promised to post some new photos – I'll post some soon!

SAY IT RIGHT

Resource centre: Unit 6
Pronunciation of *have*

Words connected with *fashion, clothes and shopping*

1 2.10 **Complete the lists with the words in the box. Listen and check.**

bill | buy | cash | change (×2) | cheque | cost | credit card | ~~customer~~ | department store | market | receipt | shop assistant | shopper | shopping centre | spend | supermarket

people	places	money (verbs)	money (nouns)
customer	______	______	______
______	______	______	______
______	______	______	______
	______	______	______
			______
			______

2 **Complete the sentences using the correct form of the words from Exercise 1.**

1 People often don't carry a lot of ______ these days because they prefer using their ______ to pay for things.

2 Take a list when you go shopping, so that you only ______ the things you need and don't ______ too much.

3 In ______ you can find everything you need in one big shop. But ______ are still popular, because all the different shops are in the same place.

4 There are lots of ______ out on the streets today but the book shop doesn't look very popular – there aren't many ______ inside.

5 After the meal, we paid the ______ and the waiter brought our ______.

6 In most shops, you get a ______ for the things you buy – it shows how much everything ______.

Verbs + prepositions

3 2.11 **Choose the correct word to complete the phrases in bold in each sentence. Listen and check.**

1 When I go shopping, I always **pay for / in** cash.
2 **Write up / down** what you want and I'll go to the supermarket for you.
3 Please **take on / off** your wet boots before you go into the house.
4 It's raining so **put on / back** your raincoat before you go out.
5 Did you **pay back / for** the online shopping by credit card?
6 Most shops give you 30 days to **take on / back** anything you don't want.

4 **Complete the sentences with some of the phrases from Exercise 3.**

1 Excuse me, did you ______ that drink? Can you show me your receipt?
2 I need to ______ these shoes. They are hurting my feet.
3 Here's the bill. Would you like to ______ cash or by credit card?
4 I always ______ what I want to buy before I go to the supermarket.

Collocations with verbs

5 2.12 **Complete the sentences with the words in the box. Listen and check.**

do | catch | for | go | keep | save

1 Do you prefer to ______ shopping with your friends or with your mum?
2 You can ______ money for a new computer game if you stop buying chocolate and cakes!
3 We usually ______ the bus when we want to go to the shopping centre.
4 The bill was £9 and 20 pence, so Dad gave the waiter £10 and told him to ______ the change.
5 'Mum, there's no milk left.' 'It's OK – I'm going to ______ the shopping later.'
6 There are some lovely clothes ______ sale in that shop.

▶ Vocabulary reference, page 158 ▶ Workbook Unit 6: Vocabulary, page 47, exercises 1, 2, 3

LISTENING | 3-option multiple choice (monologues and dialogues)

1 **In pairs or as a group, look at the photo above and answer the questions.**

1 Who usually pays for your clothes?

2 Have you ever saved your money to buy something special? What was it?

EXAM SKILL

Listening for the main idea

- You don't need to understand every word and detail to know what a speaker is saying. Often you only need to understand the main idea, message, topic, point or purpose of what you hear.
- Listen right to the end of somebody speaking to identify the main point or the overall message.

2 2.13 **Listen and decide. Which speaker talks about:**

a) a problem he/she has? ____

b) a reason for doing something? ____

c) a plan for the future? ____

d) a request to someone? ____

OPTIMISE YOUR EXAM

3-option multiple choice (monologues and dialogues)

- Before each question, you will read a sentence which tells you who the speakers are, for example, *You will hear a customer talking to a shop assistant.*
- The next question tells you what to listen for. Underline the key words in the question. For example, *What does the customer say the problem is?*
- After the question, there are three choices for your answer, A, B or C. You must choose only one. As you listen, focus on the information that relates to the words you've underlined in the question. Then choose your answer.

3 2.14 **For each question, choose the correct answer.**

1 You will hear a customer talking to a shop assistant.
What's the problem with the trousers?
A They aren't big enough.
B They aren't the right colour.
C They aren't the correct length.

2 You will hear a girl, Maisie, talking to her father.
What does Maisie want to do later?
A play the piano
B go out with her parents
C finish some school work

3 You will hear a mother talking to her son about their holiday.
What does she want her son to do?
A feed their pet
B pack his suitcase
C help put things in the car

4 You will hear two friends talking about their weekend plans.
Why is the boy happy?
A He likes making camp fires.
B He enjoys swimming.
C He loves having his dog with him.

5 You will hear a boy talking to his friend.
What does the boy need to buy?
A some new trainers
B the team's shirt
C a new racket

4 2.14 **Listen again and check your answers.**

THINK | RESEARCH | CULTURE | LEARN | ME

Work in pairs or groups and answer the questions.

- Do you think people buy more or less than in the past?
- Is this a good or bad thing? Why?

▶ **Workbook Unit 6:** Listening, page 48, exercises 1, 2, 3

GRAMMAR 2 | Present perfect simple and past simple

Grammar in context

Read these sentences from the audio in the listening lesson. Then answer the questions.

1 ***I didn't realise** until **I got back home** …*

2 ***I've** just **given** the cat some food …*

a) Which sentence tells us about a past action that is linked to the present? ____

b) Which tells us about a completed action in the past? ____

REMEMBER

- We use the present perfect to talk about an action which happened in the past and is linked to the present:
  *Katie **has put** her clothes in the suitcase.* (Her clothes are in the suitcase now. We don't know when she put them in.)
- We use the past simple to talk about a finished action:
  *Katie **put** her clothes in her suitcase last night.* (We know when she did it.)
- We use the present perfect to report information or news:
  ***I've bought** some new shoes.*
- We use the past simple to give details or explanations:
  *I **bought** some shoes at the new department store last Saturday.*

▶ **See Grammar reference, Unit 6,** page 150

1 Choose the correct verb form to complete each sentence.

1 You don't need to buy anything for the barbecue. **I've done** / **did** all the shopping already.

2 I'm sorry, we don't have that necklace anymore. A customer **has bought** / **bought** the last one this morning.

3 Oh, no! **I've lost** / **lost** my credit card. I can't find it anywhere.

4 The department store sale **has started** / **started** last week. It's been really popular with shoppers.

5 **Have you sold** / **Did you sell** many of those bags yesterday?

6 'Is that jacket new?' 'No, I **had** / **'ve had** it for years!'

2 Write pairs of sentences using the prompts. Use the present perfect in one sentence and the past simple in the other sentence.

1 I / spend / my money. I / buy / a pair of shoes.
I've spent my money. I bought a pair of shoes.

2 The boys / walk / into town. They / leave / at 2 o'clock.
____

3 I / get / Mum / a present for her birthday. I / pay / €10 for it.
____

4 He / not like / his old flat. He / live / in three different flats this year.
____

5 She / lose / an earring. She / drop / it in the street.
____

6 I / not wear / these boots before. My / old ones / be / very comfortable.
____

3 Complete the text using the correct form of the verbs in brackets.

YOUNG DESIGNER

(1) ______________ (**you ever** / **make**) your own clothes – perhaps with your mum, grandma or at school? I (2) ______________ (**start**) to design my own clothes when I was 13. At first, I (3) ______________ (**look**) at lots of different fashion magazines to see what people were wearing. But quite quickly I (4) ______________ (**decide**) to try to make my own designs. When I (5) ______________ (**tell**) my parents that I (6) ______________ (**want**) to be a designer, they (7) ______________ (**think**) it was a great idea, and they (8) ______________ (**help**) me to make my dream come true.

I (9) ______________ (**begin**) making my own clothes in 2015, and I (10) ______________ (**learn**) a lot in the last few years. Last year, I (11) ______________ (**meet**) some other young clothes designers. We (12) ______________ (**share**) a lot of ideas together online, and now we are planning to have a pop-up shop near the beach next summer.

THINK | RESEARCH | CULTURE | LEARN | **ME**

Work in pairs. Take turns to give your partner some news about something that has happened to you recently. Ask for some extra information about your partner's news.
I've bought some new jeans. *Where did you get them?*

6 SPEAKING | Discussion (pictures)

Talk2Me
I've always liked …

Flipped classroom

1 **Watch the *Talk2Me* video and answer the questions.**

1 What do Evie and Jojo decide to do to get some money?
2 What does Jojo learn when she calls the community centre?
3 How much money do they make? Why?

2 **Watch the video again. Underline the phrases in the *Phrase expert* box that you hear on the video.**

> **PHRASE EXPERT**
> I've never been to … | I've always liked … | Have you ever …? | I never knew … | I would love to do this. | I really liked …

3 **Work in pairs and answer the questions.**

1 How often do you go shopping?
2 Where do you usually go shopping?
3 Who do you usually go shopping with?

> **EXAM SKILL**
> ### Describing and expressing opinions
> - We often describe something before we give an opinion about it.
> - For objects, you can talk about what something looks like: its colour, shape or size or if it's expensive or cheap.
> - For activities, you can talk about your connection to the activity, for example, *I've never been to a big shopping centre.*

4 2.15 **Listen to two students talking about some shops. Write which shop they are talking about. What do they see to help them identify each shop?**

5 **Choose the opinion from the box that the boy and girl have about each shop.**

> boring | doesn't like | hates | interesting | likes | loves

1 **Bicycle shop:** ________
2 **Clothes shop:** ________
3 **Grocery shop:** ________
4 **Chemist:** ________
5 **Butcher's:** ________

> **OPTIMISE YOUR EXAM**
> ### Discussion (pictures)
> - You and your partner will have between one and two minutes to talk about some pictures.
> - Look at the pictures and think why you like/don't like the activities. For example, *I love clothes shopping because I like to wear different clothes every day.*
> - Give reasons for why you like/don't like something.

6 **In pairs, do the exam task. Look at the question and pictures and discuss.**

Here are some pictures of **different fashions**. Do you like these different fashions? Say why or why not.

Do you like these different fashions?

7 **Take it in turns to ask and answer these questions.**

Student A: Do you think fashion is important? Which of these fashions do you like best?

Student B: Do you think clothes are too expensive? Which of these fashions do you like best?

> THINK | **RESEARCH** | CULTURE | LEARN | ME
>
> Work in pairs or groups.
> 1 Go online and find out the name of an interesting place to shop where you live.
> 2 Note down the opening hours, address, phone number and website details. Find an interesting fact about the shop or what they sell.
> 3 Report back to the class.

▶ **Workbook Unit 6:** Speaking, page 48, exercises 1, 2

1 Work in pairs. Put the dialogue in the correct order (1–4). Then practise saying the dialogue together.

Yeah, we could really save money! ____

Do you want to go shopping tomorrow? ____

OK. I'll ask my mum for my pocket money! ____

Yes, sure. Everything's on sale now, isn't it? ____

EXAM SKILL

Identifying words that go together

- Compound nouns and collocations are two or more words that often go together. For example, *bus stop*, *have fun*, *pocket money*.
- Sometimes in an exam task, one of the missing words forms part of a compound noun or a collocation.
- It's useful to learn words as part of a whole phrase. For example, *web **page***, ***save** money*, ***catch** the bus*, etc.).

2 Read the dialogue in Exercise 1 again and underline two words that go together in each sentence.

3 Match the first part of each sentence (1–6) with the second part of the sentence (a–f).

1 I'd quite like to be a shop
2 I think online
3 Oh no – I think I left my credit
4 Very long skirts are in
5 There's a big department
6 The best place to go would be the shopping

a) store on the corner by the bank.
b) card in that new shop.
c) fashion at the moment.
d) assistant because you meet lots of people.
e) centre as it has everything you need.
f) shopping is much easier than going to the city centre.

OPTIMISE YOUR EXAM

3-option multiple-choice cloze

- Remember that some words go together to make phrases.
- Try all the answer options in the gap. If one sounds more 'right' than the others, it may be a compound noun or a collocation.
- When you have answered all the questions, read the text again with the answers you chose, to check they make sense in context.

4 For each question, choose the correct answer.

The fashion exhibition

There are a lot of museums that include fashion in their exhibitions. Many museums **(1)** ____ on special exhibitions to show things made by today's designers or designers from the past. It can be difficult to work with clothes from the past, because the materials can break easily. The clothes are kept carefully and they always have a **(2)** ____ of special people to work on the displays. Many **(3)** ____ are very interested in these exhibitions as they **(4)** ____ us how we lived in the past. One thing that often surprises people is that several **(5)** ____ ago we were all much shorter. Exhibitions of clothes designers who are still making clothes today are also very **(6)** ____ with people, as they help us to understand modern culture.

	A	B	C
1	put	have	make
2	team	band	class
3	fans	guests	visitors
4	explain	show	see
5	times	histories	centuries
6	popular	important	favourite

THINK | RESEARCH | CULTURE | LEARN | ME

Work with a partner and ask and answer the questions.

- Have you been to a good exhibition in your country?
- What was it?
- What would you like to see at an exhibition?

WRITING | Guided writing (a note)

1 In pairs or groups, answer the questions.

1 What kind of things do you like to buy when you go shopping? What do you or your family buy online?

2 Have you ever bought anything that had a problem? What was wrong with it? What did you do?

EXAM SKILL

Using a variety of tenses

- You often need to use a variety of tenses in your answer. These can include present, past, future and perfect tenses.
- Pay attention to the tenses in the instructions. If they tell you to say what you did, make sure you use a past tense in your answer; if they tell you to say what you will do, use a future tense.

2 Read the task below and the students' answers. Match the texts (A and B) to the teacher's comments (1 and 2).

You bought something, but there is a problem with it. Write a note to your English friend, Alex.

> In your note:
> - tell Alex what you bought
> - say what the problem is
> - ask Alex for advice.

Write **25 words** or more.

A

I bought a pair of trainers last week. They're really bad. There is a problem with them. I don't know what to do.

B

I bought some trainers online, but they don't fit. When I run in them, they really hurt my feet. What should I do? Do you think I should return them and ask for my money back?

1 ____

This is quite a good answer. You have used a variety of tenses, including the present perfect. You've covered all the bullet points. Your answer is longer than 25 words.

2 ____

This is not a good answer. You haven't used a variety of tenses. You haven't covered all of the bullet points. You need to write more for the second bullet point and ask Alex for advice in the third bullet point. Your answer is too short: it needs to be 25 words or more.

3 Read another student's answer to the task in Exercise 2. Choose the best words or phrases to complete the text.

(1) The last week / A week ago, I (2) bought / have bought a pair of trainers. (3) Unfortunately / Exactly, they're the wrong size and I (4) can't / didn't wear them. (5) Do you think / I'm thinking I should return them and get my money back?

OPTIMISE YOUR EXAM

Guided writing (a note)

- The points/questions you need to cover in your note will be clearly given in the exam question.
- Make sure you answer the three points in the same order as they appear in the exam task.
- Use the correct tenses in your answer.
- The main body of your note can be just three sentences long.

4 **Look at this exam task and make notes to answer the questions.**

You want to go shopping to buy a gift for one of your grandparents. Write a note to your English friend, Reese.

In your note:
- tell Reese who the gift is for
- ask Reese to come shopping
- say what you want to buy.

Write **25 words** or more.

1 Who is the gift for?
____

2 What do you want Reese to do?
____

3 What other information must you include?
____

4 How many words should you write?
____

5 Which tenses should you use?
____

6 Which words or phrases from this unit could you use?
____

5 **Plan** **Plan your note. Use the table to help you.**

	Detail	Useful language	My notes
Point 1			
Point 2			
Point 3			

6 **Write** **Write your note in an appropriate style. Write 25 words or more.**

7 **Check** **Before you hand in your note, complete this checklist.**

Checklist

- ◯ I've followed my writing plan.
- ◯ I've said who the gift is for.
- ◯ I've asked Reese to go shopping.
- ◯ I've said what I want to buy.
- ◯ I've used the correct tenses.
- ◯ I've used a good range of vocabulary.
- ◯ I've written 25+ words.
- ◯ I've checked my spelling, grammar and punctuation.

▶ **Workbook Unit 6:** Writing, page 50, exercises 1, 2, 3, 4 and Progress check 6, page 51

PROGRESS CHECK UNITS 5–6

GRAMMAR AND VOCABULARY

1 Complete the sentences using the correct form of the verbs in brackets.

1 Pria ____________ (**walk**) to school yesterday. She's never done that before!
2 ____________ you ____________ (**work**) in a shop before or is this the first time?
3 I ________________ (**buy**) a few things there last week, but there isn't much choice.
4 ____________ you ____________ (**wear**) a school uniform when you were younger?
5 I think I ________________ (**lose**) my watch. I can't find it anywhere.
6 We ________________ (**never shop**) in any of the big clothes shops in London.
7 Are those new jeans? I ________________ (**not see**) them before.
8 Alfie ____________ (**not like**) his birthday present so Mum took it back to the shop.

__/8

2 Choose the correct word to complete each sentence.

1 I sometimes find it difficult to **say** / **start** a conversation with new people.
2 Can you help me download this new **mouse** / **software**, please.
3 Do you want to try **out** / **on** this shirt? It's a really nice colour.
4 I couldn't **open** / **start** the file you sent me. Was there a problem with it?
5 How much did you pay **for** / **with** those trainers? I think they are cheaper online.
6 We haven't decided where to go this weekend. I'll **make** / **send** a text when I know the plan.
7 I'm sorry, we don't take credit cards. We only take **cash** / **change**.
8 Their new laptop has a really big **camera** / **screen** – it's great for online gaming.

__/8

3 Choose the correct word or phrase to fill each gap.

Fashion designer Dhillan Bhardwaj (**1**) ____ his first shop at the age of 18. A few months later he was a millionaire. He (**2**) ____ making clothes at home after he left school. (**3**) ____ friends saw his first designs and they asked him to make clothes for them. He put photos on social media and suddenly lots of people (**4**) ____ him to make (**5**) ____ clothes. The clothes were (**6**) ____ popular than he expected and (**7**) ____ of people bought them. Dhillan soon needed help making the clothes. Now his brand, Ratchet, is the (**8**) ____ independent clothing company in the UK.

	A	B	C
1	**A** opened	**B** opens	**C** has opened
2	**A** begin	**B** began	**C** has begun
3	**A** Much	**B** Few	**C** Some
4	**A** wanted	**B** want	**C** have wanted
5	**A** their	**B** your	**C** her
6	**A** more	**B** many	**C** most
7	**A** lots	**B** any	**C** many
8	**A** large	**B** larger	**C** largest

__/8

4 **Complete the paragraph with the words in the box.**

biggest	ever	has	in	lots	much	never	older	some	than

How are you? School (**1**) ___________ finished here for the holidays. We're visiting my cousin (**2**) ___________ Denmark. Have you (**3**) ___________ been there? I don't know (**4**) ___________ about the place, but I've looked at (**5**) ___________ of pictures online. They live in Copenhagen, which is bigger (**6**) ___________ my town. I think it's the (**7**) ___________ city in Denmark. My cousin is (**8**) ___________ than me. I've (**9**) ___________ met her. I'll send you (**10**) ___________ photos.

__/10

5 **Choose the correct word or phrase to complete each sentence.**

1 I didn't work very hard today. I sent **a few** / **much** emails, then read a magazine.
2 Not **much** / **many** people buy things in that shop – it's very expensive.
3 I'm going on holiday next week. I need to get **lots** / **any** of new clothes before I go.
4 There were too **many** / **much** people in the shopping centre, so we left.
5 **Some** / **A little** people say that this is the best computer game ever.
6 I could only understand a **few** / **little** of what he was saying. He speaks really quickly.
7 How **many** / **much** money do you usually spend on clothes in a year?
8 Excuse me, do you have **any** / **much** of these trainers in a size 10?

__/8

6 **Read the descriptions. What is the word for each one? The first letter is given.**

1 A large shop where people buy food is a s_ _ _ _ _ _ _ _ _ _ .
2 A program that makes computers do different things is a piece of s_ _ _ _ _ _ _ .
3 When you use the internet you are o_ _ _ _ _ .
4 The people who buy things in a shop are called c_ _ _ _ _ _ _ _ .
5 You can use this to pay for things you buy: c_ _ _ _ _ c_ _ _ .
6 Pictures made by computers are called g_ _ _ _ _ _ _ .
7 When you write on a computer, you use a k_ _ _ _ _ _ _ .
8 You do this when you copy programs or music from the internet: d_ _ _ _ _ _ _ .

__/8

Total score __/50

EXAM SKILLS

Tick the statements that are true for you. Review the skills in the unit if you need more help.

I can …	Unit/page
☐ understand the text type	Unit 5 p48
☐ understand when things happen	Unit 5 p52
☐ talk about preferences	Unit 5 p54
☐ use determiners	Unit 5 p55
☐ use linking words in a story	Unit 5 p56
☐ understand linking words and phrases	Unit 6 p58
☐ listen for the main idea	Unit 6 p62
☐ describe and express opinions	Unit 6 p64
☐ identify words that go together	Unit 6 p65
☐ use a variety of tenses in a note	Unit 6 p66

7 The future of learning

READING | 3-option multiple choice (long text) | A news article

1 In pairs or as a group, answer the questions.

1 Do you use technology in your classroom? What do you use it for?

2 What do you think the students in the picture on page 71 are using the laptop for?

EXAM SKILL

Multiple-choice questions

- Look at the question. Before reading the three options, try to answer the question by yourself.
- Then read the three options and look for one that is similar to your idea/answer.
- Check the other options and decide why they are wrong.
- Finally, read the text again and make sure that the answer you have chosen is correct.

2 Read the paragraph and answer the question.

School of the Air is a school for children in Australia who live far away from cities and towns and can't get to school. When School of the Air started, the teachers and students had special radios for their lessons, but now internet technology is helping students to learn. They use video chat in their homes to have their lessons and it feels like they're all in a normal classroom because they can see each other on their screens.

How does technology help children in Australia?

____

3 Look at the answers below. Is there one that is similar to your answer?

a) Technology helps them feel part of a school.

b) Students who live far away from cities and towns can now have lessons.

c) They can chat with other students in their class.

OPTIMISE YOUR EXAM

3-option multiple choice (long text)

- The order of the questions follows the order of the information in the text, unless there is a global question which will often be the final question (question 5).
- Underline the answers to the questions in the text and write the number of the question in the margin to help you find any answers you aren't sure about.

TECHNOLOGY FOR ALL

1 In classrooms around the world, many students now have computers or tablets on their desks instead of books. Technology is helping young people to learn about the world, and preparing them for work. But in poorer countries, there aren't any computers available for students.

2 That was a problem for schools in the countryside in Uganda, in East Africa. But since 2007, the Mobile Solar Computer Classroom has helped many classes of children and adults at schools and libraries to use computers. There are two mobile computer classrooms, and they travel all over the country in two large cars, going to schools to give computer lessons. Later today, one of them is going to visit a village in the west of the country.

It's a long way down a difficult road, but the drivers are lucky because it isn't going to rain, and that helps. In the car, there are 15 laptop computers, desks and chairs, two ICT* teachers and a large battery. This produces solar energy for the computers, because many of the villages don't have electricity.

3 More than 200 people a day can have computer lessons from the two mobile classrooms. This means over 5,000 people have these lessons each year! What are they going to do next? Well, over the next few years, they are going to build computer classrooms in 55 Ugandan schools. Teachers and students know how important computers will be in the future and these classrooms will really help students prepare for a job in tomorrow's world.

* Information and Communications Technology

4 2.16 **Read the article about mobile classrooms. For each question, choose the correct answer.**

1 How does technology help young people?
   A They don't need to buy books.
   B It teaches them about important things.
   C It shows them how to find jobs.
2 What is special about the Mobile Solar Computer Classroom?
   A It brings technology to the countryside.
   B It has two classrooms.
   C It gives lessons in libraries.
3 Where in the country does the mobile classroom go?
   A to villages in the west
   B the whole of Uganda
   C to the eastern part of the country
4 Why is there a large battery in the car?
   A to give energy to the villages
   B so the car can travel far and fast
   C so the computers can work
5 What is the plan for the future?
   A to teach more students each year
   B to put computer classrooms in schools
   C to teach students why computers are important

5 Write a highlighted word from the text to match each definition.

1 older people, not children ____________
2 an object in a car, radio, etc. that gives it electricity ____________
3 small, mobile computers that are bigger than mobile phones but smaller than laptops ____________
4 work that you do to make money ____________
5 places where you can borrow books ____________
6 when something good happens as a result of good luck ____________
7 the people who drive vehicles like trains, buses and cars ____________
8 the area outside towns and cities ____________

THINK | RESEARCH | CULTURE | LEARN | ME

Work in pairs. Make a list of the different ways you can use computers to help you learn.

▶ **Workbook Unit 7:** Reading, pages 52–53, exercises 1, 2, 3, 4

Grammar in context

Find these sentences in the text on page 71 and then answer the question.

1 *Later today, one of them* ***is going to visit*** *a village in the west of the country.* (paragraph 2)

2 *... but the drivers are lucky because it* ***isn't going to rain****, and that helps.* (paragraph 2)

3 *What* ***are they going to do*** *next?* (paragraph 3)

What are these sentences about? Choose the correct answer.

a) the present ____

b) the past ____

c) the future ____

REMEMBER

- We use *going to* to talk about future plans: *I'm* ***going to buy*** *a new bike next week.*
- We also use *going to* when we predict something because of what we see now: *She's playing very well. I think she'****s going to win****.*

▶ **See Grammar reference, Unit 7,** page 150

1 **Complete the conversation with the correct form of *going to*.**

Teacher: You need to finish your project about the town by Friday. What are your plans?

Alicia: Well, I (**1**) ___am going to___ write the introduction today and then Demir (**2**) ______________ check it tomorrow.

Demir: After I've checked it, Alicia and I (**3**) ______________ take some pictures for the cover.

Teacher: But you can't do that tomorrow, because Alicia (**4**) ______________ be at school. She (**5**) ______________ go on a school trip.

Demir: Yes, I know. We (**6**) ______________ do it on Wednesday.

Alicia: Then on Thursday, Demir (**7**) ______________ write about the history of the town.

Teacher: (**8**) ______________ use the internet, Demir?

Demir: Yes, I am, because I need to get some more information.

Alicia: I (**9**) ______________ use the internet. I don't need it for my part of the project.

Teacher: Well, you seem to have everything organised. I think your project (**10**) ______________ be really good!

2 **Complete the sentences using the correct form of *going to* and the verbs in brackets.**

1 Giulio ______________ (**study**) English in London next summer. He's very excited.

2 Maria and Marco ______________ (**not win**) the race – they're right at the back.

3 What ______________ she ______________ (**do**) next year?

4 I ______________ (**not go**) to school tomorrow because it's a holiday.

5 My sister ______________ (**be**) a doctor when she finishes university.

6 It's very cold today. I think it ______________ (**snow**).

3 **Complete the text with the verbs in the box and the correct form of *going to*.**

be (× 3)	have	meet
not go	not use	study

BIG School

I'm a student at City Montessori School in Lucknow, the largest school in the world. There are over 50,000 students at the school. At the moment, there are 45 students in my class, but next term there (**1**) ______________ more because it's very popular. This morning we have maths. We often use computers in class, but today we (**2**) ______________ them because we (**3**) ______________ a test. After that, I (**4**) ______________ in one of the libraries. I love the libraries here. They're always quiet and there are thousands of books to read.

There are also lots of events at my school. Next month, there (**5**) ______________ a children's film festival here. Unfortunately, I have exams so I (**6**) ______________ , but my friends are. They (**7**) ______________ children from all over the world at the festival. It (**8**) ______________ great.

SAY IT RIGHT

Resource centre: Unit 7
Pronunciation of *going to*

Words connected with *school and studying*

1 2.17 **Put the words in the box into the correct category. Listen and check.**

biology | ~~board~~ | bookshelf | desk
dictionary | eraser | geography | history
learn | maths | music | physics
practise | remember | study | teach

things in the classroom	school subjects	verbs for things people do at school
board	____	____
____	____	____
____	____	____
____	____	____
____	____	____
	____	

2 **Read the sentences. Which subject from Exercise 1 is each one about?**

1 Today we're going to learn about the kings and queens of France.
____
2 The longest river in Europe is the Volga.
____
3 All animals need water to live.
____
4 What is 12 × 6?
____
5 In today's lesson, we're going to look at how aeroplanes fly.
____
6 Now, let's sing that again.
____

Words + prepositions

3 2.18 **Choose the best word (A, B or C) for each gap. Listen and check.**

1 You can learn a lot ____ books.
A on **B** for **C** from
2 You need to use technology when you study or are ____ work.
A at **B** to **C** for
3 Today we're going to learn ____ how the stomach works.
A for **B** on **C** about
4 Do you need any help ____ your homework?
A to **B** with **C** at
5 I usually arrive ____ school just before 9am.
A to **B** for **C** at
6 You can borrow three books ____ the library at one time.
A from **B** to **C** for

Collocations with verbs

4 2.19 **Match the nouns (a–f) to the verbs (1–6) to make phrases. Listen and check.**

1 do _d_ **a)** a course
2 draw ____ **b)** to university
3 take ____ **c)** school
4 leave ____ ~~**d)** homework~~
5 go ____ **e)** a foreign language
6 learn ____ **f)** a picture

5 **Complete the sentences using phrases from Exercise 4.**

1 In our art lesson today we're going to ____________ of these flowers.
2 Jess is going to live in a different country for the summer so that she can ____________ .
3 I'm going to ____________ in photography.
4 Would you like to ____________ when you finish school?
5 The students have to ____________ every evening.
6 Most students in the UK ____________ when they're 18.

THINK | RESEARCH | CULTURE | LEARN | ME

Work in pairs and answer the questions.

- What do you like most about school? Why?
- What are your favourite subjects? Why?
- How much time do you spend doing homework every day?

7 LISTENING | Gap fill

1 Work in pairs and answer the questions.

1 Who do you ask when you need help with your homework?
2 Would you like to have someone to talk to about it online? Why / Why not?

EXAM SKILL

Thinking about the missing information

- Look carefully at the words before the gaps.
- If there is a preposition before the gap, think about which words can and can't follow it.
- For example, in Exercise 4, question 3, you need to listen for a period of time – probably a month or year because the gap follows the preposition *in*.

2 Complete the table with the words in the box.

afternoon | Amsterdam | Halloween
March | night | Paris | Wednesday
2018 | 3:20

in	months and years, e.g. in September, in 1850, __________, __________ towns and countries, e.g. in Manchester, Spain, __________, __________ time of the day, e.g. in the morning, in the __________
on	days of the week, e.g. on Tuesday, on your birthday, __________
at	time of the day, e.g. at 10:30, at midday, __________, __________ holiday time, e.g. at New Year, at half term, __________

3 Delete the word or phrase that CANNOT complete the sentence.

1 Alice lives in:
England | a city | a village | a computer
2 She teaches on Mondays and:
Tuesdays | Wednesdays | evenings | Fridays
3 She started teaching online in:
December | January | 2017 | London
4 The subjects she helps with are:
history | geography | study | English
5 She has photos of:
online | flowers | trees | her family

OPTIMISE YOUR EXAM

Gap fill

- Before you listen, read the information carefully and decide what sort of word you need to write for each answer.
- Don't worry if you don't hear all the answers the first time you listen.
- When you listen again, write any answers you missed and check that your spelling is correct.

4 2.20 For each question, write the correct answer in the gap. Write one word or a number or a date or a time.

You will hear a woman talking about how she helps children in Argentina.

Alice

Lives in: *England*
Works for: (1) __________
Helps: (2) __________
Started job in: (3) __________
Biggest class size: (4) __________ *students*
Teaches: (5) *English and* __________

5 2.20 Listen again and check your answers.

THINK | RESEARCH | CULTURE | LEARN | ME

Write down five questions you would like to ask someone your age who lives in India.

▶ **Workbook Unit 7 :** Listening, page 56, exercises 1, 2

GRAMMAR 2 | *will* and *going to*

Grammar in context

Look at these sentences. Match the descriptions (a–e) to the sentences (1–5).

1 *So, what **am I going to teach** them today?* ____
2 *I know! **I'll talk** about this interview.* ____
3 *They'**ll** probably **ask** lots of questions …* ____
4 ***I'm going to teach** a new class now.* ____
5 ***I'll tell** you all about it next time.* ____

a) offering to do something
b) asking about a plan that has already been made
c) saying/predicting what you think will happen
d) deciding to do something
e) saying what you know is going to happen

REMEMBER

- We use *will* when we decide to do something at that moment: *It's cold. **I'll close** the window.*
- We use *will* when we make offers: ***I'll go** and buy the bread and milk.*
- We use *will* when we say/predict what we think will happen: *The lesson **will be** interesting. We **won't be** bored.*
- We use *going to* when we already have a plan: ***I'm** not **going to be** at home on Saturday morning. **I'm going to play** tennis with Ali.*
- We use *going to* when it is something we can see or know about: *It says on the radio that there's been an accident. He**'s going to be** late.*

▶ **See Grammar reference, Unit 7,** page 150

1 Choose the correct answer to complete each sentence.

1 I'll / **'m going to** study English at summer school in July. I've got my plane tickets already.
2 The teacher has just given us lots of homework. **I'll / 'm going to** stay at home tonight and study.
3 I'm new here. **Will you / Are you going to** show me where the library is, please?
4 'Are you going to be away in July?' 'No. We **aren't going to go / won't go** on holiday until August this year.'
5 'Who wants to read the first sentence?' '**I'll / 'm going to** do it.'
6 We've got tickets for the school concert on Friday so we **aren't going to / won't** go to the party.

2 Complete the conversation using *will* or *going to* and the verbs in brackets.

Daniel: So, we need a plan for the end-of-term garden party on Friday.
Casilda: The teacher said we **(1)** ____________ (**make**) the posters in art class tomorrow.
Pete: And everyone knows I **(2)** ____________ (**sell**) the tickets.
Magda: What can I do?
Daniel: Hmm, let me think … **(3)** __________ you __________ (**choose**) the music, please?
Magda: Yes, of course. I **(4)** ____________ (**buy**) the drinks as well.
Daniel: Good idea. Thanks. What about the food?
Pete: My mum **(5)** ____________ (**prepare**) some pizzas. I asked her yesterday.
Casilda: Great! Everyone is talking about it, so I think lots of people **(6)** ____________ (**come**).
Pete: Oh, and **(7)** __________ you __________ (**check**) the weather forecast for Friday, Daniel?
Daniel: I checked my phone earlier, Pete. It says it **(8)** ____________ (**be**) sunny.

3 Read the article about how children get to school in a village in China. Complete the text with one word in each gap.

It's Monday morning and 12-year-old Yi Feng Li is **(1)** __________ to go to school. But he isn't **(2)** __________ to walk or take a bus. He and the other children in Atuler **(3)** __________ going to climb 800 metres down the side of a mountain, using a ladder. It takes 90 minutes and it is one of the most dangerous journeys to school in the world.

However, some of the people in the village believe this **(4)** __________ change soon. A Chinese photographer visited the village and took some photos of the journey. 'We want people to see how dangerous it is for the children. And we think they **(5)** __________ help.'

Lots of important people have now seen the photos and have discussed what they can do to help. Next year, they are going **(6)** __________ build some new steps for the children to use. The journey **(7)** __________ still take a long time, but it **(8)** __________ be a lot safer.

▶ **Workbook Unit 7:** Grammar 2, page 55, exercise 1

7 SPEAKING | Questions

Talk2Me
I've always liked …

Flipped classroom

1 **Watch the *Talk2Me* video and answer the questions.**

1 Why do the twins look sad?
2 How much will they earn a day?
3 When do they start work?

2 **Watch the video again. Underline the phrases in the *Phrase expert* box that you hear on the video.**

> **PHRASE EXPERT**
> In (one year's) time / the future
> One day, I plan to … | Next week/month/year | tomorrow | tonight | When I (leave school) …

3 **Work in pairs and answer the questions.**

1 What are the best and worst things about going to school?
2 How old are students when they leave school in your country?
3 How will school prepare you for the future?

> **EXAM SKILL**
> ### Talking about the future
> - Remember to use *going to* and not *will* when talking about your plans for the future.
> - Use *will* when you decide to do something while you're speaking. For example, *I'll open the door for you.*
> - You can also use *I would like to … / I'd like to …* to talk about hopes and desires or the future. For example, *I'd like to be a teacher.*

4 2.21 **Write the questions in the correct order. Listen and check.**

1 you / to / going / exams / term / Are / take / this / ?
____
2 pass / classmates / Will / the / your / test / ?
____
3 study / will / languages / you / What / year / next / ?
____
4 study / summer holidays / Are / to / in / going / you / the / ?
____

5 2.21 **Listen again and complete the responses.**

1 No, we're not going to take any exams until ________.
2 Yes, they are studying really hard, so I think they ________ pass.
3 I think I'll study French and English ________ .
4 No, when school finishes for the holidays, I ________ work at a summer camp.

> **OPTIMISE YOUR EXAM**
> ### Questions
> - Listen carefully to the questions the examiner asks you. Make sure you use the correct structure or phrase to talk about the future.
> - If you're unsure of your answer about the future, you can say *I think…* or *Perhaps …*
> - There are no right or wrong answers in this part of the exam, so you can invent an answer if necessary.

6 **Work in pairs. Take turns asking and answering the questions below. Make notes of your partner's answers.**

1 What are your favourite subjects at school?
____
2 What subjects are you going to study in the future?
____
3 How many hours of homework are you going to do this week?
____
4 What are you going to do when you finish school today?
____
5 Tell me something about what you will do when you leave school.
____

THINK | **RESEARCH** | CULTURE | LEARN | ME

Talk to some students about what they are going to do when they finish school.

1 **Work in pairs. Look at the photo in Exercise 5 and answer the questions.**

1 What do you think is happening?
2 Can you do this in your school?

EXAM SKILL

Commonly confused words

- Sometimes the answer options are both from the same topic. For example, *teach* and *learn* are both to do with school and education.
- Although some words may seem similar, their meanings are often very different or they may even be opposites, for example *lend* and *borrow*.
- If you're not sure what the answer is, think of example sentences where you can use the words and see if that helps you to choose the correct word.

2 **Choose the correct word to complete each sentence.**

1 I **made** / **did** an English test this morning.
2 Do you usually **have** / **do** lunch at 2pm?
3 I'm going to **learn** / **make** French next year.
4 Please **do** / **does** Exercise 3 for homework.
5 He doesn't want to **make** / **do** a mistake.
6 It's a good idea to **do** / **take** notes in class.

3 **Complete the sentences with the words in the box.**

did	do	had	make	take

1 How often do you ____________ sport at school?
2 I ____________ dinner for everyone on Saturdays because I enjoy cooking.
3 Everyone ____________ very well in yesterday's test.
4 We ____________ an English class at 9:30 this morning.
5 Lots of students ____________ the bus to school.

4 **Work in pairs. Read the text in Exercise 5 quickly and answer the question.**

Who do students work with?

a) the teacher **b)** other students **c)** their parents

OPTIMISE YOUR EXAM

3-option multiple-choice cloze

- Many everyday phrases are formed with *make* and *do* and can be confused so they are often tested in the exam.
- Learn collocations with these verbs to get them right. For example, *do homework*, *do an exercise*, *make a mistake*, *make a cake* etc.
- Keep a list of collocations and test yourself regularly.

5 **For each question, choose the correct answer.**

Playing is learning

There are now many computer games that students can play in the classroom. For some games, students can work in small teams and can (**1**) ____ points for their team. There is usually a prize for when they do something like answering questions in lessons or helping classmates with their homework. They can also lose points when they (**2**) ____ something wrong. Most games are designed so that when students do (**3**) ____ in class they can move up a level in the game. Working in (**4**) ____ helps students to (**5**) ____ friends with other students and gets them to work together. In games like *Classcraft*, parents can also (**6**) ____ online and see how their children are doing in the game and in class.

	A	B	C
1	**A** have	**B** get	**C** take
2	**A** do	**B** decide	**C** act
3	**A** fine	**B** good	**C** well
4	**A** classes	**B** families	**C** teams
5	**A** get	**B** find	**C** make
6	**A** go	**B** run	**C** turn

THINK | RESEARCH | CULTURE | LEARN | ME

Work in groups. Imagine you are going to play a class computer game. Think of three good things you can do to get points and two bad things you can do to lose points. Share your ideas with the class.

WRITING | Picture story

1 In pairs or groups, answer the questions.

1 How often do you go on trips with your school?

2 What was the best school trip you've been on? Why?

2 Look at the picture story. In pairs or groups, say what you think the story is about.

3 Look at the story in Exercise 2 again. Complete the table with suitable nouns, verbs and adjectives that can describe what you see in the pictures.

	nouns	verbs	adjectives
Picture 1	*museum ...*		
Picture 2		*watch ...*	
Picture 3			*interesting ...*

EXAM SKILL

Using adjectives

- Adjectives make your writing more interesting. Use adjectives ending in *-ed* to describe how people feel, and adjectives ending in *-ing* to describe what something is like. For example, *Lily was bor**ed** because the film was bor**ing***.
- Think how you would feel if you were in the same situation you are writing about. Make a note of adjectives to describe your feelings and then use them in your story.

4 Circle the correct adjectives to complete the sentences.

1 We were **surprised** / **surprising** when our teacher told us about the school trip.

2 The children were **excited** / **exciting** about their school trip.

3 Henry said that the Science Museum was very **interested** / **interesting**.

5 Write the adjectives in the correct group.

afraid | awesome | awful | bored | excited | fantastic | great | interesting | sad | scary | strange | tired | unusual | worried

1 Adjectives to say how someone feels:

____

2 Adjectives to describe what something is like:

____

6 Complete the story from Exercise 2 with suitable adjectives from Exercise 5.

On Saturday, Alex and Lucy went to the Science Museum. They were very (**1**) __________ to be there. First, they saw some (**2**) __________ old TVs and phones. Then, Lucy played chess with a robot! She had a (**3**) __________ time. Finally, they went to the gift shop and they bought a souvenir. They had an (**4**) __________ time at the museum!

OPTIMISE YOUR EXAM

Picture story

- Choose a time in the past to set your story. For example, *Yesterday …*, *Last summer …*, *On Saturday …*, etc.
- You can start your story with a time expression, or you can put the time expression at the end of a sentence. For example, *Last Saturday, …* or *Alex … last Saturday*.
- Write about what is happening in the pictures, not the small details. For example, *The students were having a lesson*. (this is the main action) / *There were books on their desks*. (this is a small detail)

7 **Look at the story in Exercise 8. Choose the best introductory sentence to set the scene.**

a) The bus was waiting at the school for the students.
b) Last Friday, Lisa and her class went on a school trip.
c) The students were happy about the school trip.

8 **Read the exam task. Write two adjectives to describe each picture.**

Look at the three pictures.
Write the story shown in the pictures.
Write **35 words** or more.

Picture 1 ______________ Picture 2 ______________ Picture 3 ______________

9 Plan

Plan your story. Use the table to help you.

	Who?	**Where?**	**What?**
Picture 1			
Picture 2			
Picture 3			

10 Write

Write your story in an appropriate style. Write 35 words or more.

11 Check

Before you hand in your story, complete this checklist.

Checklist

- ◯ I've followed my writing plan.
- ◯ I've included an introductory sentence.
- ◯ I've written about the three pictures.
- ◯ I've used the correct tenses.
- ◯ I've used linking words.
- ◯ I've used a good range of adjectives.
- ◯ I've written 35+ words.
- ◯ I've checked my spelling, grammar and punctuation.

▶ **Writing reference,** page 164 ▶ **Workbook Unit 7:** Writing, page 58, exercises 1, 2, 3, 4, 5, 6 and Progress check 7, page 59

8 It's only a game

READING | 3-option multiple choice (short texts) | Notices and messages

1 **In pairs or as a group, answer the questions.**

1 What's your favourite sport?
2 How often do you practise?
3 Tell your partner about any sports competitions you have entered.
4 Tell your partner about any prizes you have won.

2 **In pairs, think of different sports. Write the sports in the correct list below.**

Team sports	Sports you play alone
______	______
______	______
______	______
______	______
______	______

EXAM SKILL

Finding ideas that mean the same

- Sometimes you need to understand the overall meaning of a text rather than specific information.
- Look for ideas that have a similar meaning to ideas in the text, for example, *half-price tennis shoes* has the same meaning as *pay less for something to wear*.

3 **Read the notice. Then tick the sentences (a–d) that are true.**

> **Learn to play basketball**
> Lessons every Tuesday and Thursday, 6–7pm.
> Call Max

a) There are lessons twice a week.
b) Call Max between 6 and 7 o'clock.
c) Max can give you information about the lessons.
d) Max is learning to play basketball.

4 **Read the email and match (1–4) with (a–d) to make sentences.**

> From: Bruce
> To: Sheila
>
> I have tickets for the match. It starts at 3, but let's get to the stadium earlier.
>
> Don't forget your scarf!

1 Bruce and Sheila
2 They shouldn't
3 Sheila should
4 Bruce thinks it is a good idea

a) get there after 3 o'clock.
b) bring something with her.
c) are going to watch a sport.
d) to be at the stadium before the match begins.

OPTIMISE YOUR EXAM

3-option multiple choice (short texts)

- If you don't understand a new word, read the whole sentence and try to guess what it means.
- Remember to think about where the message is taken from, who it's for and why it was written. This will help you to understand the meaning of any new words.

5 2.22 **Read the texts. For each question, choose the correct answer.**

1

Hi Tim

Sorry, but I can't practise for the match today. I'm tired and I haven't finished my homework. Can we go tomorrow?

Adele

A Adele has to study today.
B Adele is tired because she did some sport.
C Adele and Tim will practise tomorrow.

2

From: Alex
To: Sue

We are the winners!

My team won the competition, so I'm having a party on Saturday. Can you and Karen come?

What should Sue do?
A Tell Karen the winners of the competition.
B Check if Karen wants to go to the party.
C Ask Karen to plan a party.

3

Hi Rob

Are you feeling better? Do you want me to visit you? I can show you what we did in art class today.

Helena

A Rob couldn't go to art class because he was ill.
B Helena is giving Rob art lessons.
C Rob doesn't have many visitors.

4

From: Alice
To: Marc

Thanks for the book, I love it! As you know, I'm Usain Bolt's biggest fan. The photos are amazing!

Marc has
A borrowed a book from Alice.
B sent Alice some photos.
C given Alice a present.

5

Tennis coach
Beginners: £10 a lesson
Can lend rackets to students
Must bring trainers

A Only beginners pay for the tennis lessons.
B You must take a racket to all the tennis lessons.
C You need to wear the right type of shoes.

6

Sailing trip
To go on the trip, you must be able to swim well.

A Swimmers of all levels may go on the trip.
B The trip is only for good swimmers.
C People on the trip must know about sailing.

6 **Write a highlighted word from the text to match each definition.**

1 finished first in a competition ____________
2 objects used to hit a ball in tennis, badminton, etc. ____________
3 this person teaches you how to play a sport ____________
4 this team is the best ____________
5 needing rest or sleep ____________
6 a sport you do in a boat ____________

THINK | **RESEARCH** | CULTURE | LEARN | ME

Find out about a famous sports person in your country. Make a poster about him or her.

▶ **Workbook Unit 8:** Reading, pages 60–61, exercises 1, 2, 3, 4, 5

8 GRAMMAR 1 | Modals (1): ability, necessity, obligation, possibility

Grammar in context

Find these sentences in Exercise 5 on page 81 and then choose the correct words to complete sentences a–e.

1 *People on the trip* ***must*** *know about sailing.*
2 *You* ***need to*** *wear the right type of shoes.*
3 *Swimmers of all levels* ***may*** *go on the trip.*
4 ***Can*** *you and Karen come?*
5 *Adele* ***has to*** *study today.*
6 *Rob* ***couldn't*** *go to art class because he was ill.*

a) We use *can* to talk about **ability / necessity**.
b) We use *have to* to talk about **possibility / obligation**.
c) We use *may* to talk about **possibility / ability**.
d) We use *must* to talk about **possibility / obligation**.
e) We use *need(n't)* to talk about **necessity / ability**.

REMEMBER

- Modal verbs do not change their form and are followed by the bare infinitive (without *to*) of another verb.
- We use *can/can't (cannot)* to talk about ability in the present and *could/couldn't* to talk about ability in the past.
- We can use *must / have to* for rules made by other people or when the person doing the action believes it is necessary. There is no past form of *must*, we use *had to*. The negative form is *don't have to*.

▶ **See Grammar reference, Unit 8,** page 151

1 Choose the correct words.

1 When my dad was at school, he **can't / couldn't** understand maths.
2 All football players **may / must** follow the rules of the game.
3 The weather forecast says it's going to snow tomorrow so we **might / needn't** go snowboarding.
4 Sports people **could / have to** train every day.
5 We **couldn't / needn't** go for a run today if we don't want to.
6 You **can't / must** tell the sports teacher if you don't feel well.

2 Complete the conversation with the words in the box.

can | can't | don't have
have | might | needn't

Robert: (1) ___________ you see who's got the ball?
Anna: No, I (2)___________. I think it's number 10.
Robert: Oh, that's Harry Kane. He's an amazing player. But dad says he (3) ___________ move to a different team next year. I hope not.
Anna: Oh, you (4) ___________ worry. He loves this team so I don't think he'll want to leave.
Robert: Look! He's scored a goal! That's 1-1.
Anna: That's great! There's only a few more minutes left, so shall we go now?
Robert: No way! We (5) ___________ to stay until the end. There's still time for another goal.
Anna: OK, then. We (6) ___________ to hurry, anyway. We've got lots of time until the next bus.
Robert: That's good. Now let's enjoy the end of the game!

3 Complete the text with the correct form of the modals *can('t), could(n't), had (to), have (to), may/might, need(n't)*.

Keep on running...!

At 15, Emil Zátopek was a young Czech who worked in a shoe factory. When he was younger he **(1)** ___________ do any sports particularly well, so he **(2)** ___________ never have become a runner. However, one day, the factory sports coach told him he **(3)** ___________ to run in a race. Everyone was surprised when he came second. Zátopek then started to think that he **(4)** ___________ work in the factory forever. He thought maybe he could be a runner instead!

Everyone knows that to be the best at any sport you **(5)** ___________ to train hard, and he did. Zátopek ran in the 1952 Olympic Games, and he won the 5,000- and 10,000-metre races. He also ran in the marathon, the longest race in the Games. It was his first marathon, but he ran the 42-kilometre race and won! Today most people still **(6)** ___________ believe he did this ... but he did! Zátopek showed that if you really want something, you **(7)** ___________ worry about what other people **(8)** ___________ think. Just believe in yourself.

 ▶ **Workbook Unit 8:** Grammar 1, page 62, exercises 1, 2, 3

Words connected with *sport*

1 2.23 **Write a word from the box to match each definition. There are two extra words you do not need. Listen and check.**

badminton	cricket	kit	pool
skiing	stadium	table tennis	winner

1 You need a small plastic ball to play this game. ______
2 You can go swimming here. ______
3 You can do this sport on snow in the mountains. ______
4 You can watch a football game here. ______
5 This is the person who is first in a competition or race. ______
6 You need a racket to play this game. ______

2 2.24 **Choose the best word to complete each sentence. Listen and check.**

1 The ______ told us what exercises to do and helped us play better.
A team **B** coach **C** member
2 Can you ______ a horse?
A play **B** skate **C** ride
3 You need a ______ to go to the basketball game tonight.
A ticket **B** bat **C** club
4 I can't go swimming because I haven't got my ______ .
A swimsuit **B** beach **C** pool
5 Ed was the winner of the 800-metre ______ .
A race **B** bat **C** club
6 They played in a rugby ______ yesterday, and won 35-3!
A club **B** goal **C** match

Verbs/nouns

3 2.25 **Complete the table. Listen and check.**

verb	noun
win	winner
(1) ______	surfer
swim	(2) ______
(3) ______	runner
play	(4) ______

4 **Complete the sentences with the correct form of some of the words from Exercise 3.**

1 There are over 50 ______ in the pool today!
2 Novak Djokovic ______ the tennis match.
3 The eight best ______ waited in the stadium to start the 500-metre race.
4 Who do you think is the best football ______ in the world this year?
5 If you want to learn to ______ , it's important that you can swim.

Collocations with verbs

5 2.26 **Complete the sentences with the correct form of the verbs in the box. Listen and check.**

climb	enter	go	play	throw	win

1 Greg ______ the ball into the road.
2 My class ______ swimming at the city pool every Wednesday.
3 Everyone can ______ the competition but only one person can win.
4 In the summer, lots of people in England ______ cricket.
5 Do I need to practise a lot before I ______ a mountain?
6 Emil Zátopek was very happy when he ______ the 5,000-metre race at the Olympic Games.

1 **Work in pairs. Look at the poster for a summer camp and answer the questions.**

1 What sports are the young people doing?
2 Would you like to do the sports in the poster? Why / Why not?
3 What other sports would you like to do at a summer camp?

EXAM SKILL

Listening for important information

- You don't need to understand every word to answer the questions.
- The first time you listen, think about the important words.
- When you listen again, think carefully about what the speakers mean.

2 2.27 **Listen to five people talking about sports. Match each speaker to a sport.**

Speaker 1 ____	**a)** running
Speaker 2 ____	**b)** windsurfing
Speaker 3 ____	**c)** badminton
Speaker 4 ____	**d)** cycling
Speaker 5 ____	**e)** table tennis

3 2.27 **Listen again and write the names of the other sports the people talk about in each conversation.**

Conversation 1 _football..._
Conversation 2 ____________
Conversation 3 ____________
Conversation 4 ____________
Conversation 5 ____________

OPTIMISE YOUR EXAM

Matching

- Read the question and all the possible answers carefully.
- Remember that there are three possible answers that you don't need.
- When you listen again, check the three possible answers you didn't choose, to make sure they aren't correct.

4 2.28 **You will hear Bea talking to her dad about her summer camp. What sport did she do on each day?**

Example:
Monday morning _H_

1 Monday afternoon	____	**A**	swimming
2 Tuesday	____	**B**	badminton
3 Wednesday	____	**C**	volleyball
4 Thursday	____	**D**	tennis
5 Friday	____	**E**	sailing
		F	football
		G	cricket
		~~**H**~~	~~running~~

5 2.28 **Listen again and check your answers.**

THINK | RESEARCH | **CULTURE** | LEARN | ME

Work in pairs and answer the questions.
- How popular are summer camps in your country?
- What sports and other activities can you do there?

▶ **Workbook Unit 8:** Listening, page 64, exercises 1, 2, 3

GRAMMAR 2 | Modals (2): advice, permission, polite requests, prohibition

Grammar in context

Look at these sentences from the audio in the listening lesson and then match them to the descriptions (a–e).

1 *You **should** start playing again, Dad – it's good exercise ...*

2 *Camp rules say we **mustn't** swim if there's a strong wind ...*

3 *... **could** you take some photos of the boats, please?*

4 *Well, you **shouldn't** be out all day in the sun if it's very hot.*

5 *The camp leader says we **can** go to the pool today instead.*

a) something is not allowed ____

b) we have permission ____

c) someone is making a request ____

d) something is a good idea ____

e) something isn't a good idea ____

REMEMBER

- We use modals to:
  - ask for / give advice: *should/shouldn't*
  - ask for / give permission: *can/could*
  - refuse permission: *can't/couldn't*
  - make a polite request: *could*
  - say something is prohibited: *mustn't*
- To make the negative form, you add 'not' after the modal verb and this is usually contracted, e.g. *need not = needn't.*
- Sometimes the negative form changes the modal's meaning: *In the UK, you **must** drive on the left.* (obligation) *In the UK, you **mustn't** drive on the right.* (prohibition)
- To make a question, the subject and modal swap position: ***Could you** pass me my racket, please?*

▶ **See Grammar reference, Unit 8,** page 152

1 **Choose the correct words.**

1 We're very happy because the teacher says we **shouldn't** / **can** all watch a video for the last half hour this afternoon.

2 'Amber, come back and get your helmet! You **could** / **mustn't** ever go out on your bike without it.'

3 Ed, **should** / **could** you help me with my school project, please?

4 Please turn the computer off. You **shouldn't** / **can** play video games all evening. It's not a good thing to do!

5 You look very tired. You **mustn't** / **should** go to bed earlier.

2 **Choose the correct words (a, b or c) to complete each sentence.**

1 I'm not sure how to do this. ____ you help me, please?
a) Could **b)** Should **c)** Shouldn't

2 You ____ eat for 30 minutes before you go swimming.
a) could **b)** can **c)** shouldn't

3 I think you ____ try learning a new sport. It's fun!
a) mustn't **b)** couldn't **c)** should

4 The teacher says we ____ use her tennis rackets. That's kind of her.
a) can **b)** shouldn't **c)** couldn't

5 The boys ____ go to the match last night because their dad said no.
a) shouldn't **b)** couldn't **c)** mustn't

6 The rule here is that you ____ do any water sports if you ____ swim 500 metres.
a) should, can **b)** mustn't, can't **c)** could, mustn't

3 **Complete the text about a summer camp with the phrases from the box.**

can use | can't do | could you bring
mustn't leave | should bring (×2)
shouldn't arrive | could you ask

A WELCOME
from our Camp Manager

We're really excited about meeting everyone at Super Sports Summer Camp next month. Before you come, I want to give you some important information.

- **What to bring** First of all, everyone (**1**) ________________ these things to camp: a pair of trainers, shorts or leggings and a T-shirt. You (**2**) ________________ sports without them. Secondly, don't bring your best clothes, because we don't want them to get dirty. So (**3**) ________________ some old clothes for art activities, please? People often ask us if they (**4**) ________________ their own rackets, bats or balls. The answer is no. We have all the equipment here and you (**5**) ________________ it whenever you want.

- **When to arrive** The camp starts at 11:30 on Saturday 7th July. You (**6**) ________________ too early, as the leaders won't all be here until 10, so please try to arrive at about 10:30 if possible.

- **And finally ...** When you arrive, (**7**) ________________ your parents to park in the Rees Lane car park. There's plenty of room there for everyone. And, one last thing ... always remember the camp rule while you're here – you (**8**) ________________ the camp at any time without permission. See you on Saturday!

8 SPEAKING | Discussion (pictures)

Talk2Me
Never mind!

Flipped classroom

1 **Watch the *Talk2Me* video and answer the questions.**

1 What can the twins' new phones do?
2 What question does Jojo ask her phone?
3 What surprising thing do the phones do at the end?

2 **Watch the video again. Underline the phrases in the *Phrase expert* box that you hear on the video.**

PHRASE EXPERT

I think … | Never mind! | It's rubbish. | In my opinion … | I believe …

EXAM SKILL

Giving opinions

- Often in an exam, you will be asked to give your opinion. For example, the examiner will ask questions like *Do you think playing a team sport is fun? Which of these sports do you like best?* etc.
- There are many phrases you can use to give your opinion. For example, *Yes, I think …, For me, …, In my opinion …, No, I don't believe that …, … is my favourite.*

3 **Complete the table to say if you like or don't like the activity.**

Activity	Opinion	Why?
ice hockey	*don't like*	*very cold, too fast*
skateboarding		
surfing		
volleyball		

4 **Work in pairs. Ask and answer questions about the activities in Exercise 3 and give a reason for your opinion.**

Student A: Do you like ice hockey?
Student B: No. For me, it's too fast and very cold.

SAY IT RIGHT

Resource centre: Unit 8
Intonation in questions

OPTIMISE YOUR EXAM

Discussion (pictures)

- Make sure you reply to the examiner's question. For example, if he/she asks *Do you think …?* you must give a reason. If you're asked *Which … do you like best?* you must give a preference.
- Remember to use suitable phrases to show the examiner how much language you know.

5 2.29 **In pairs, do the exam task. Then listen to two students doing the task. Did you agree with any of their ideas?**

Do you like these sports? Say why or why not.

6 **Take it in turns to ask and answer these questions.**

Student A: Is it better to play sports in a team or do sports alone?
Do you think playing tennis is difficult?

Student B: Do you prefer doing sport in the summer or winter?
Do you think playing football is fun?

▶ **Workbook Unit 8:** Speaking, page 64, exercises 1, 2, 3

LANGUAGE IN USE | Open cloze

1 **In pairs or as a group, answer the questions.**

1 What different places can you do sports in?
2 Do you prefer to do sports inside or outside?

EXAM SKILL

Using modal verbs

- Remember that modal verbs add meaning to the main verb. For example, they are used to express ability (*can/can't*), advice (*should/shouldn't*), obligation (*must/mustn't*), etc.
- Their form changes to express the present, past or future tense and they are usually followed by the infinitive without *to*.
- You need to understand the meaning of the text and the time when the action takes place (present, past, etc.) in order to select the correct modal verb.

2 **Complete the sentences with a modal verb from the box.**

can	could	may	must	shouldn't

1 You ____________ do sport after eating a big meal.
2 Running is popular because you ____________ do it everywhere.
3 We ____________ go swimming later today if we have time.
4 The whole class ____________ run round the field twice for being late.
5 ____________ you pass me the ball, please?

3 **In pairs, read the text in Exercise 4 quickly and answer the questions.**

1 What does Street Games do?
A It organises football competitions.
B It gives money to young people.
C It helps young people do sport.

2 Where do most games happen?
A inside
B outside
C inside and outside

OPTIMISE YOUR EXAM

Open cloze

- As you read the text in the exam, ask yourself what type of information the writer is trying to communicate. For example, if the writer is talking about an ability or a possibility, or giving some advice, then the sentence may need a modal verb.
- If you think the sentence needs a modal verb, think carefully if it should be in the present or the past.
- Most modal verbs aren't followed by *to*, except for *need to* and *have to*.
- Remember to write only <u>one</u> word in each gap. Negative contractions are two words, for example, *mustn't* = *must not*. However, the word *can't* = *cannot* (one word) can be used.

4 **For each question, write the correct answer. Write ONE word for each gap.**

Subject: Street Games

Hey Sally

I was reading about this great idea ___*called*___ Street Games. It's a way to get young people to do more sport and **(1)** ____________ fit. They organise sports events in areas **(2)** ____________ people don't get to a sports centre because they live **(3)** ____________ far away. The events are held in the streets and people play sports **(4)** ____________ basketball, football and tennis. Street Games believes all young people **(5)** ____________ have the chance to play sports, and that children who do sport can live healthier lives. You don't **(6)** ____________ to be good at sports, so why don't we try it out?

THINK | **RESEARCH** | CULTURE | LEARN | ME

Find out about the sports that young people played in the streets in your country in the past. Are they similar to the sports of today?

8 WRITING | Guided writing (an email)

1 **In pairs, answer the questions.**

1 What sports do you do at your school:
- in the winter?
- in the summer?

2 Do boys and girls do sports together or separately?

3 How many hours a week do you do sport?

EXAM SKILL

Writing in an informal style

- When you write an email to a friend or family member, use informal language, for example, *Hello!, Hi, See you soon, Write soon, Bye.*
- In informal writing we can use contractions, for example, *I'm, he can't, we've got, they didn't.*
- We often also use more exclamation marks than we do in formal writing, for example, *I've got a great idea!*

2 **Write the contractions of the words in bold in each sentence.**

1 **I would** like to learn how to play golf next year.
I'd

2 **Sally has** got a new pair of trainers.
____

3 **They will** start playing baseball in May.
____

4 Those two teams **were not** good enough to win the competition. _______________

5 He **did not** score any goals in the match.
____

6 **Who is** the new player in the cricket team?
____

7 **I am** excited because my team is winning! _______________

8 **We have** trained really hard this winter.
____

3 **Write F (formal) or I (informal) next to the words and phrases, as in the example.**

Example: Dear _F_ Hi _I_

1 I suggest we … ____
2 How about … ____
3 Can't wait to … ____
4 I would like to thank you for … ____
5 See you soon ____
6 Love ____
7 I am looking forward to … ____
8 Yours sincerely, ____
9 Thanks a lot for … ____
10 Best wishes ____

4 **Read the email from Chris to his English friend Sam. Then answer the questions.**

From: Chris
To: Sam

Hi Sam,

Thanks for your email. My school is really cool!

We play football, cricket, hockey and basketball and do athletics at school. Yes, everyone's got to do at least one sport each term! We often go to the park to do sports when the weather is good, but when it rains we use the gym.

Write soon,
Chris

1 What sports does Chris have at his school?
2 How many sports do you have to play each term?
3 When do they go to the park?
4 What do they do when it rains?

5 **Find examples of informal style in the email in Exercise 4. Write them in the correct place below.**

1 informal words or phrases
_______________ , _______________

2 a contraction _______________

OPTIMISE YOUR EXAM

Guided writing (an email)

- In the exam, you can invent details in your emails – what you write doesn't have to be true.
- Use your imagination and use a variety of adjectives to make your email interesting to read.
- Remember that your email should be short. You only need to write one paragraph of 25 words or more.

6 Look at this exam task. What information do you need to include in your email? Choose the correct answers.

You want to join your English friend Lee's tennis club this summer.
Write an email to Lee.

In your email:
- tell Lee you have all the kit
- say your dad will give you the money
- ask Lee how often they practise.

Write **25 words** or more.

1 **the clothes he has / the clothes he needs to buy**
2 **the person who will give you the money / how much the club costs**
3 **the amount of time / the places where** they practise

7 Plan **Plan your email. Use the table to help you.**

	Details	My notes
First line	use informal language to greet the person you are writing to	
Point 1	Tell	
Point 2	Say	
Point 3	Ask	
Last line	use informal language to say goodbye	

8 Write **Write your email to Lee in an appropriate style. Write 25 words or more.**

9 Check **Before you hand in your email, complete this checklist.**

Checklist

- ◯ I've followed my writing plan.
- ◯ I've started and ended my email in the right way.
- ◯ I've used all three points.
- ◯ I've used a good range of vocabulary.
- ◯ I've used an informal style.
- ◯ I've written 25 words or more.
- ◯ I've checked my spelling, grammar and punctuation.

▶ **Writing reference,** page 163 ▶ **Workbook Unit 8:** Writing, page 66, exercises 1, 2, 3, 4 and Progress check 8, page 67

PROGRESS CHECK UNITS 7–8

GRAMMAR AND VOCABULARY

1 Complete the conversation using the correct form of *will* or *going to*.

Simona: What **(1)** __________ you __________ do in the summer holidays?

Martin: I **(2)** __________ stay with my cousins in France for two weeks. After that, I **(3)** __________ visit my grandparents. **(4)** __________ you __________ go on holiday?

Simona: No, I'm not. I **(5)** __________ study English at a summer school in London. But I need to pass an exam first.

Martin: You're one of the best students in the class. I'm sure you **(6)** __________ pass.

Simona: I hope so. I have to go now. I **(7)** __________ do my history homework in the library.

Martin: I'm really bad at history. **(8)** __________ you help me?

Simona: OK. I **(9)** __________ help you find the information you need, but I **(10)** __________ tell you the answers.

Martin: That's great. Thanks a lot.

__/10

2 Choose the correct answers (A, B or C).

1 What do I need to play tennis?
A It's a good idea.
B A racket and some trainers.
C Don't forget your bat and ball.

2 I want to take an English course in September.
A You should speak to my teacher. He's great.
B I don't think so.
C Can you help me?

3 Have you seen my dictionary?
A I have to go.
B It's on the bookshelf.
C It's after lunch.

4 Who won the race?
A Not at the moment.
B It doesn't take long.
C I don't know. They're still running.

5 I'm going to enter this competition.
A I hope you win.
B You don't have to run.
C Wait until it finishes.

__/5

3 Choose the correct modal verb to complete each sentence.

1 My sister **could / may / should** play tennis when she was five.
2 My cousin **can't / couldn't / shouldn't** read or write until he was eight.
3 I **can / have to / may** need your help with my homework, but I'm not sure yet.
4 You **can't / needn't / couldn't** use your mobile phone during the exam. Leave it in your bag.
5 You **don't have to / should / may** wear a coat to school because it might be cold later on.
6 In football, only goalkeeper **doesn't have to / has to / can** touch the ball with their hands.
7 You **have to / shouldn't / couldn't** eat too much before you do sport.
8 The runners **don't have to / can / shouldn't** stop for water, but it's a good idea.
9 You **can / needn't / have to** use a dictionary during French lessons if you want to find a word.
10 Everyone **could / may / has to** wear a swimsuit in the pool.
11 You **can / may / don't have to** go to school in the holidays.
12 I **may / couldn't / can't** come to the match on Saturday, but at the moment I don't know. I'll tell you tomorrow.

__/12

4 **Complete the blog post with one word in each gap.**

I'm Paz Nevado, I'm 14 years old, I'm from Spain (**1**) ___________ I love sport. I (**2**) ___________ tennis three times a week and I'm also in the school team. Every year, we enter a big competition (**3**) ___________ May. This year, it's (**4**) ___________ to be in Madrid. We have (**5**) ___________ practise a lot (**6**) ___________ we go to the competition. We've never won it, (**7**) ___________ last year we came second. It's great fun and I always (**8**) ___________ lots of new friends there. I also love swimming. I can't swim very often (**9**) ___________ there isn't a pool in my town. Every summer, we (**10**) ________ to the beach and I swim in the sea. I love it!

__/10

5 **Complete the sentences with the verbs in the box.**

climb	do	go	make	ride	take	throw	win

1 When you're at school, you need to ___________ homework every night.
2 It's really useful to ___________ notes when the teacher is talking.
3 Cora wants to ___________ a really high mountain when she is older.
4 Who do you think will ___________ the 10,000-metre race at the Olympics?
5 Lots of young people ___________ to university when they're 18.
6 Don't ___________ the ball into the road. It's dangerous.
7 It's OK to ___________ mistakes when you're learning something new.
8 I'd really like to learn how to ___________ a horse next year.

__/8

6 **Read the descriptions about sports. What is the word for each one? The first letter is already there.**

1 Two or four people play this game with a ball and rackets. t_ _ _ _ _
2 You hit a ball with a bat in this English summer game. c_ _ _ _ _ _
3 Moving through water. s_ _ _ _ _ _ _
4 You hit a ball with your hands in this team game. v_ _ _ _ _ _ _ _ _
5 Riding a board on the sea. s_ _ _ _ _ _

__/5

Total score __/50

EXAM SKILLS

Tick the statements that are true for you. Review the skills in the unit if you need more help.

I can ...	Unit/page
☐ develop strategies to answer the question in multiple-choice activities	Unit 7 p70
☐ think about the missing information I need to listen for	Unit 7 p74
☐ talk about the future and make predictions	Unit 7 p76
☐ identify commonly confused words	Unit 7 p77
☐ use adjectives in a story	Unit 7 p78
☐ find ideas that mean the same in the text	Unit 8 p80
☐ listen for important information	Unit 8 p84
☐ give opinions in a discussion	Unit 8 p86
☐ use modal verbs	Unit 8 p87
☐ write an email using an informal style	Unit 8 p88

9 Whatever the weather

READING | 3-option multiple matching | Blog posts

1 In pairs or as a group, answer the questions.

1 What is the weather like today?
2 What is the weather like in January, April, July and October in your country?
3 What is your favourite time of the year? Why?

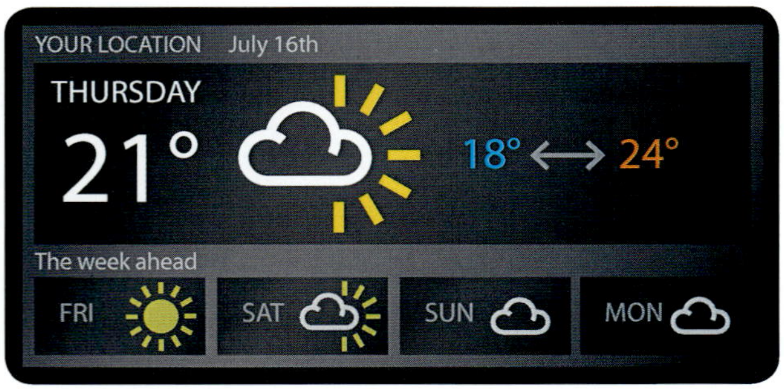

EXAM SKILL

Thinking logically

- Sometimes, if the answer isn't immediately clear, it helps to think logically about the information given in a text.
- For example, if you read in a text *The weather in the area isn't good*, it's logical to say that *People spend a lot of time indoors there*.

2 Match each sentence with a logical conclusion, a or b.

1 The sun is shining this morning.
a) It's usually warm here in May.
b) It's going to be a warm day.

2 There was ice on the ground.
a) It was difficult to walk without falling over.
b) It was on the roads and on the grass.

3 A thunderstorm woke me up last night.
a) It was very loud.
b) There was a lot of rain.

3 Read the blog posts on page 93 quickly and tick the events that are mentioned.

1 a very hot day in a cold country ☐
2 a bad snowstorm ☐
3 foggy weather ☐
4 a sudden storm ☐
5 moving ice ☐
6 thunder and lightning ☐

Crazy WEATHER!

Max

Do you like snow? I do, but sometimes it can cause problems! One morning when I woke up, there was snow. It covered our car and the garden. Because of the snow, we were without electricity, and it was dark and cold in the house. For me, it was an adventure, but my parents were very worried. We couldn't go outside for three days. Now that I'm older, I think I would be scared if it happened again.

Ian

If you go sailing often, be careful! One Saturday, it was warm and sunny, so my family decided to go out in our boat. We spent the morning sailing. Then we stopped at a beach to have lunch. But very quickly, it became windy and dark as clouds covered the sky. Then the storm started. It wasn't safe to sail, so we waited in the rain until it finished. We were lucky that we weren't at sea when it happened!

Joe

My village is near a lake and, a few winters ago, something very dangerous happened: strong winds began to slowly push the ice on the lake towards the village! Nothing could stop it. The ice went into people's houses, covered the roads and moved their cars. People were afraid, but luckily nobody was hurt. It was the strangest thing I've ever seen. If it happens again, I'll film it and put it on YouTube!

OPTIMISE YOUR EXAM

3-option multiple matching

- For each question, underline the key idea. Then scan the text looking for similar idea(s).
- Look out for similar words in the question and the text. For example, *It was cloudy* is the same as *The sky was grey*.
- The answer to the question may be a logical conclusion. For example, if the question is *Who spends a lot of time outdoors?* a logical statement in the text would be *I'm always at the beach*.

4 3.01 **Read the blog posts again. For each question, choose the correct answer.**

		Max	Ian	Joe
1	Who says what happened to the weather was very unusual?	A	B	C
2	Who got wet during a storm?	A	B	C
3	Who had to stay in his house because the weather was bad?	A	B	C
4	Who gives advice about an activity?	A	B	C
5	Who says it was dark indoors?	A	B	C
6	Who describes how the weather came indoors?	A	B	C
7	Who was enjoying himself before the bad weather began?	A	B	C

5 **Match the definitions (a–h) to the highlighted words in the article (1–8).**

1 village ____
2 finish ____
3 worried ____
4 clouds ____
5 covered ____
6 dangerous ____
7 ice ____
8 lake ____

a water that is below 0° C
b to think and feel unhappy about bad things that could happen
c a very small town in the countryside
d white or grey things in the sky which are made of water
e to come to an end
f the opposite of safe
g a large area of water
h was on top of something so that thing can't be seen

THINK | **RESEARCH** | CULTURE | LEARN | ME

Find out about some unusual weather that has happened in your country. Make a poster about it.

Grammar in context

Find the sentences in the text on page 93 and then answer the questions

1 *If you **go** sailing often, **be** careful!*

2 *If it **happens** again, **I'll film** it and put it on YouTube!*

Which sentence talks about:

a) something that is a fact or is always true? ____

b) something that is possible in the future? ____

REMEMBER

Zero conditional

- We use present tenses in both parts of the sentence: *If the weather **is** bad, he **stays** at home.*
- We use the zero conditional to talk about things that are true and scientific facts: *If you **heat** water to 100° Celsius, it **boils**.*

First conditional

- We use ***If*** + the present simple in one part of the sentence and ***will*** in the other: ***If** the weather **is** good tomorrow, we**'ll have** a barbecue.*
- We use the first conditional to talk about real, likely or possible situations in the future: ***If** the weather **is** bad **tomorrow**, he**'ll stay** at home.*

Note: in zero conditional sentences, *If* can be changed to *When* with no change in meaning.

▶ **See Grammar reference, Unit 9,** page 152

1 Choose the correct words to complete the zero conditional sentences.

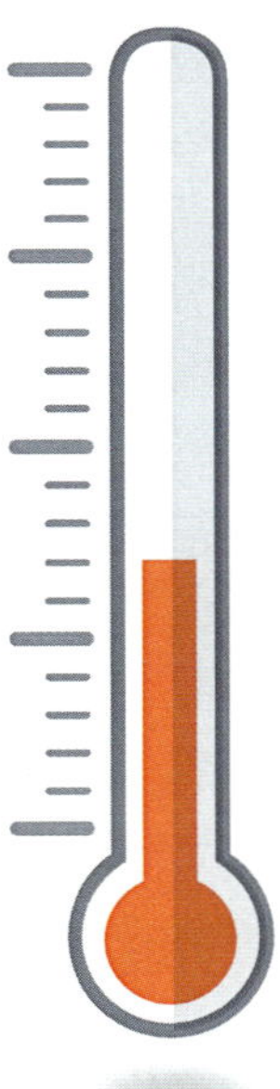

1 If the temperature **is** / **will be** below 0° Celsius, water **changes** / **will change** to ice.

2 When it **is** / **will be** very windy, trees sometimes **will fall** / **fall** down.

3 I always **will feel** / **feel** better when the sun **shines** / **will shine**.

4 If plants **don't** / **won't** have enough air and water, they **don't** / **won't** grow.

5 **Do** / **Will** you usually go out for long walks in the forest when it **will snow** / **snows**?

6 When I **will have** / **have** a bad cold, I **won't** / **don't** go to school.

2 Choose the correct words to complete the first conditional sentences.

1 If it **rains** / **will rain** this afternoon, I **don't** / **won't** go and play football in the park.

2 If the weather **gets** / **will get** very cold tonight, some of the flowers in our garden **will die** / **die**.

3 There **isn't** / **won't be** any cars on the road if it **snows** / **will snow** a lot later.

4 **Will** / **Do** you come with me if I **will go** / **go** out to make a snowman?

5 If you **go** / **will go** out in this cold weather, you **need** / **will need** a warm jacket.

6 We **are not** / **won't** go out if there **is** / **will be** a storm tonight.

3 Complete the article using the correct form (present simple or *will*) of the verbs in brackets.

Using plants in science

When you **(1)** ____________ **(go)** to bed tonight, will you take your mobile phone with you? And if you **(2)** ____________ **(keep)** it with you, will it be near your bed? If your phone **(3)** ____________ **(be)** usually near your head during the night, how do you feel in the morning? If you **(4)** ____________ **(feel)** tired and don't do well at school, this **(5)** ____________ **(not be)** unusual.

Five teenagers from Denmark found that on nights when they **(6)** ____________ **(sleep)** with their phones near their heads, they can't **(7)** ____________ **(think)** very well at school the next day. They wanted to know why, so they did an experiment with plants. They grew plants in two rooms. In one room there was a wi-fi router and in the other room there wasn't. Before they started, the girls thought, 'If wi-fi and mobile phones **(8)** ____________ **(be)** totally safe, then the plants **(9)** ____________ **(grow)** normally.'

After 12 days, they were surprised. The plants near the router didn't grow, and many of them died. But the plants in the other room were healthy and grew well. So, if wi-fi **(10)** ____________ **(stop)** plants from growing, what does it do to us? Because of what these girls did at school, scientists now want to find out.

THINK | RESEARCH | CULTURE | LEARN | **ME**

Work in pairs and discuss the questions.

What will you do if …

- it rains all weekend?
- it is sunny tomorrow?
- it snows on Sunday?

▶ **Workbook Unit 9:** Grammar 1, page 70, exercises 1, 2, 3

Words connected with *weather and nature*

1 3.02 **Look at the weather map of Europe and choose the correct word to complete each sentence. Listen and check.**

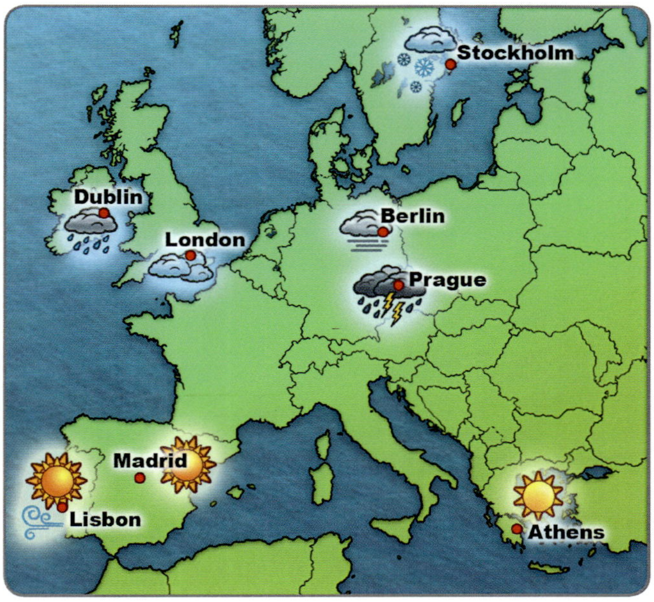

1 It is warm and **foggy** / **sunny** in Madrid.
2 There is **snow** / **sun** in Stockholm.
3 It is **rainy** / **sunny** in Dublin.
4 It is **rainy and windy** / **sunny and windy** in Lisbon.
5 There is **ice** / **fog** in Berlin.
6 There **is ice** / **are thunderstorms** in Prague.
7 It's **foggy** / **cloudy** in London.

2 3.03 **Complete the descriptions with the words in the box. Listen and check.**

beach | forest | hill
mountain | river | sky

1 A large area of trees and other plants.
____
2 It is very tall and sometimes there is snow on the top.
____
3 It takes water from the mountains to the sea.
____
4 It's by the sea and people go there in the summer.
____
5 The space above you that you see when you look up into the air.
____
6 It is smaller than a mountain.
____

Words + prepositions

3 3.04 **Match the first part (1–6) of each sentence with the end (a–f). Listen and check.**

1 The students did experiments ____
2 It is important ____
3 The students were good at ____
4 Scientists want to ____
5 Summer is the best time ____
6 They learnt about animals by ____

a) to visit the beach, because it's sunny.
b) to protect our forests and rivers.
c) to see if wi-fi was dangerous.
d) visiting the zoo.
e) thinking of new science experiments.
f) find out why things happen.

Nouns/adjectives

4 3.05 **Complete the table with a noun or adjective. Listen and check.**

noun	adjective
cloud	*cloudy*
fog	(1) __________
(2) __________	icy
rain	(3) __________
(4) __________	snowy
sun	(5) __________

5 **Complete the sentences using the correct form of some of the words from Exercise 4.**

1 There are lots of __________ in the sky. I think it's going to rain.
2 It was very cold and wet and the path was very __________ . Lots of people fell down.
3 If it's __________ tomorrow, we will go to the beach.
4 When there is lots of __________ , you can't see very far.
5 A lot of __________ fell in the night and now everything outside is white.
6 It was a __________ day and everyone at the volleyball game got wet.

SAY IT RIGHT
Resource centre: Unit 9
/əʊ/ and /aʊ/

9 LISTENING | 3-option multiple choice (pictures)

1 Work in pairs and answer the questions.

1 What do you like doing in your free time in the summer?

2 What are you going to do in the next summer holiday?

EXAM SKILL

Understanding the speakers' questions

- It is important to understand exactly what the speakers mean when they ask a question.
- When the speakers agree or disagree with someone, they don't always say *yes* or *no*.
- Listen carefully to the words the speakers use and try to decide exactly what they mean.

2 3.06 Listen to five short conversations. Are the answers *yes, no* or *don't know*? Tick the correct box for each conversation (1–5).

	yes	no	don't know
1			
2			
3			
4			
5			

3 Complete the conversations with the words in the box.

idea | maybe | really | sure

1 **A:** Do you want to go skiing next winter?
B: Good ____________ ! I love skiing.

2 **A:** I'm going to the lake on Sunday. Can you come?
B: I'm not ____________ . I think my cousins are coming to visit me.

3 **A:** Do you want to go horse-riding in the forest?
B: Not ____________ . It's too cold today.

4 **A:** Would you like to go to the countryside on Saturday?
B: ____________ . But I need to ask my mum first.

OPTIMISE YOUR EXAM

3-option multiple choice (pictures)

- When you choose the correct picture, you may need to listen for numbers, descriptions or the correct word for something.
- Be careful. Sometimes you will hear more than one possible answer.
- When you listen again, check that the picture you chose is correct.

4 3.07 For each question, choose the correct picture.

1 Where does Sophie want to go at the weekend if the weather is good?

A B C

2 What's the weather like today?

A B C

3 Which place is the boy not going to visit this summer?

A B C

4 What's the weather going to be like here tomorrow afternoon?

A B C

5 Which season does the girl like the best?

A B C

5 3.07 Listen again and check your answers.

THINK | RESEARCH | CULTURE | LEARN | ME

What are the most popular free-time activities for young people in the winter in your country?

▶ **Workbook Unit 9:** Listening, page 72, exercises 1, 2, 3

GRAMMAR 2 | Second conditional

Grammar in context

Look at these sentences from the audio in the listening lesson and answer the questions.

1 *If it was sunny, I would go to the beach today.*
   a) Is it sunny? ___________
   b) Is the speaker going to the beach today? ___________

2 *We'd go to the beach in Spain if we had more money.*
   a) Is the speaker going to the beach in Spain? ___________
   b) Does the speaker have a lot of money? ___________

3 *If I didn't have a guitar lesson at 1 o'clock, I'd come with you.*
   a) Does the speaker have a guitar lesson at 1 o'clock? ___________
   b) Can the speaker go with his friends at 1 o'clock? ___________

REMEMBER

- We use ***If*** + past simple in one part of the second conditional, and ***would*** in the other part: ***If*** *my brother* ***were*** *here right now, he* ***would*** *know what to do.*
- We use the second conditional to talk about unlikely or impossible situations now, generally or in the future: *If I* ***lived*** *in England, I'****d eat*** *fish and chips every day.*

Note: we use *were* for the first and third person singular in second conditional sentences using the verb *to be*: *If I* ***were*** *you, I'd stay at home until the rain stops.*

▶ **See Grammar reference, Unit 9,** page 153

1 **Choose the correct word to complete the sentences.**

1 If there **is** / **was** lots of snow outside, we would go skiing in the mountains.
2 If there were no rivers, we **won't** / **wouldn't** have fresh water to drink.
3 If the grass **won't** / **didn't** grow in spring, the cows in the field wouldn't have any food.
4 If it wasn't warm and sunny in the summer, **will** / **would** the fruit grow on the trees?
5 If there **are** / **were** no people, what would the world be like?

2 **Complete the second conditional sentences using the correct form of the verbs in brackets.**

1 If he ______________ (**can**) travel into space, he ______________ (**visit**) the moon.
2 If Harry ______________ (**not own**) a bike, he ______________ (**not cycle**) to school and back every day.
3 Would you ______________ (**go**) swimming every day if you ______________ (**live**) by the beach?
4 If they ______________ (**have**) a lot of money, they ______________ (**buy**) a big house.
5 If everyone ______________ (**stop**) driving cars, the air ______________ (**be**) cleaner.

3 **Work in pairs. Complete the second conditional sentences using your own ideas.**

1 If I owned a plane, I ______________________________.
2 If I were famous, I ______________________________.
3 If I lived in a forest, I ______________________________.
4 If I were good at singing, I ______________________________.
5 If I could live anywhere, I ______________________________.

4 **Complete the text by making second conditional sentences using the correct form of the verbs in the box.**

be | be able to | can | do | not have | wash

LIVING WITH NATURE

When you wake up in the morning, what do you usually do? Perhaps you turn on the light and have a warm shower. But what do you think you would (**1**) ___________ if you didn't have electricity? How would you (**2**) ___________ if you (**3**) ___________ hot water to use? Well, if you wanted to know, you (**4**) ___________ always ask 16-year-old Zeki Basan. Zeki lives by himself in a forest on the island of Skye, near Scotland.

Zeki is a student at the School of Adventure Studies on Skye and he decided to live in a tent in the forest to learn more about life in the countryside. He gets up at six every morning and lights the fire. If he didn't have a fire, he wouldn't (**5**) ___________ cook food or keep warm. He washes his clothes in the river. He doesn't use the internet and can't watch TV.

If he lived in a normal house, his life (**6**) ___________ a lot easier. But out here in the forest, Zeki loves the fresh air, the highland cows and living close to nature.

THINK | RESEARCH | CULTURE | LEARN | ME

If you lived in a forest by yourself, what would you eat and drink? Do you think you would be happy?

9 SPEAKING | Questions

Flipped classroom

1 Watch the *Talk2Me* video and answer the questions.

1 Who has a French exchange partner?
2 Where does Anouk live?
3 Why are the twins excited at the end?

2 Watch the video again. Underline the phrases in the *Phrase expert* box that you hear on the video.

PHRASE EXPERT

I live in a village/town/city. | In my … there is/are … | It's a (beautiful/fun/quiet) place to live. The thing I like the most/least about … is …

3 Work in pairs and answer the questions.

1 What's your favourite time of year for the weather? Why?
2 Do you travel more in the summer or the winter? Why?
3 What do you enjoy eating on a hot day? Why?

EXAM SKILL

Talking about a topic

- Sometimes we need to give a longer answer to a question. To ask someone to give more information on a topic, we can say: *Tell me something about …*
- To add information you can include examples from your daily life and say what you like or what your interests are.
- To give an example, you can use phrases such as *For example*, *Such as …*, *Let me give you an example*, *An example is …*

4 3.08 Listen to four students and match each one to a topic. There is one extra topic you do not need.

city where you live | family and friends
hobbies | places you go on holiday | technology

5 3.08 Listen again and write down the examples each student gives.

Student 1 ______________________
Student 2 ______________________
Student 3 ______________________
Student 4 ______________________

6 3.09 Listen to another student. Write down the topic, the examples given and the phrase used to correct a mistake.

Topic: ______________________
Examples: ______________________
Correction phrase: ______________________

OPTIMISE YOUR EXAM

Questions

- Sometimes you might make a mistake when you are speaking, especially in a long response.
- Use phrases such as *Sorry, I mean …*, *Sorry, I'll say that again.*, or *No, that's wrong. I mean/meant …* to show that you know you made a mistake and want to correct it.
- These phrases show the examiner your understanding of language and this gives you another chance to get it right.

7 Spend one minute planning your answers for the topics (1–3) below. Then, in pairs, take turns to talk about the topics.

1 Tell me something about the place where you live.
____
2 Tell me something about your friends.
____
3 Tell me something about your family.
____

THINK | **RESEARCH** | CULTURE | LEARN | ME

Find out what the weather is like today in the following cities:

Bangkok, Buenos Aires, London, Melbourne, Oslo and Tokyo.

▶ **Workbook Unit 9:** Speaking, pages 72–73, exercises 1, 2

LANGUAGE IN USE | 3-option multiple-choice cloze

1 Work in pairs and answer the questions.

1 Would you like to live in the mountains? Why / Why not?
2 Do you like going to the countryside? Why / Why not?

EXAM SKILL

Identifying conditional sentences

- We use different types of conditional sentences to express different things.
- When we use present tenses, we say something true, for example, *If you heat water, it boils.*
- When we use present and future tenses, we say something will probably happen, for example, *If you go to school late, you will get into trouble.*
- When we use the past tense and *would* we say something is less possible or impossible, for example, *If I had a lot of money, I would travel the world.*

2 Match the first part of each sentence (1–5) with the end (a–e).

1 If we lived near the beach, ____
2 They will be completely out of breath ____
3 We could live by the beach ____
4 If the train is crowded, ____
5 I wouldn't spend all my pocket money ____

a) if your father didn't work in the city.
b) if I didn't love sweets and chocolates.
c) we would go swimming every day.
d) you can never get on it.
e) if they try to climb the hill.

3 In pairs, say if the sentences in Exercise 2 are F (fact), L (likely) or U (unlikely). Give reasons for your answers.

4 Complete the sentences with the correct word.

1 I'll be very surprised __________ he passes the exam.
2 If we don't buy the concert tickets now, they __________ sell out.
3 I __________ definitely like to live in Canada if I could go skiing every day!
4 If you __________ decide quickly, I'm going to leave.
5 If there __________ clouds, it always rains in the afternoon.

OPTIMISE YOUR EXAM

3-option multiple-choice cloze

- There are different places where you may find a gap in a conditional sentence. For example, the gap for *if* can be at the start of the sentence or in the middle e.g. *I'll arrive at 6pm __ the train is on time.* or *__ the train is on time, I'll arrive at 6pm.*
- The verb that is missing can also come in the first or second part of the sentence. For example, *I would go out if I had time.* or *I would go out if I had time.*
- Remember to look at both parts of the conditional sentence and think about how likely the situation is before choosing the answer (A–C).

5 For each question, choose the correct answer.

Is the weather good for you?

Many people complain about the weather and how it makes them feel. They may be **(1)** ____ ! There is a lot of research which shows the different **(2)** ____ that the weather can change how we feel. For example, it is very **(3)** ____ for people to get headaches, especially in hot weather. Traffic and factories are also a **(4)** ____ . If there is no wind, the bad air stays in the city or town and this can make it hard for some people to breathe. Another example is when it's cold or wet, then more people will **(5)** ____ colds. In fact, it seems most people **(6)** ____ that the weather changes how they feel and many of us are happier when it is sunny.

	A	B	C
1	**A** real	**B** true	**C** right
2	**A** ways	**B** types	**C** sorts
3	**A** correct	**B** normal	**C** sure
4	**A** question	**B** problem	**C** puzzle
5	**A** catch	**B** become	**C** receive
6	**A** explain	**B** achieve	**C** find

THINK | RESEARCH | CULTURE | LEARN | ME

What is the worst weather you have ever been in? Write a few sentences then tell your partner.

WRITING | An email

1 In pairs or as a group, answer the questions.

1 Have you been on a trip with your friends? Did you enjoy it? Why / Why not?
2 Would you prefer a trip to the countryside or the beach? Why?
3 Have your plans ever been affected by the weather? What happened?

EXAM SKILL

Expressing preferences

- Sometimes when you write to a friend, you need to reply to a question about what you prefer to do. For example, *I prefer to spend sunny days outdoors, I think … is better, I like … more.*
- When you express a preference for something, explain why you prefer it. For example, *I prefer staying at home in the winter because I don't like cold weather.*

2 Read the dialogues and then choose the correct words to complete the sentences.

A: Do you prefer summer or winter?
B: I prefer winter because I love skiing in the mountains.

A: Would you prefer to go swimming or to walk in the countryside?
B: It's hot today so I'd prefer to go swimming.

1 We use ***prefer*** / ***would prefer*** to talk generally about what we like and what we want.
2 We use ***prefer*** / ***would prefer*** when we are talking about something more specific.

3 Read the teacher's email and the notes Annie has made on it. Discuss in pairs what you think Annie's notes mean.

From: Diana Smith
Subject: School trip

Dear Class,

It's time to think about our end-of-year trip next month. — *Brilliant!*

The weather will be warm, so we could either go to the beach or to the countryside. Where would you prefer to go? — *Explain …*

Which day should we go on our trip? — *Suggest …*

Should we have a picnic or go somewhere for lunch? — *Tell Mrs Smith*

Reply by Thursday!
Diana Smith

4 Read the email and notes in Exercise 3 again and complete the sentences.

1 Annie thinks the trip ________________.
2 Annie must choose between ________________.
3 She must say which day ____________ and why.
4 She must decide what she ________________.

5 Read Annie's reply and answer questions 1–4.

Underline the parts of Annie's email where she explains the following opinions and preferences.

1 Why it's a good idea for the class to go on a trip.
2 Why she would prefer to go to the beach.
3 Why they should go on their trip during the week.
4 Why a picnic is a good idea.

From: Annie
To: Mrs Smith
Subject: School trip

Dear Mrs Smith,

I'm really excited that we're going to go on a school trip. That's the best way to end the year!

The weather is usually very nice in June, so I'd prefer to go to the beach. We could swim and play games there.

Lots of people go to the beach at the weekend, so it's always very crowded then. That's why I think we should go during the week.

I think a picnic is a good idea. Then everyone could bring different dishes to share. I think it'd be great fun!

I'm really looking forward to the trip!

Annie

OPTIMISE YOUR EXAM

An email

- In the exam, you must respond to each note in your email. If you don't, you'll lose marks.
- Respond to the notes in the same order as they appear in the email you read.
- Use a different paragraph in your email for each note you respond to.
- Your email must be about 100 words or more.

6 Look at the exam task below. Tick the things that John asks about.

Read this email from your English friend John, and the notes you have made.

From: John

Subject: Summer camp

Hi,

My parents say I can come on the summer camp. Are you? — *Great!*

The website says we can sleep in beds or in a tent. Which would you prefer? — *Explain …*

I think it will be cold in the evening. What should we bring to stay warm? — *Suggest …*

Shall we take the train to the camp or should we catch the bus? Which do you think is better? — *Tell John*

See you on Saturday,

John

Write your **email** to John using **all the notes**.

John asks about

- the best way to get to the camp ☐
- the time to meet ☐
- the weather ☐
- what clothes to take ☐
- where to sleep ☐
- how you feel about going on the trip ☐

7 Plan Plan your email. Use the table to help you.

	Useful language	My notes
First line	*Hello …,* *Hi …,*	
Question 1	*Yes, it's going to be …! That's …*	
Question 2	*I'd prefer …*	
Question 3	*If I were you, I'd …*	
Question 4	*I think …*	
Last line	*See you soon.*	

8 Write Write your email to John in an appropriate style. Write about 100 words.

9 Check Before you hand in your email, complete this checklist.

Checklist

- ◯ I've followed my writing plan.
- ◯ I've started and ended my email the right way.
- ◯ I've written about all four notes in the exam task and developed them further.
- ◯ I've expressed preferences correctly.
- ◯ I've used a good range of vocabulary.
- ◯ I've written about 100 words.
- ◯ I've checked my spelling, grammar and punctuation.

▶ Writing reference, page 163 ▶ Workbook Unit 9: Writing, page 74, exercises 1, 2, 3, 4 and Progress check 9, page 75

10 Looking after yourself

READING | 3-option multiple choice (short texts) | Notices and short messages

1 In pairs or as a group, answer the questions.

1 When was the last time you felt ill?
2 What did you do?
3 Do you usually take medicine when you're ill? Do you do anything else?

EXAM SKILL

Deciding the general message

- Short messages like emails, notices and text messages, often give people instructions, that is, they tell or ask them to do something.
- Read the text and decide what the general message is. For example, does it ask someone to do something? Does it tell someone what (not) to do?

2 Look at the phrases and decide if they are used to A (ask) or T (tell) people to do something.

1 You should … . ____
2 Could you …? ____
3 Don't … . ____
4 Can you …? ____

3 Read the texts and use your own words to complete both sentences about the general message.

1 Ivan, text me when you get home. Don't just order a pizza for dinner. Cook something healthy, there's food in the fridge! Love Mum

a Ivan must ______________.
b Ivan mustn't ______________.

2 You must see a nurse before you leave the hospital.

a Don't go home before ______________.
b You mustn't leave the hospital if ______________ first.

OPTIMISE YOUR EXAM

3-option multiple choice (short texts)

- We often use modals and imperatives to give instructions, for example, *Could you …, Will you…, You should…, You must/mustn't …, Don't go …, Check the website …*, etc.
- Decide what the meaning of the message is before choosing your answer.
- Often the correct answer will say the same thing as the message, but in a different way.

4 3.10 **Read the notices and short messages. For each question, choose the correct answer.**

1 Students who are ill should stay at home and have their parents contact the school.

A Students should call the school to tell them why they will miss school.
B Parents need to let the school know when their child won't be in class.
C Parents should contact the school before their child returns to school.

2
From: Anna
To: Julie

I've just remembered I have an appointment today. Can we go to the cinema at 8 instead of 6?

A Anna wants to change their plans.
B Anna has decided not to watch the film.
C Anna is inviting Julie to the cinema.

3
Ben,
Tina has been in hospital since Saturday. Let's visit her and buy her a present. Have you got any ideas?
Rob

What should Ben do?
A take Rob to the hospital on Saturday
B tell Rob about the gift he has bought Tina
C say what they should get for Tina

4 42 km Running Competition
Have you entered the race yet? You must be fit.

A Anyone can enter this competition.
B This competition is for people who are healthy.
C The competition will be easy.

5
Hi Joe,
Did you know that the local hospital has had first-aid courses for six months? I'm interested. Are you? Let me know.
Cathy

What should Joe do?
A look for information about the course
B tell Cathy if he wants to join her on the course
C find out from the hospital when the course starts

6
From: Meg
To: Lorna

I'm so upset! The doctor's checked my eyes and I can't swim this Saturday. I've already missed so many races this year!

Meg

What does Meg want to do?
A take part in a sports event
B see a doctor about her eyes
C watch the next swimming race

5 **Write a highlighted word from the text to match each definition.**

1 examined someone/something to make sure everything is as it should be ______
2 in the area where you live ______
3 communicate with someone to tell them something ______
4 an arrangement to meet someone at an agreed time ______
5 healthy and strong ______
6 unhappy because something you don't like has happened to you ______

▶ **Workbook Unit 10:** Reading, pages 76–77, exercises 1, 2, 3, 4

10 GRAMMAR 1 | Present perfect simple: *for, since, already, just, yet*

Grammar in context

Find the sentences in the texts on page 103 and then answer the questions.

1 *... the local hospital has had first-aid courses* ***for*** *six months?*
2 *I've* ***just*** *remembered I have an appointment today.*
3 *Tina has been in hospital* ***since*** *Saturday.*
4 *I've* ***already*** *missed so many races this year!*
5 *Have you entered the race* ***yet****?*

Which sentence (1–5) talks about

a) when something started? ____
b) a length of time? ____
c) something that has happened at that same moment? ____
d) something that has not happened up to now? ____
e) something that has happened before this time ____

REMEMBER

- We use *for* to talk about a period of time.
- We use *since* to talk about when something started in the past.
- We use *already* to talk about something that has happened earlier. *Already* can go between *have/has* and the main verb, or at the end of the sentence.
- We use *just* to talk about something that happened a short time ago. *Just* goes between *have/has* and the main verb.
- We use *yet* with negative sentences and questions, to talk/ask about 'any time up to now'. *Yet* usually goes at the end of the sentence.

▶ **See Grammar reference, Unit 10,** page 153

1 Complete the sentences with the words in the box.

already (x2) | for | just | since (x2) | yet (×2)

1 Can you help me, please? I've ___________ hurt my hand.
2 Have you seen the doctor ___________ ?
3 Sara's had a headache ___________ last night.
4 I've ___________ taken some medicine today so I don't need any more until tomorrow.
5 Max hasn't been to the doctor ___________ over a year.
6 Where's the ambulance? It hasn't arrived ___________ .
7 I've had this pain in my stomach ___________ Friday, so maybe I should see the doctor.
8 He's ___________ been to the dentist twice, but his tooth is still sore.

2 Complete the sentences using the present perfect simple form of the verbs in brackets and choose the correct word.

1 I ___________ (**not / see**) the doctor about the pain in my legs **since / yet**.
2 How long ___________ you ___________ (**have**) toothache **for / since**?
3 Dad ___________ **just / yet** ___________ (**hurt**) his back.
4 The children ___________ (**not eat**) anything **for / since** 7 o'clock this morning.
5 The nurse ___________ **already / yet** ___________ (**take**) my temperature.

3 Complete the article with the correct present perfect form of the verbs in brackets. If there is no verb, use *already*, *for*, *just*, *since* or *yet*.

Lessons for life

Imagine this – you've been on a bike ride with your friends, but one of them (1) ___________ (**fall**) and hit their head. You (2) ___________ (**phone**) for an ambulance (3) ___________ , but it (4) ___________ (**not arrive**) (5) ___________ . Would you know what to do next?

Something like this happened to Lily Kent a few weeks ago when she was out cycling. Her friend, Annie, fell and hurt her leg, but Lily (6) ___________ (**be**) on a first-aid course, so she knew exactly what to do. She phoned for an ambulance and then sat with Annie and held her hand while they waited for help to arrive. Annie felt safe knowing Lily was there.

Annie is fine now, but the accident (7) ___________ (**change**) her views about first aid. 'I've wanted to learn about first aid (8) ___________ a long time, but (9) ___________ the accident, I've been even more interested.' said Annie. 'So I've (10) ___________ started a first-aid course – and it's really interesting!'

THINK | RESEARCH | CULTURE | LEARN | **ME**

Write a sentence about a time when you've recently hurt yourself and needed help.

Words connected with *health*

1 3.11 **Write the names for the different parts of the body. Use the words in the box. Listen and check.**

ankle | arm | back | ear | eye | face
finger | foot | hand | knee | leg
neck | nose | stomach | throat

2 **Choose the correct word or phrase to complete each sentence.**

1 If I eat too quickly, I usually get **neck** / **stomach** ache.
2 Sarah has hurt her **ankle** / **eye** and now she can't walk.
3 I hurt my **face** / **foot** when I kicked the ball during the football match.
4 Alex can't talk because he has a problem with his **finger** / **throat**.
5 My mum has hurt her **neck** / **nose** and she can't move her head very well.
6 If you can't read the board, maybe you should get your **ears** / **eyes** checked.
7 I've run 10 kilometres and now my **fingers** / **knees** hurt.
8 Arthur threw the ball so fast that it hurt Dan's **foot** / **hand** when he caught it.

Words + prepositions

3 3.12 **Complete the sentences. Choose the best word (A, B or C) for each gap. Listen and check.**

1 I had a bad pain ____ my foot this morning.
A with **B** for **C** in
2 Ashley has a problem ____ his stomach so he can't eat bread.
A for **B** with **C** to
3 This is a hospital ____ children and babies.
A with **B** for **C** to
4 Sitting down all day can be a danger ____ your health.
A to **B** in **C** with
5 I'd like an appointment ____ the doctor, please.
A for **B** with **C** to
6 Have you got any medicine ____ a bad cold?
A with **B** in **C** for
7 What's the matter ____ you?
A with **B** in **C** for
8 I hope to do a course ____ nursing.
A of **B** in **C** at

Collocations with verbs

4 3.13 **Match the nouns (a–f) to the verbs (1–6) to make expressions about health. Listen and check.**

1 take ____ **a)** your leg
2 make ____ **b)** ill/better
3 break ____ **c)** a cold
4 brush ____ **d)** an appointment
5 catch ____ **e)** your temperature
6 feel ____ **f)** your teeth

5 **Complete the sentences using the correct form of the expressions from Exercise 4.**

1 I ______________ from one of my friends at school and had to stay in bed for two days.
2 Jack couldn't walk for eight weeks after he ______________ during a skiing holiday last year.
3 Have you ______________ to see the doctor yet?
4 Your head feels very warm. I think I need to ______________ to see if you are ill.
5 It's important to ______________ every morning and evening so they are clean and healthy.
6 If you ______________ at school, you should tell the school nurse.

1 **Work in pairs and do the following:**

1 Make a list of all the health problems you can think of.

2 Look at the list together and decide which health problems you should go to hospital for.

EXAM SKILL

Identifying incorrect answers

- Sometimes the speaker says something that looks very similar to an answer option. This doesn't mean the answer option is correct unless it means exactly the same as what you hear.
- Listen carefully to who says what. An answer may sound correct, but it may be completely wrong or contain only some of the important information.

2 3.14 **Listen to four people talking about their health and choose the correct answers.**

1 The boy is visiting the doctor because
A his head hurts. **B** his ear hurts.

2 The girl had an accident
A on her way home. **B** on her way to school.

3 The boy hurt his ankle when he was
A running. **B** playing tennis.

4 The girl is having problems
A seeing. **B** hearing.

OPTIMISE YOUR EXAM

3-option multiple choice (monologues and dialogues)

- Read the questions and the answer options carefully before you listen.
- Remember, just because you hear one or more of the words that are written in the answer options, it doesn't mean it is a correct answer. For example, you may hear a teacher say *You may choose your own topics, but check with me before you begin your projects*, and the option answer says *The teacher will check the students' projects*. The words *check* and *projects* are included, but the answer is incorrect.

3 3.15 **For each question, choose the correct answer.**

1 You will hear two friends talking about their plans.
What do they decide to do at the weekend?
A play tennis
B watch football
C go swimming

2 You will hear a boy, Sam, talking to his football coach about his health.
What mustn't Sam do?
A He mustn't play sports for a week.
B He mustn't take medicine.
C He mustn't eat sugar.

3 You will hear a father talking to his daughter, Sarah.
What is Sarah's dad asking her to do?
A clean her room
B help her mother
C look after her pet

4 You will hear two friends talking about their friend David.
How did Anna try to help her friend?
A She took him to a concert.
B She wanted to take him to the doctor.
C She gave him some medicine.

5 You will hear a teacher talking to Peter's mother.
Why is the teacher talking to his mum?
A to discuss his homework
B to tell her about his health
C to say why he was late

4 3.15 **Listen again and check your answers.**

THINK | RESEARCH | CULTURE | **LEARN** | ME

Complete the words and phrases from the audio to show interest or to agree with something.

1 G_ _ _
2 Y_ _ _, OK
3 … what a _ _ _ _ !
4 Oh _ _ _ _ !

 ▶ **Workbook Unit 10:** Listening, page 80, exercises 1, 2, 3

GRAMMAR 2 | Verb patterns: verb + infinitive / *-ing*

Grammar in context

Look at these sentences from the audio in the listening lesson and answer the questions.

1 *I **offered to take** him to the doctor.*
2 *… he **hates taking** medicine.*
3 *What do they **decide to do** at the weekend?*
4 *I **told** him **to drink** lots of water …*
5 *… he **keeps getting** ill.*

a) Which verbs are followed by the infinitive?
________ , ________ , ________

b) Which verbs are followed by the *-ing* form?
________ , ________

REMEMBER

- When we use two verbs in a sentence, there isn't a rule about whether the second verb is in the infinitive or ends in *-ing*. You have to learn the verb patterns.
- Common verbs followed by the infinitive are: *agree, choose, decide, help, hope, try* and *want*.
- Common verbs followed by the *-ing* form are: *don't mind, enjoy, keep, spend time* and *stop*.

▶ **See Grammar reference, Unit 10,** page 153

1 Choose the correct verb to complete each sentence.

1 My dad **decided** / **enjoyed** to do more exercise.
2 The nurses wanted **helping** / **to help** my grandmother when she was in hospital.
3 My brother **didn't mind** / **agreed** taking the medicine.
4 Paul **hoped** / **kept** to visit his best friend in hospital.
5 Pippa **chose** / **stopped** eating unhealthy food when she felt ill.
6 Yasmin **wanted** / **kept** getting stomach aches when she ate bread.

2 Complete the sentences using the correct form of the verbs in brackets.

1 Leo decided ________ (**make**) an appointment to see the doctor.
2 Laura stopped ________ (**take**) the medicine after she felt better.
3 The students enjoyed ________ (**hear**) about what the nurses did at work.
4 They wanted ________ (**eat**) healthier food and do more exercise.
5 My grandfather didn't mind ________ (**take**) the medicine for his stomach problem.
6 The nurse spent time ________ (**put on**) a new bandage for me.

3 Complete the article using the infinitive or *-ing* form of the verbs in brackets.

Everyday solutions for everyday problems

When we feel ill or have a health problem most of us decide (**1**) ________ (**visit**) a chemist or doctor. But sometimes the things we have at home can help us too.

Do you feel sick when you travel by car or bus? It happens to a lot of people. Many hope (**2**) ________ (**feel**) better after taking expensive medicines, while other people just stop (**3**) ________ (**travel**) in cars and buses. Before you do that, you might want (**4**) ________ (**try**) this. Scientists have found that the smell of fresh lemon can stop you feeling sick. So the next time you travel by car, just cut a lemon in half and put it under your nose. It will help you (**5**) ________ (**enjoy**) the journey.

We all know that it's important to exercise regularly. A lot of people try (**6**) ________ (**get**) fit by running or going to the gym once or twice a week. This is usually a good thing. However, it can sometimes be a problem. One surprising thing happens to a few people when they stop (**7**) ________ (**run**) and take off their shoes. Smelly feet! If this happens to you, the solution is to put your feet in a bowl of warm black tea. There is something in the tea that stops the smell. If you keep (**8**) ________ (**do**) this every day for a few weeks, your feet will smell much nicer!

SAY IT RIGHT

Resource centre: Unit 10
/ɪ/ and /iː/

THINK | RESEARCH | CULTURE | LEARN | **ME**

Write sentences about things …
- you enjoy doing now to get fit.
- you would like to do to be healthier.

▶ **Workbook Unit 10:** Grammar 2, page 79, exercises 1, 2

Talk2Me
Let me think …

Flipped classroom

1 Watch the *Talk2Me* video and answer the questions.

1 How much are the tickets for students?
2 What time is it when their call is answered?
3 How many tickets do they buy?

2 Watch the video again. Underline the words and phrases in the *Phrase expert* box that you hear on the video.

PHRASE EXPERT

Just a minute, please. | Let's have a look at … | Let me think … | Let's see … | Looking at the information, it says … | OK. | Well …

3 3.16 Listen to four students answering questions. Circle opinion or example to show how they extend their answers. One student does both.

1 opinion / example
2 opinion / example
3 opinion / example
4 opinion / example

4 3.16 Listen again and write down the expressions which helped you answer Exercise 3.

1 ____________________
2 ____________________
3 ____________________
4 ____________________

5 In pairs, give your opinion on each activity. Give an example to support your opinion.

A

B

C

EXAM SKILL

Giving yourself time to think

- Sometimes you may need a little time to think before you answer.
- If you can't think of an answer immediately, use phrases like *Let me think*, *Let me see* or *Well, …* to give yourself more time to think before answering.

6 3.16 Listen again and note down the phrases you hear two of the speakers use to give themselves time to think.

1 ____________________
2 ____________________

OPTIMISE YOUR EXAM

Discussion

- In this part of the test, the examiner will ask you and your partner the same questions.
- Listen carefully to what your partner says and try not to repeat his/her answer.
- Give yourself time to think and use your own ideas. If you have the same opinion as your partner, say something like *I agree with … . I also think/prefer … because … .*

7 Take it in turns to ask and answer these questions.

Student A to Student B:
How often do you play sport?
Which is more important – doing a sport or eating healthily?

Student B to Student A:
Do you think it's important to keep fit?
What do you do to keep healthy?

THINK | RESEARCH | CULTURE | LEARN | ME

Keep a diary in English for a day. Note down everything you eat and the physical activities you do.

▶ **Workbook Unit 10:** Speaking, page 81, exercises 1, 2, 3, 4

1 Work in pairs. Look at the photos and answer the questions.

1 What do you think about the food in these two photos?
2 Which food would you rather eat? Why?
3 Do you usually follow a healthy diet?
4 Have you ever had stomach ache?

EXAM SKILL

Using the present perfect

- Remember that the present perfect is used to show a link between the present and the past. We use it to talk about an unfinished time. For example, *He's been at the hospital* ***since*** *seven o'clock.* (He went there and he's still there.)
- We use the time expressions *for*, *since*, *already*, *just* and *yet* with the present perfect. We use *for* with a period of time and *since* with a specific event or date.
- Remember to check the spelling of the past participles, especially if they are irregular.

2 Match the answers (a–g) to the questions (1–6). There is one extra answer you do not need.

1 How long have you eaten a healthy diet for? ____
2 Where's your lunch? ____
3 Have you made dinner? ____
4 Have you had a stomach ache for long? ____
5 Has Dad done the shopping? ____
6 Have you tried Italian food? ____

a) Yes, but it's still too hot to eat.
b) Yes, already.
c) For three years.
d) Not yet, he's just left work.
e) I've already eaten it.
f) Yes, but only once.
g) No, just since this afternoon.

3 Complete the sentences with the correct word.

1 I've __________ called the ambulance three times.
2 I haven't had a headache __________ over a week now.
3 __________ you seen the doctor yet?
4 I've __________ the medicine every day for a week.
5 How long __________ you had backache for?
6 I've eaten a lot of fruit __________ I was small.

OPTIMISE YOUR EXAM

Open cloze

- In this part of the exam, the missing word could be a time expression linked to the present perfect.
- Remember:
  - we use *yet* in a negative sentence or a question. For example, *The doctor has**n't** arrived **yet**. / Has the doctor arrived **yet?***
  - we use *already* or *just* between *have/has* and the main verb. For example, *They have **already/just** been to the gym three times this week.*
  - we use *for* or *since* after *have/has* and the main verb. For example, *I have known Tim **for** a long time / **since** 2012.*

4 For each question, write the correct answer. Write ONE word for each gap.

Hi Marty,

Have I told you that I went ___to___ hospital last week? I have (1) __________ a stomach ache every day (2) __________ a week, so last Sunday my dad took me to the hospital. The doctor asked me what I eat every day and he told me I have to eat healthy food. I haven't had any chips or chocolate (3) __________ Sunday. It's very hard! I've already eaten a salad and a lot (4) __________ fruit today but I'm still hungry. I can't wait (5) __________ feel better. I think I'm going to go for a cheese burger then!

Kerry

THINK | RESEARCH | CULTURE | LEARN | ME

Find out about which types of food are the best and worst for your:
a) stomach **b)** throat **c)** eyes.

WRITING | Picture story

1 In pairs or groups, answer the questions.

1 Do you do anything to keep fit? What do you do?
2 Have you ever hurt yourself while playing sport? What happened?
3 Have you ever been in an accident? What happened?
4 Have you ever broken your arm or leg? What happened?

2 Look at the picture story. In pairs or groups, say what you think the story is.

EXAM SKILL

Writing a good ending

- After you have written your story, it's a good idea to finish with a conclusion, that is, a short sentence that sums it up. For example, *It was the best football game!*
- Ask yourself how the people felt at the end of the story – did they have fun? / was it a great day? Then write the last sentence. For example, *They had a lot of fun and Anna was very happy!*

3 Look at the story in Exercise 2. Write S for the sentences that can start a story and E for the sentences that can end it.

1 Jason was sad and upset. ____
2 Last weekend, Jason was in the park with his friend. ____
3 It was the worst day ever! ____
4 It wasn't a good day for Jason. ____
5 On Sunday, Jason and Ben decided to ride their skateboards. ____

4 Read the story about Jason and Ben. Add a sentence to start and end the story as well as linking words.

____

____

They were skateboarding when Jason fell and hurt his arm.

__________ Ben called an ambulance because he was worried.

__________ , the ambulance took Jason to the hospital.

____

____

OPTIMISE YOUR EXAM

Picture story

- Make sure you say enough about each picture in the story. For example, don't just write *They went to the park*. Give more details to reach the word length needed and make your sentences more interesting. For example, *They went to the park because it was a nice day.*
- Use *because* to explain the reasons for something happening, and *so* to explain the results of something. For example, *He went to the dentist because he had toothache., Julie hurt her foot so she couldn't walk.*

5 Look at the pictures and read the exam task. Write three adjectives to describe each picture.

Look at the three pictures.
Write the story shown in the pictures.
Write **35 words** or more.

6 Look at the pictures in Exercise 5 again. Circle the correct words to complete the sentences about the boy in the story.

1 He was walking quickly **because** / **so** it was raining.
2 It was raining, **because** / **so** he was walking quickly.
3 He stayed at home **because** / **so** he was sick.
4 He was sick, **because** / **so** he stayed at home.

7 Plan Plan your story. Use the table to help you.

	Who?	Where?	What?
Picture 1			
Picture 2			
Picture 3			

8 Write Write your story in an appropriate style. Write 35 words or more.

9 Check Before you hand in your story, complete this checklist.

Checklist

- ◯ I've followed my writing plan.
- ◯ I've written an introductory sentence.
- ◯ I've written about the three pictures.
- ◯ I've used the correct tenses.
- ◯ I've used linking words.
- ◯ I've written a good ending.
- ◯ I've used a good range of vocabulary.
- ◯ I've written 35+ words.
- ◯ I've checked my spelling, grammar and punctuation.

Writing reference, page 164 ▶ **Workbook Unit 10:** Writing, page 82, exercises 1, 2, 3, 4, 5, 6, 7 and Progress check 10, page 83

PROGRESS CHECK UNITS 9–10

GRAMMAR AND VOCABULARY

1 Complete the zero, first and second conditional sentences using the correct form of the verbs in brackets.

1 If we _______________ (**live**) in a warmer country, we could go to the beach every day.
2 When I have a headache, I _______________ (**lie**) on my bed and rest.
3 My mum always _______________ (**give**) me lots to drink if I have a temperature.
4 If my legs were longer, I _______________ (**be**) really good at volleyball.
5 If they get up early tomorrow, they _______________ (**go**) to the mountains.
6 How would you feel if you _______________ (**win**) a race at the Olympics?
7 If I _______________ (**pass**) all my exams, I'll become a dentist.
8 They _______________ (**enjoy**) their holiday in India more if they learn about the culture.
9 She _______________ (**feel**) a lot better if she stopped watching so much TV.
10 If you brush your teeth twice a day, you _______________ (**not need**) to see the dentist so much.

__/10

2 Choose the correct word to complete each sentence.

1 Afonso Mendes works in a hospital **for** / **of** / **to** children in Liverpool.
2 This morning, he is **giving** / **having** / **taking** the temperature of Eddie, a 10-year-old boy.
3 Eddie has a problem **on** / **with** / **for** his ears.
4 He **feels** / **catches** / **takes** pain when he opens his mouth.
5 Afonso spends a long time **tries** / **try** / **trying** to help Eddie feel better.

__/5

3 Read the descriptions. What is the word for each one? The first letter is given.

1 It is between the eyes and the mouth. n__ __ __
2 You listen with these. e__ __ __
3 Food goes here. s__ __ __ __ __ __
4 You walk on these. f__ __ __
5 This joins your head to your body. n__ __ __
6 You hold your pen with this. h__ __ __
7 You move these fast when you run. l__ __ __
8 The person who checks your teeth. d__ __ __ __ __ __
9 It's behind you. b__ __ __
10 You can put this round your knee if you hurt it. b__ __ __ __ __ __

__/10

4 Choose the correct word or phrase to complete each sentence.

1 Mark has been a doctor **since** / **for** ten years.
2 Charlotte hopes **to work** / **working** in a children's hospital when she finishes university.
3 Jack wants to be a nurse, but he hasn't left school **yet** / **already**.
4 It's **just** / **since** stopped raining, so we can go outside now.
5 Mrs Oliver keeps **to go** / **going** to see the doctor with her back pain.
6 I've **already** / **just** been swimming and done my homework this morning.
7 My dad has just stopped **to eat** / **eating** unhealthy food. I'm really happy about it.
8 Tim didn't enjoy **to take** / **taking** the medicine, but he knew it would make him feel better.
9 I haven't been to the doctor **since** / **for** last January.
10 My sister has always been interested in **to learn** / **learning** about animals and birds.

__/10

5 **Complete the dialogue between two friends. Choose from the list (A–H) what Fiona says to Jake. Use the letters only once. There are three extra letters you do not need.**

Jake: I've just heard some news about Sophie.
Fiona: (1) ____
Jake: She's got a problem with her leg. She's in hospital now.
Fiona: (2) ____
Jake: If it is, I don't think she'll be able to go anywhere.
Fiona: (3) ____
Jake: I don't know what they said. I haven't spoken to her yet.
Fiona: (4) ____
Jake: She fell off her bike.
Fiona: (5) ____
Jake: Good idea. Me too.

A I think I'll go and see her tonight.
B Where did she go?
C I think she'll be fine. It's nothing serious.
D What have the doctors said?
E How did it happen?
F She's going skiing on Saturday. I hope it isn't broken.
G What is it?
H Can I borrow your phone?

__/5

6 **Complete the sentences with the words in the box.**

clouds	foggy	forest	hill	ice	river	snow	sunny	thunderstorm	wet

1 I prefer to go to the beach when it's warm and __________ .
2 The Thames is a __________ that takes water through London to the sea.
3 There is lots of __________ on the mountains. We can go skiing.
4 Did you hear the __________ last night? It woke me up.
5 There are lots of __________ in the sky. I think it's going to rain.
6 You shouldn't drive when there is __________ on the road. It's dangerous.
7 It is so __________ today I can't see anything outside.
8 If you walk to the top of that __________ you can see the whole of the city.
9 You'll need an umbrella because it's very __________ today.
10 Take your jacket when you go for a walk in the __________ . It can be cold under the trees.

__/10

Total score __/50

EXAM SKILLS

Tick the statements that true for you. Review the skills in the unit if you need more help.

I can ...	**Unit/page**
☐ think logically about the information in a text	Unit 9 p92
☐ understand a speaker's questions	Unit 9 p96
☐ talk about the weather	Unit 9 p98
☐ identify conditional sentences	Unit 9 p99
☐ express preferences	Unit 9 p100
☐ decide the general message of a text	Unit 10 p102
☐ identify incorrect answers in multiple-choice activities	Unit 10 p106
☐ give myself time to think in a discussion	Unit 10 p108
☐ use the present perfect	Unit 10 p109
☐ write a good beginning and ending to a story	Unit 10 p110

11 The world of work

READING | 3-option multiple choice (long text) | A magazine article

1 In pairs or as a group, answer the questions.

1 What job did you want to do when you were six years old?
2 What do you want to do now? Why?

EXAM SKILL

Identifying incorrect answer options

- Sometimes, two answer options both seem to be correct. When this happens, ask yourself how they are different.
- Then look at the text again and decide which one is correct and which one doesn't quite answer the question. For example, an answer which seems correct may not have all the necessary information.

2 Look at the question and answers below. How many answers seem correct?

Which is a job that people do on trains?

A They check the tickets.
B They make sure passengers get on the train on time.
C They make sure the trains aren't dirty.

3 Now read paragraph 1 of the article on page 115 carefully and answer the questions about Exercise 2.

1 Which is the best answer in Exercise 2? ____
2 Which answer is incorrect because the information isn't in the paragraph? ____
3 Which answer seems correct, but doesn't match the information in the paragraph? ____
4 What extra information is needed to make it correct? ____________________

OPTIMISE YOUR EXAM

3-option multiple choice (long text)

- When you are not sure of an answer, cross out the answer option that is definitely wrong. This option is usually completely wrong because the text doesn't say this.
- When you are left with two possible answer options, read them carefully and check the part of the text that answers the question. Make sure that every part of the option you think is right answers the question. Then make your final choice.

ALL ABOARD THE CHILDREN'S RAILWAY

1 Are you interested in trains? Have you ever thought about all the jobs people do on a railway? It isn't easy. All the trains have to be clean, the engineers need to check everything is working, someone needs to sell the tickets and take the money, and the trains mustn't be late. The trains must leave and arrive on time and this must match the timetable. And, very importantly – the trains must be safe. Almost everywhere in the world, railway staff are adults. But in Budapest, there is a special railway and nearly everyone who works there is a child.

2 The Gyermekvasút, or Children's Railway, in Hungary, first opened to customers in 1948. And it is still taking passengers on journeys from a few hundred metres to 11 kilometres, through the hills in the west of the city. The train drivers and engineers are adults, but all the other staff, from the ticket sellers to the station managers, are between 10 and 14 years old. All the workers have to wear a smart uniform, and they are all volunteers, which means they don't get paid. Every year, lots of children want to work on the railway, but they don't give jobs to everyone. Anyone who doesn't get good marks at school won't get a job. The children who get jobs have two days off school every month to work on the railway.

3 The Children's Railway isn't a toy or a model railway. It is part of the national railway system of Hungary and an important part of Budapest's transport system. Each year over 300,000 customers use the railway to get to work, visit friends or just to see how well the children do their jobs!

4 3.17 **Read the article and the questions. For each question, choose the correct answer.**

1 Why is the railway in Budapest unusual?
A Adults work there only two days a week.
B Most people who work there are children.
C Only children work there.

2 What is the longest journey on the Children's Railway?
A a few hundred metres to the city
B through some hills in the city
C to the countryside near the city

3 Which staff wear a uniform?
A the people who work on the railway
B some of the children
C only the volunteers

4 How are children selected to work on the railway?
A They must have clean school uniforms.
B They have to be teenagers.
C They must do well at school.

5 Why do some people use the Children's Railway?
A to travel to their jobs
B to meet their friends there
C to see Hungary by train

5 **Match the highlighted words from the article to a definition.**

1 clothes that all people who work or study at the same organisation wear ____________
2 the opposite of 'dirty' ____________
3 the ways of moving people or things from one place to another ____________
4 a piece of paper or online text that allows you to enter a place, travel on a bus or train, etc. ____________
5 the opposite of 'early' ____________
6 the people who work somewhere ____________
7 a list of times that says when all buses, trains, etc. arrive or leave ____________
8 the opposite of 'dangerous' ____________

Grammar in context

Find the sentences in the text on page 115 and then do the task below.

1 *... the engineers need to check* ***everything*** *is working, ...* (paragraph 1)
2 *...* ***someone*** *needs to sell the tickets and take the money, ...* (paragraph 1)
3 *Almost* ***everywhere*** *in the world, railway staff are adults.* (paragraph 1)
4 *... but they don't give jobs to* ***everyone.*** (paragraph 2)
5 ***Anyone*** *who doesn't get good marks at school won't get a job.* (paragraph 2)

Complete the sentences with *-one*, *-thing* or *-where*.

a) We use ___________ to talk about objects and actions.
b) We use ___________ to talk about people.
c) We use ___________ to talk about places.

REMEMBER

- We use indefinite pronouns to talk about people or things without saying exactly who or what they are.
- We use *every-* to talk about all of the things, places or people: ***Everyone*** *in my family likes trains.*
- We use *some-* in positive sentences: *I want* ***something*** *to eat, but I'm not sure what.*
- We use *any-* in negative sentences and questions: *Does* ***anyone*** *in your family like trains? I don't want* ***anything*** *to eat.*

► **See Grammar reference, Unit 11,** page 154

1 Choose the correct word to complete each sentence.

1 We've looked **everywhere** / **everything** but we can't find the car keys.
2 Is there **everything** / **anything** about the job that you don't like?
3 I didn't listen to **everything** / **everywhere** the manager said.
4 They are looking for **anyone** / **someone** who can cook and clean.
5 My mum's new office is **somewhere** / **anywhere** in the city centre.
6 There's **something** / **anything** I need to ask my boss today.

2 Complete the sentences with the words in the box.

anything	anywhere	everyone
everywhere	someone	something

1 ___________ who visits the office must speak to the receptionist.
2 Is there ___________ I can do to help?
3 They have customers ___________ in the country, in all the towns and cities.
4 ___________ in the office is going to be the next manager.
5 I can't find my mobile phone and diary ___________ .
6 There's ___________ I need to do before I leave today, so don't wait for me.

3 Complete the text. Choose the best word (A, B or C) for each gap.

News | Home

PLAN ahead

In all schools and colleges, students (**1**) ____ in the UK, have a chance to do work experience before they finish school. This means they spend one or two weeks working to learn what it's like to have a job. Of course, (**2**) ____ has different experiences, and two weeks isn't long enough to learn (**3**) ____ there is to know about a job. But most students say they definitely learnt (**4**) ____ while they were on work experience, and there was always (**5**) ____ there to help them.

However, there is a school in London that wants to make work experience even better for its students. Lister Community School uses technology called the *Life Skills Pod* to help students choose work experience. Inside the *pod* (a room with a large screen), students choose (**6**) ____ they want to work, for example a factory or a hotel. Then they have to answer questions, which could be about (**7**) ____ that's connected to the place and job they've chosen. Students who use the *Life Skills Pod* usually find it helps them to decide where to work and it also helps to make sure they don't go (**8**) ____ they won't enjoy.

	A	B	C
1	**A** everything	**B** everywhere	**C** everyone
2	**A** everyone	**B** anyone	**C** someone
3	**A** anything	**B** everything	**C** something
4	**A** somewhere	**B** something	**C** someone
5	**A** anyone	**B** someone	**C** everyone
6	**A** something	**B** somewhere	**C** someone
7	**A** somewhere	**B** everyone	**C** anything
8	**A** anywhere	**B** something	**C** everyone

SAY IT RIGHT

Resource centre: Unit 11
/θ/

THINK | RESEARCH | **CULTURE** | LEARN | ME

How do young people in your country learn about and get ready for the world of work?

Words connected with *work and jobs*

1 3.18 **Match the jobs in the box to the descriptions. Listen and check.**

actor | cleaner | engineer | firefighter | journalist | pilot | police officer | shop assistant

1 someone who writes articles for a newspaper ______________
2 someone who flies planes ______________
3 someone who cleans an office or a home ______________
4 someone who is a member of the police ______________
5 someone who works in a theatre or in films ______________
6 someone who helps you in a shop ______________
7 someone who stops fires ______________
8 someone who designs or builds things such as roads, bridges or machines ______________

2 3.19 **Complete the text with the words in the box. Listen and check.**

career | companies | customer | earn | managers | meetings | social media officer | staff | worker

Thousands of us love using social networking. But have you ever thought of it as a (**1**) ______________ ? There are jobs for young people in most of the big social media (**2**) ______________ . As a new (**3**) ______________ , you might be a (**4**) ______________ , for example – working with some of the social media (**5**) ______________ , working on the website and going to (**6**) ______________ . And if you're good at what you do, you'll get the chance to do different jobs and (**7**) ______________ more money. So instead of being a social media (**8**) ______________ , why not think about becoming a member of (**9**) ______________ ?

Words with *-ian / -ress / -ist / -er / -r*

3 3.20 **Write the word stems in the correct column to make the names of jobs. Some words can go in more than one column.**

art | chem | clean | dent | drive | engine | explore | farm | football | journal | manage | music | photograph | reception | wait | write

-ian	-ress	-ist	-er	-r

4 **Complete the sentences using the jobs from Exercise 3.**

1 Jo's a ______________ . She looks after animals and grows vegetables.
2 Phil's an excellent ______________ . He plays the piano, guitar and violin.
3 The ______________ answers the phone and helps visitors when they arrive at the office.
4 The ______________ made a mistake. I didn't order a chicken salad.
5 When I have toothache, I usually visit my ______________ .
6 If you are late to work, the ______________ won't be happy.

Words + prepositions

5 3.21 **Complete the sentences. Choose the correct preposition (A, B or C) for each gap. Listen and check.**

1 Alex is the manager ____ a clothes shop in the city centre.
A of **B** on **C** with
2 Charlie hopes to get a diploma ____ music from a college in London.
A from **B** in **C** to
3 Steph is a receptionist and she works ____ a company that makes computers.
A with **B** for **C** to
4 Judy is the singer ____ a local rock band.
A at **B** on **C** in
5 Michael is a writer ____ children's books.
A in **B** to **C** of
6 We have an important meeting today ____ the manager.
A of **B** with **C** to

▶ Vocabulary reference, page 162 ▶ Workbook Unit 11: Vocabulary, pages 86–87, exercises 1, 2, 3

1 **Work in pairs and answer the questions.**

1 Think about things you like doing in your free time. Could you start a business doing any of these things?
2 If you could start a business, what would you do?

EXAM SKILL

Taking notes

- Don't write down everything you hear, just write the important words.
- Be careful with spelling, especially when the word is spelt out for you.

2 3.22 **Listen to the names of people and places being spelt out and write them down.**

1 ______ 4 ______
2 ______ 5 ______
3 ______

3 3.23 **Listen to Ed talking about his business idea and correct the notes.**

The concert

When? (1) in June
Where? (2) in Dan's large house
Number of people: (3) 18 _people and_ six _bands played_
Best band: (4) _Jaybeeland_
Earned: (5) _£_ 220

OPTIMISE YOUR EXAM

Gap fill

- You should only write one word in each gap. Remember, in the exam, contractions such as *isn't* and *weren't* count as two words.
- Remember to write the exact word you hear.

4 3.24 **For each question, write the correct answer in the gap. Write one word or a number or a date or a time.**

You will hear a boy telling people about his business.

ZI YANG'S BUSINESS

Started at age of: _14_
Father works near: (1) ______
Sells: (2) ______
No orders on: (3) ______
Orders by: (4) ______ pm
Delivers to: (5) ______ customers

5 3.24 **Listen again and check your answers.**

THINK | **RESEARCH** | CULTURE | LEARN | ME

Find out about a young business person from your country who has earned a lot of money. What was their idea? How did they make money?

GRAMMAR 2 | Relative clauses: *who, which, that*

Grammar in context

Look at these sentences from the audio in the listening lesson and do the task below.

1 *Altogether there are 52 people* ***who*** *buy from us every week.*

2 *... my dad works in a big factory* ***which*** *is near Guangzhou ...*

3 *... a business* ***that*** *I started a year ago.*

Choose the correct word.

a) In sentence 1, *who* is about the person **buying / selling** fruit.

b) In sentence 2, *which* is about **the dad / the factory**.

c) In sentence 3, *that* is about **a business / a person**.

REMEMBER

- Relative clauses give us more information about someone or something we have already mentioned earlier in a sentence.
- We use relative pronouns (*who, which, that*) at the beginning of relative clauses.
- We use the relative pronoun *who* to talk about a person or people, and *that* or *which* to talk about a thing or things: *Henry's the man* ***who*** *works in the new offices in town. Reading is something* ***that/which*** *I like doing in my spare time.*

▶ **See Grammar reference, Unit 11,** page 154

1 Choose the correct words to complete the sentences.

1 It's a question **which / who** no-one has the answer to.

2 The secretary **who / which** works in our office is away today.

3 Kelly has got a job **that / who** she is enjoying a lot.

4 The message **who / which** you sent yesterday hasn't arrived yet.

5 I want to get a job in the new office building **who / which** has just been built.

6 Is that the mechanic **who / which** repaired your car last week?

7 One of the men **which / who** works in our London office is coming to visit us today.

8 Where's the shop assistant **which / who** works in the food department?

2 Make one sentence from these two sentences using *who, which* or *that* to replace the underlined words.

1 Alex is a manager. He works in my dad's office.
Alex is a manager who works in my dad's office.

2 There is a factory near here. It makes cars.
____

3 Fred is the waiter. He took our order.
____

4 I would like a desk. It is near the window.
____

5 They had a meeting. It was with the new manager.
____

3 Complete the article with *who, which* or *that*.

I'm a firefighter (**1**) __________ works in a large city in the north-east of England. I love my job, but it's really hard work. We work in teams (**2**) __________ are called watches, and there are eight of us in each team. I've known the people (**3**) __________ are in my team for a long time.

The hours (**4**) __________ I work are not the same every day. Today I started work at 8am and will finish at 6pm, but next week I will work through the night. Every day, we need to check everything at the fire station is working. It's an important job (**5**) __________ usually takes about an hour.

At any time, we can get a call from someone (**6**) __________ needs help. This morning we went to a hotel (**7**) __________ was on fire. There were over 100 guests there and a lot of them were very afraid. Inside the hotel, there was fire everywhere. It was really hot and very dangerous, but we helped all the people (**8**) __________ were there to get outside safely. It's all in a day's work!

11 SPEAKING | Questions

Flipped classroom

1 **Watch the *Talk2Me* video and answer the questions.**

1 Whose birthday is it soon?
2 Where is the party going to be?
3 How many people can go to the party?

2 **Watch the video again. Underline the phrases in the *Phrase expert* box that you hear on the video.**

PHRASE EXPERT

I have (two) brothers and (two) sisters.
I'm an only child, but I have (three cousins).
In my family there are (five) people.
My dad/mum is a (job) …

3 **Work in pairs. Follow the instructions.**

1 Write down as many jobs as you can in one minute.
2 Write down as many family members as you can in one minute.
3 Tell your partner about the jobs people in your family do.
Example: *My uncle is a builder.*

4 3.25 **Listen to a student talking about her family and decide if the statements are T (True) or F (False).**

1 She's got two brothers and a sister. T / F
2 Her older brother is an actor. T / F
3 Matthew works in an office. T / F
4 Her dad works in Manchester. T / F
5 Her mum is a lawyer. T / F

EXAM SKILL

Talking about jobs

- Sometimes, you have to talk about jobs. It could be about a job you want to do in the future or perhaps a question about your parents' jobs. You can say *My mum/dad works for* + company; *He/She works as a/an* + job; *He/She works in* + place.
- Remember to use the present simple to talk about someone's daily routines. For example, *She checks her emails when she gets to work.*
- When we talk about situations that last for a short time, we also use the present continuous. For example, *He usually works in Barcelona, but this week he's working in Madrid.*

5 3.25 **Choose the correct form to complete each sentence. Listen and check.**

1 Marta **works** / **is working** in a theatre. She's worked there for ten years.
2 Matthew often **meets** / **is meeting** his manager in the morning.
3 Anna **cooks** / **is cooking** lunch at the moment.
4 Jane usually works in an office, but this month she **visits** / **'s visiting** customers.

OPTIMISE YOUR EXAM

Questions

- In this part of the test, the examiner may ask you about your family.
- Learn to describe and talk about things such as your parents' jobs, family routines, etc.
- Remember to answer the questions in full sentences or use short answers and then add more information.

6 **Work in pairs. Take turns asking and answering the questions. Make notes of your partner's answers.**

1 What's your name?
______
2 Where do you live?
______
3 What jobs do people in your family do?
______
4 What job do you want to do after school or university?
______
5 What's more important to you – earning lots of money or helping people? Why?
______

▶ **Workbook Unit 11:** Speaking, pages 88–89, exercises 1, 2, 3

LANGUAGE IN USE | Open cloze

1 **Work in pairs. Look at the photo in Exercise 4 and answer the questions.**

1 What job do you think the woman in the photo is doing?

2 What do you think are the good and bad things about doing a job like this? Make a list and then discuss with your partner.

EXAM SKILL

Using indefinite and relative pronouns

- We use indefinite pronouns to talk about people (*someone, anyone, everyone, no-one/nobody*), places (*somewhere, anywhere, everywhere, nowhere*) or things (*something, anything, everything, nothing*) without saying exactly who or what they are.
  For example, *I want **something** to drink.*
- We use relative pronouns after a noun, to make it clear which person or thing we are talking about.
  We use *who* to talk about people, for example, *The woman **who** works in that shop is my aunt.*
  We use *which* and *that* to talk about places and things, for example, *France is a country **that/which** I want to visit.*

2 **Choose the correct word to complete the gap.**

1 Linda is someone __________ likes working at weekends.
a) who **b)** which

2 I think __________ is going to the party on Saturday.
a) someone **b)** everyone

3 My cousin works in a company __________ is in Madrid.
a) where **b)** that

4 Ethan is looking for __________ new to live.
a) somewhere **b)** anywhere

5 I would like a job __________ is interesting.
a) who **b)** which

3 **Complete the sentences with the correct word.**

1 He is the journalist __________ asked me a lot of questions.

2 I want to go __________ hot for my holiday.

3 I like to travel to places __________ have lovely beaches!

4 I can't believe that __________ has a suitcase I can borrow!

5 I love Italy, __________ I go people are always very friendly.

OPTIMISE YOUR EXAM

Open cloze

- Remember that an indefinite pronoun is used instead of a noun. If there is no noun in the gapped sentence, the missing word could be an indefinite pronoun.
- If there is a gap between a noun and a verb, the missing word could be a relative pronoun.
  For example, *Helen is the girl **who** lives in my street.*

4 **For each question, write the correct answer. Write ONE word for each gap.**

From: Sara
To: Dany

Hi Dany,

I work for ___a___ travel magazine. I'm lucky because I have travelled almost **(1)** __________ in the world. I write stories about the amazing places I've visited. If you are **(2)** __________ who enjoys travelling, this is a great way to see the world **(3)** __________ you work. I like **(4)** __________ new people, but I'm always away from home. I've met people in big cities and people **(5)** __________ live in trees in the forest. I don't earn much money **(6)** __________ it's a very exciting job and I get to see the world for free!

Good luck!

Sara

THINK | RESEARCH | CULTURE | LEARN | ME

Which country in the world would you most like to work in? Why?

▶ **Vocabulary reference,** page 162 ▶ **Workbook Unit 11:** Language in Use, page 89, exercises 1, 2, 3

11 WRITING | An article

1 **In pairs or as a group, look at the adverts below and answer the questions. Use the adjectives in the box to help you.**

easy | boring | dangerous | difficult | interesting | safe

1 What do you think you have to do in each job?
2 Which job would you prefer to do? Why?

Dog walkers needed!
We're looking for people who love dogs … and exercise!
Interested? Call us on 06295 332131

WAITER WANTED
Friday and Saturday 5–8pm
£10 per hour
Phone for details: 022435 8181

2 **Tick the statements that you agree with and then discuss them in groups.**

Students should work because …

- they'll learn to be more responsible. ☐
- it's a good way to use their free time. ☐
- it teaches them the value of money. ☐

Students shouldn't work because …

- they'll have less time to study. ☐
- they won't see their friends enough. ☐
- they'll have less time for hobbies and exercise. ☐

EXAM SKILL

Planning an article

- Read the exam task and underline the things you need to write about in your article.
- Don't just start writing – think first. Write down ideas for each of the points you have underlined. Then choose the best ones.
- Use a new paragraph for each new idea.

3 **Read the advert in an English-language magazine and answer questions 1–4.**

Articles wanted!

TEENAGERS WHO WORK

Write an article telling us if students should work.
What jobs are best for teenagers?
Do you think it's good for students to work?
Why should/shouldn't students work?

The best articles will be published next month.

1 How many things are you asked to write about in the task? ________
2 What are they? Underline them.
3 How many paragraphs do you need to write? ________
4 Which points can go in the same paragraph?
____

4 **Read the article that was written in reply to the magazine advert in Exercise 3 and circle the correct words.**

STUDENTS WITH JOBS

Should students work? That's an interesting question. A job leaves less time for homework, **(1) while / however**, students can work in the summer or at weekends.

There are many different jobs for teenagers. They can walk dogs or be babysitters for families they know. If they **(2) prefer / would prefer** to work with lots of people, they can get a job in a shop or a café.

(3) For / In my opinion, work is a good way for students to use their free time. First, they learn important skills. **(4) Also / After that**, they earn their own money. Finally, working can make young people more responsible. For these reasons, I think it's good for students to work.

5 **Read the article in Exercise 4 again and decide if the statements are T (True) or F (False).**

1 The article begins in a way that makes people want to read on. ____
2 The writer has answered all the questions in the exam task. ____
3 The article ends with a conclusion. ____

OPTIMISE YOUR EXAM

An article

- When you write an article, it's important to make it interesting for your readers. Think of an interesting way to start your article so your readers want to continue reading.
- End your article with a short sentence that refers back to what you have written. For example, *That's why I think part-time jobs are great for teenagers.*

6 **Look at this writing task and underline the things you need to write about.**

You see this announcement in your school English-language magazine:

Articles wanted!

WHAT'S THE PERFECT JOB FOR YOU?

Write an article telling us which job you'd like to do and why you think it's a good job.

Do you think it's better to do a job that pays well or one that you enjoy? Why?

The best articles will be published next month.

Write your **article**.

7 **Plan** **Plan your article. Use the table to help you.**

	Details	My notes
Paragraph 1	*Think of an interesting way to start your article*	
Paragraph 2	*Say what job you would like and why it's a good job*	
Paragraph 3	*Say which is better – a job that pays well or one you enjoy – and why*	
Conclusion	*Write a short sentence that refers back to what you've written*	

8 **Write** **Write your article in an appropriate style. Write about 100 words.**

9 **Check** **Before you hand in your article, complete this checklist.**

Checklist

- ◯ I've followed my writing plan.
- ◯ I've responded to the four points.
- ◯ I've used a good range of vocabulary.
- ◯ I've written about 100 words.
- ◯ I've checked my spelling, grammar and punctuation.

▶ Writing reference, page 166 ▶ Workbook Unit 11: Writing, page 90, exercises 1, 2, 3, 4, 5, 6 and Progress check 11, page 91

12 Home time

READING | 3-option multiple matching | Blog posts

1 In pairs or as a group, answer the questions.

1 What do you like most about the area where you live?

2 Is there anything in your home that you couldn't live without?

2 Read the statements. Write C if they describe city life or V if they describe village life.

1 It's surrounded by countryside. ____

2 A lot of people live in flats and apartments. ____

3 People can walk everywhere they need to go. ____

4 The air is fresh and clean. ____

5 People have pets and walk them in parks. ____

6 There is noise and traffic. ____

7 People have working animals. ____

8 There are lots of things to do in the evening. ____

3 Where would you prefer to live – in a city or in a village? Give three reasons for your answer and then discuss as a group.

____

____

____

EXAM SKILL

Understanding words with opposite meanings

- Sometimes the correct answer is expressed with an opposite word or phrase in the text. For example, *It's difficult to …* is the same as *I don't think it's easy to … .*
- Don't just look for words or phrases in the texts that mean the same as the words in the questions. Also look for words with opposite meanings and check if they answer the question.

4 Read the blog posts on page 125 quickly. Look for the words and phrases which have the opposite meaning of those below.

1 dirty ____________

2 large ____________

3 interested ____________

4 ugly ____________

5 old-fashioned ____________

6 cold ____________

This is where I Live

Gala, Russia
My village is in a beautiful forest. I love it because I wake up to the sounds of birds and the wind in the trees. Our house isn't modern, but it has everything we need. There's one big room with the kitchen and living area, a bathroom and two bedrooms – one for my parents and another that I **share** with my sister. In my bedroom there are **shelves** for books and our beds have lots of **blankets**. In winter, the house is **heated** by a fire and it stays nice and warm.

Luiza, Brazil
There are many towns in Brazil. Mine is near the Amazon river. It's a big town with fantastic new houses and some older ones too that aren't as nice. The older houses are made from **wood** and they're tiny. My house is new and it's very comfortable. I live here with my parents and my two brothers. My best friend lives next door. It's great here. There's a nice square in the **middle** of the town with cinemas and cafés. We also have a big festival every year. I don't want to live anywhere else!

Lara, UK
I live on a farm, far away from a town or city. My parents are farmers and they grow lots of fruit and vegetables on the **land**. On Fridays they are sold in the local market by my parents. We also have some sheep and cows – they're my pets! Everything we eat is healthy and the air we **breathe** is fresh and clean. Life on a farm isn't for everyone. But if you want to live close to nature and don't need to turn on the TV or use a laptop every time you're bored, life on a farm is great!

OPTIMISE YOUR EXAM

3-option multiple matching

- Words from the questions may appear in the texts, but don't choose a text just because it contains the same words as the question.
- Remember that the idea in the question may be expressed with words or phrases that have opposite meanings in the text.
- When you think you have found the answer read that part of the text again carefully. Check that it really does answer the question.

5 3.26 **Read the blog posts again. For each question, choose the correct answer.**

		Gala	Luiza	Lara
1	Who says this life is good for people who don't use computers a lot?	A	B	C
2	Who explains why she doesn't feel cold in her house?	A	B	C
3	Who has fun things to do where she lives?	A	B	C
4	Who thinks some people don't like living in the countryside?	A	B	C
5	Who doesn't have her own bedroom?	A	B	C
6	Who explains how some people earn money?	A	B	C
7	Who says the new houses are better where she lives?	A	B	C

6 Complete the sentences with highlighted words from the blog posts.

1 There are a lot of shops and offices in the ___________ of the city.
2 They are going to make a park on the ___________ behind my house.
3 ___________ comes from trees.
4 Our living room is ___________ by a fire.
5 If you're cold, you can put more ___________ on your bed.
6 It's hard to ___________ when there is a lot of pollution.
7 I keep my school books on ___________ in my room.
8 Let's ___________ the chocolates so everyone gets one.

THINK | **RESEARCH** | CULTURE | LEARN | ME

Find out about a group of people who live in unusual homes. Make a poster about them which answers these questions:

- Who lives there?
- Where do they live?
- Where do they get their food?

▶ **Workbook Unit 12:** Reading, pages 92–93, exercises 1, 2, 3, 4

Grammar in context

Look at these three passive sentences from the texts on page 125 and then answer the question.

*... the house **is heated** by a fire.* (Gala)

*The older houses **are made** from wood ...* (Luiza)

*... they**'re sold** in the local market ...* (Lara)

Are these sentences right (R) or wrong (W)?

a) We can only use the passive if we know who does the action. ____

b) In passive sentences, we don't have to say who does the action. ____

c) We can use the passive when it is not important who does the action. ____

REMEMBER

- We use the present simple form of the verb *be* and the past participle of the main verb to make the present simple passive.
- We use the passive when the action is more important than who does the action.

▶ **See Grammar reference, Unit 12,** page 155

1 Choose the correct verb form to complete these active and passive sentences.

1 We **grow / are grown** lots of flowers in the garden.
2 These carpets **make / are made** in Turkey.
3 The rooms **clean / are cleaned** by the hotel staff.
4 The children sometimes **stay / are stayed** at their grandparents' house.

2 Put these words into the correct order to make present simple passive sentences.

1 is / month / The / cut / grass / every

____

2 made / houses / from / are / wood / The

____

3 every / This / week / is / kitchen / cleaned

____

3 Complete the present simple passive sentences about a house using the correct form of the verbs in brackets.

1 Meals ______________ (**cook**) in the kitchen.
2 The car ______________ (**keep**) in the garage.
3 The front door ______________ (**open**) with a key.
4 The garden ______________ (**not use**) very often in the winter.
5 These fridges ______________ (**make**) in Germany.
6 The heating ______________ (**not turn on**) in the summer.

4 Complete the article using the present simple passive form of the verbs in brackets.

MOVING HOUSES

Have you ever moved house? It can be very tiring. Before the move, all your things (**1**) ______________ (**pack**) into boxes. Next, everything (**2**) ______________ (**carry**) out of your house and put into a big lorry. Then someone drives everything to your new home.

But in some countries, when people say they are going to move house, they mean it. Their whole house (**3**) ______________ (**move**) to a different place!

In the villages in Indonesia, the houses (**4**) ______________ (**make**) from wood. Sometimes there is a lot of rain, which makes it difficult to live in some areas. When this happens, the houses (**5**) ______________ (**pick up**) and moved away from the rainy areas.

In the USA, people usually leave one house to go and live in another one. But sometimes 'old' houses (**6**) ______________ (**take**) to new places. If the people who want to do this are Amish and they don't believe in using modern technology, they might do it by hand. This (**7**) ______________ (**not do**) very often, because it is very difficult and can be dangerous. But it is amazing to watch when it does happen.

THINK | RESEARCH | **CULTURE** | LEARN | ME

Find out how many people in your class have moved house. Ask ...

- where did they move from and to?
- how did they move?
- how long did it take?

Words connected with *houses and homes*

1 3.27 **Write the words on the correct lines. Some words can go on more than one line. Listen and check.**

armchair | bath | bed | blanket bookcase | chair | cooker | fridge lamp | pillow | shower | sink sofa | table | toilet | towel

kitchen: ____________________

living room: ____________________

bathroom: ____________________

bedroom: ____________________

2 **Work in pairs. Decide which is the odd one out in each group (1–5) and why.**

1 bath | sink | sofa | towel ________
2 pillow | lamp | blanket | fridge ________
3 sofa | bookcase | cooker | armchair ________
4 sink | table | chair | bed ________
5 blanket | cooker | fridge | sink ________

Phrasal verbs

3 3.28 **Complete the sentences. Choose the best word (A, B, or C) for each gap. Listen and check.**

1 My dad grew ____ in a small wooden house in a village.
A up **B** out **C** down

2 In the evenings, I often lie ____ on my bed and read a book.
A in **B** down **C** to

3 If you go ____ tonight, take a front door key.
A in **B** out **C** up

4 My bed is really comfortable so I find it very difficult to get ____ in the morning.
A on **B** up **C** in

5 Please tidy the dining room and wash ____ your things in the sink before you leave.
A off **B** in **C** up

6 Can you find ____ how much those new flats cost?
A of **B** for **C** out

4 **Complete the text about Albert Parker with the correct form of some of the phrasal verbs you completed in Exercise 3.**

I (**1**) ____________ in Liverpool in the 1930s. Our family didn't have much money. My mum worked in the kitchen of a restaurant. She had to (**2**) ____________ hundreds of dishes every day. My dad (**3**) ____________ early every morning and sold newspapers. I went to school and studied hard. After doing my homework, I would often (**4**) ____________ on my bed for a rest. I usually fell asleep so never (**5**) ____________ with my friends during the week as I was always tired.

Collocations with verbs

5 3.29 **Match the nouns (a–f) to the verbs (1–6) to make things you do at home. Listen and check.**

1 wash	____	**a)** house
2 tidy	____	**b)** my bed
3 make	____	**c)** the washing-up
4 do	____	**d)** your room
5 have	____	**e)** the floor
6 move	____	**f)** a shower

6 **Complete the sentences with the correct form of the collocations from Exercise 5.**

1 My mum doesn't like leaving dirty dishes around so we always ____________ after dinner.
2 My sister always listens to music in the bathroom when she ____________ in the morning.
3 Can you ____________ before you go out? There are clothes and books everywhere.
4 If you go into the kitchen with dirty shoes on, you'll have to ____________ .
5 Next year, we're going to ____________ because we want to live somewhere bigger.
6 Mum sometimes ____________ for me.

▶ **Vocabulary reference,** page 162 ▶ **Workbook Unit 12:** Vocabulary, pages 94–95, exercises 1, 2, 3

12 LISTENING | 3-option multiple choice (dialogue)

1 **Work in pairs and answer the question.**

Would you like to live on a boat?
Why / Why not?

EXAM SKILL

Checking your answers

- The speakers may talk about all the possible answers but only one is correct.
- When you listen the second time, check that the possible answers you didn't choose aren't correct.

2 3.30 **Read the question and possible answers. Then listen and choose the best answer.**

Where does Gabriel live now?

a) on a boat **b)** in an apartment **c)** in a house

3 3.30 **Work in pairs and discuss the following question: What does Gabriel say about the other answers in Exercise 2? Listen again and check.**

4 **Read the questions (1–5) in Exercise 5 and match them to the ideas below (a–e).**

a) the room that isn't on the boat ____
b) the thing that Heidi doesn't like on the boat ____
c) the type of people who like living on a boat ____
d) something Heidi really likes on the boat ____
e) how long Heidi has lived on a boat ____

OPTIMISE YOUR EXAM

3-option multiple choice (dialogue)

- Read the questions and all the possible answers carefully.
- The first time you listen, make a note of the words you hear that are in the possible answers.
- When you listen again, think carefully about what the speakers are saying about those words.

5 3.31 **You will hear Heidi talking to her friend Jed about living on a boat. For each question, choose the correct answer.**

1 Heidi has lived on a boat
A for ten years.
B for four years.
C all her life.

2 On the boat, there isn't
A a kitchen.
B a bathroom.
C a dining room.

3 Heidi's favourite thing about the boat is
A the fire.
B her bedroom.
C the views.

4 She doesn't like
A the heating.
B that there isn't a washing machine.
C where the boat is.

5 Jed says that life on a boat is for
A people who don't like noise.
B everyone.
C people who want lots of space.

6 3.31 **Listen again and check your answers.**

SAY IT RIGHT

Resource centre: Unit 12
/b/ and /v/

▶ **Workbook Unit 12:** Listening, page 96, exercises 1, 2, 3

GRAMMAR 2 | Past simple passive and *by*

12

Grammar in context

Look at these sentences from the audio in the listening lesson and answer the questions.

*But four years ago, when I was ten, my parents **were given** a boat **by their cousins**. It **was built** about 30 years ago, but it **wasn't finished**, …*

a) Did Heidi's parents buy the boat? ____

b) Do we know who gave her parents the boat? ____

c) Do we know who built the boat? ____

REMEMBER

- We use the past simple form of the verb *be* and the past participle of the main verb to make the past simple passive.
- When we want to say who did something, we use *by*: *The house was built **by** my grandfather.*

▶ **See Grammar reference, Unit 12,** page 155

1 **Underline who did the action in these past simple passive sentences.**

1. The pictures were given to me by my grandmother.
2. The man was interviewed for the waiter's job by the manager.
3. The essays were written by the pupils in Year 8.
4. The children were taught English by my mother.
5. The furniture was made by a man from Scotland.
6. The house was moved by a team of 30 men.

2 **Look at the sentences in Exercise 1 again and circle the passive verbs.**

3 **Put these words into the correct order to make past simple passive sentences.**

1. bought / my father / The fruit trees / by / were

   ____

2. driven / a taxi driver / home / were / My parents / by

   ____

3. made / The / were / by / every / beds / morning / the hotel staff

   ____

4. designed / a man called Jasper / was / new house / Our / by

   ____

5. weren't / The English tests / teacher / our / by / marked

   ____

4 **Complete the article about a teenager who built a house, using the correct past or present passive form of the verbs in brackets.**

BUILD YOUR OWN HOME

When he was 15, and most of his friends were playing video games, Austin Hay was building his own house!

Austin first became interested in house building at school, but he **(1)** ______________ **(not give)** the chance to build a house there, so he decided to build one at home. He wanted to build a tree house, but when he **(2)** ______________ **(tell)** that he could build a house on wheels, that seemed like a better idea. He bought a trailer, which is a metal floor on wheels, for $2,000 and started building.

Austin **(3)** ______________ **(help)** by his dad and his friends. Lots of pieces of wood and glass **(4)** ______________ **(give)** to him by friends and family, and they **(5)** ______________ **(use)** for different parts of the house.

Inside the house there is a kitchen, shower and toilet, a very small living room, and a bed. There is also electricity. A total of about $12,000 **(6)** ______________ **(spend)** on the house. After the house **(7)** ______________ **(finish)**, Austin became quite famous and a documentary **(8)** ______________ **(make)** about him by the journalist, Kirsten Dirksen. Quite often, Austin **(9)** ______________ **(ask)** by local schools to help with their building projects, and in his town the house **(10)** ______________ **(know)** as the house built by a boy.

5 **Look at the highlighted examples of *by* in the text and answer the questions.**

1. Who helped Austin build his house?
2. Who gave him some glass and wood?
3. Who made the documentary about him?
4. Who does Austin help with their building projects today?

THINK | RESEARCH | CULTURE | LEARN | **ME**

Design your own small home on wheels. Draw a plan of your home and include different rooms.

12 SPEAKING | Discussion (pictures)

Talk2Me

Just a minute, please.

Flipped classroom

1 **Watch the *Talk2Me* video and answer the questions.**

1 What is Evie asked to buy?
2 Who was the picture in Jojo's room painted by?
3 Who was the strawberry cake made by?

2 **Watch the video again. Underline the phrases in the *Phrase expert* box that you hear on the video.**

> **PHRASE EXPERT**
> But can I just say … | Can I just add … |
> I remember you … | Just a minute, please. |
> Oh yes, I forgot to say …

3 **Work in pairs. Read the dialogues and look at the gaps where Speaker B interrupts. Which phrase from the *Phrase expert* box would you use in each gap?**

1 **A:** I'd really like to decorate my room because the paint is very old now but …
B: ______________ I've got to answer my phone.
2 **A:** Can you help me choose a desk for my bedroom please because …
B: ______________ , I think you should look online first.
3 **A:** I'm so bored with the colours in my bedroom …
B: ______________ said last year you wanted to paint it.

EXAM SKILL

Agreeing and disagreeing

- During a discussion, you need to show that you agree or disagree with the other speaker.
- To show that you agree, use phrases such as *Yes, I agree*, *That's right*, *I see what you mean* or *That's a good point*.
- When you disagree, you may want to interrupt someone to say or to add something. You can do this politely by using expressions such as *I'm afraid I don't agree* or *I'm not sure about that*.

4 3.32 **Listen to two students talking about places to live. Decide if they A (agree) or D (disagree) on these points.**

1 Cities are more fun than the country. ____
2 The country is nice in the summer. ____
3 It's better to live in the middle of a city. ____
4 Transport is bad in the country. ____
5 Living in the city is better. ____

OPTIMISE YOUR EXAM

Discussion (pictures)

- In a discussion, don't only give your own opinion, but also respond to what your partner says by agreeing or disagreeing.
- Don't worry if you don't agree with your partner. Say what you really think and explain why you think that.

5 **In pairs, look at the question and pictures and discuss.**

Do you like these different homes? Why / Why not?

6 **Take it in turns to ask and answer these questions.**

Student A: Do you think living in a boat is comfortable?
Which of these homes do you like best?

Student B: Do you think living in the city centre makes life easy?
Which of these homes do you like best?

▶ **Workbook Unit 12:** Speaking, pages 96–97, exercises 1, 2, 3, 4

1 **Work in pairs. Tell your partner about all the different homes you know, e.g. your house, your grandparents' house, etc.**

EXAM SKILL

Identifying words that show the order of events

- Words like *first*, *then* and *finally* help us to understand the order in which things happen.
- Other words like *while* and *during* tell us that things are happening at the same time.
- We use these linking words to tell a story, describe events in the past, or to give the steps we need to follow when we do something.

2 **Put the events (a–e) in order (1–5) to tell the story.**

a) Then my dad had an idea to build two extra rooms at the back of the house.
b) My family wanted to buy a small house by the river in Oxford.
c) Finally, Mum and Dad decided to buy it, and I am really happy they did as I love living here.
d) First, we went to see the house but it was smaller than we thought.
e) While my parents were trying to decide whether or not to buy the house, my dad was thinking about ways to make the house bigger.

1 ___ **2** ___ **3** ___ **4** ___ **5** ___

3 **Complete the email with the words in the box.**

by | finally | first | while | then

From: Maria
To: Paula
Subject: My room!

Hi Paula,

How are you? So you've decorated your bedroom! I hated the colour of my room too. I wanted to paint it but **(1)** ____________ I had to ask my mum. She said OK so **(2)** ____________ we went to the paint shop to choose a colour. Honestly, there were so many colours there I couldn't decide. **(3)** ____________ I was thinking about which colour to choose, Mum and I went to a café for some tea and cake. **(4)** ____________ I decided to paint it pale blue but **(5)** ____________ the time we left the café, the shop had closed. We will have to go back tomorrow.

OPTIMISE YOUR EXAM

3-option multiple-choice cloze

- As you read the text, underline the different events and write 1, 2, 3, etc. above each one so you can clearly see the order they happen in.
- Look at the gap and try to work out if the missing word shows the order of events or shows that two events are happening at the same time.
- Try the different answer options in the gap and see which one is the most logical.

4 **For each question, choose the correct answer.**

Changing homes

The **(1)** ____ of houses we live in are always changing. My home is a good example. There's always been a house on this land, but it's changed over the years. First, the house was **(2)** ____ of a farm and was built from wood. After many years the farm was sold and the next family built a modern house. Over the years, many people left the village and went to work in the city, so the house was empty. During the 1970s the village started to **(3)** ____ again and a new family **(4)** ____ . When they left, the house was **(5)** ____ to a rich family who started a really big garden and then finally we bought it! I love living here because there's lots to **(6)** ____ .

1	**A** groups	**B** sorts	**C** types
2	**A** part	**B** bit	**C** piece
3	**A** grow	**B** plant	**C** collect
4	**A** went	**B** arrived	**C** entered
5	**A** offered	**B** bought	**C** sold
6	**A** make	**B** do	**C** prepare

THINK | RESEARCH | CULTURE | LEARN | ME

Writing your own sentences is a great way to learn vocabulary. Write six sentences describing your own house, using some of the words and ideas from this lesson.

▶ **Vocabulary reference,** page 162 ▶ **Workbook Unit 12:** Language in Use, page 97, exercises 1, 2, 3

12 WRITING | A story

1 In pairs or as a group, look at the photos and answer the questions.

1 Which of the two places in the photos would you prefer to live in?
2 What would be the good and bad things about living in the place in photo 1?
3 What would be the good and bad things about living in the place in photo 2?

EXAM SKILL

Writing a story

- Remember to make a plan before you write. Organise your plan in three paragraphs:
  - think about where and when the story takes place and set the scene.
  - make notes about the main part of the story.
  - think about how the story will end.
- Read your notes about what you will write in each paragraph and write down any useful vocabulary.
- Remember to use linking words and phrases to tell your story, for example, *at first, in the end*, etc.

2 Match (1–3) to (a–c) to complete the sentences about the structure of a story.

1 The beginning ____
2 The middle ____
3 The end ____

a) explains the action or events in a story.
b) is about the things that happen to the people or in the place in a story.
c) introduces the people, place and time of a story.

3 Read the story and answer the questions.

Nick got out of his parents' car and looked at the house. It was amazing and it had a huge garden that was full of beautiful flowers and trees. It was like something in a magazine.

It all started a month ago when his parents won the house in a competition. They wanted to surprise him, so yesterday they drove to the countryside and they stopped outside the house. When they told him, Nick couldn't speak because he was very surprised!

Then they went inside and explored the house. It had everything they needed. They were all excited and they knew they would be very happy living there.

1 Underline the sentences that introduce the beginning, the middle and the end of the story.
2 Which words does the writer use to show a reason and a result? ______________________
3 Find and circle the six adjectives used in the story.
4 Which linking word does the writer use to start a paragraph? __________

OPTIMISE YOUR **EXAM**

A story

- You will be given a sentence that you must start your story with. Use the sentence to plan your story.
- Use the first sentence to help you think about ideas for your story. For example, if the first sentence is *Ben read the text message and smiled*, ask yourself *Who sent Ben the message? Why did Ben smile? What did the message say? What did Ben do after that? How did the story end?*
- Remember to use adjectives to make your story more interesting for the reader.

4 Read the exam task and answer the questions with your own ideas.

> Your English teacher has asked you to write a story.
> Your story must begin with this sentence:
> *Lucy sat on her bed and looked around her room.*
>
> Write your **story**.

1 Who is the main character in the story?
____

2 When did the story take place?
____

3 Did Lucy share her room?
____

4 Why was she in her room?
____

5 What did she have in her room?
____

6 What was she thinking?
____

5 Plan

Plan your story. Use the table to help you.

	First sentence	Adjectives	Linking words	My notes
Paragraph 1	*Lucy sat on her bed and looked around her room.*			
Paragraph 2				
Paragraph 3				

6 Write

Write your story in an appropriate style. Write about 100 words.

7 Check

Before you hand in your story, complete this checklist.

Checklist

- ◯ I've followed my writing plan.
- ◯ I've used the correct tenses.
- ◯ I've used linking words.
- ◯ I've used adjectives.
- ◯ I've used the sentence I was given to start my story.
- ◯ I've used a good range of vocabulary.
- ◯ I've written about 100 words.
- ◯ I've checked my spelling, grammar and punctuation.

▶ **Writing reference,** page 164 ▶ **Workbook Unit 12:** Writing, page 98, exercises 1, 2, 3, 4, 5, 6 and Progress check 12, page 99

PROGRESS CHECK UNITS 11–12

GRAMMAR AND VOCABULARY

1 Write the job each person does.

1 I fly planes all over the world. I'm a ______________ .
2 I write articles for a local newspaper. I'm a ______________ .
3 I grow vegetables and keep cows and pigs. I'm a ______________ .
4 I serve customers in a shop. I'm a ______________ .
5 I repair engines and machines. I'm an ______________ .
6 I look after people's teeth. I'm a ______________ .
7 I help when there is a fire. I'm a ______________ .
8 I serve people meals in a restaurant. I'm a ______________ .
9 I clean the floors in an office. I'm a ______________ .
10 I talk to people when they come into the office, and answer the phone. I'm a ______________ .

__/10

2 Read the descriptions. What is the word for each one? The first letter is given.

1 We can bake cakes in this. c_ _ _ _ _
2 We keep food and drink cold in this. f_ _ _ _ _
3 We do the washing-up in this. s_ _ _
4 We can use this to read in the dark. l_ _ _
5 We put our heads on this in bed. p_ _ _ _ _
6 We eat dinner sitting around it. t_ _ _ _
7 We sit and relax on this. a_ _ _ _ _ _ _
8 We can fill this with water and sit in it. b_ _ _
9 We keep dishes, cups and food in this. c_ _ _ _ _ _ _
10 We can put this on our bed to keep warm. b_ _ _ _ _ _

__/10

3 Choose the correct word to fill each gap.

I'm the manager **(1)** __________ a famous pop group. I travel **(2)** __________ with them. It's a job **(3)** __________ I've done for years. The main thing I do is to make sure that they have **(4)** __________ they need. I work with people **(5)** __________ are great singers. But they don't enjoy talking on TV, so I talk for them. When **(6)** __________ goes wrong, I have to help. Once there wasn't **(7)** __________ to eat after a concert. So I had to cook dinner for **(8)** __________ . It's all in a day's work!

	A	B	C
1	**A** of	**B** in	**C** to
2	**A** somewhere	**B** everything	**C** everywhere
3	**A** what	**B** where	**C** which
4	**A** something	**B** everything	**C** everywhere
5	**A** who	**B** that	**C** where
6	**A** everything	**B** something	**C** someone
7	**A** anything	**B** everything	**C** something
8	**A** someone	**B** anyone	**C** everyone

__/8

4 **Complete the sentences using the correct passive or active form of the verbs in brackets.**

1 The swimming pool ______________ (**close**) by the manager last week.
2 Last year, Camilla ______________ (**give**) a job in a large company that makes computers.
3 My parents ______________ (**buy**) the house when they first moved to England.
4 Teenagers ______________ (**not teach**) enough about healthy eating.
5 The engineer ______________ (**not repair**) the fridge very well and it stopped working again.
6 The woman's bag ______________ (**take**) while she was talking to the receptionist.
7 The workers ______________ (**not tell**) that the factory was closed.
8 Everyone ______________ (**move**) their picnic tables and chairs closer to the river.
9 Uniforms ______________ (**wear**) by all the staff while they are working.
10 Everyone ______________ (**pay**) more money after the company did very well.
11 He ______________ (**write**) the book while living in France for a year.
12 Most of the clothes we buy ______________ (**make**) in Asia.

__/12

5 **Complete the blog post about Domenico's home with one word in each gap.**

I live in a small town (**1**) ___________ is about 20 km from Naples. We have a large house and a garden (**2**) ___________ is full of flowers. I share a bedroom with my brother, (**3**) ___________ is two years older than me. My parents work in Naples. My dad is the manager (**4**) ___________ a shoe shop and my mum works (**5**) ___________ a company that sells holiday apartments. My grandparents help around the house. My grandmother is always cooking and my grandfather does the gardening. My brother and I have (**6**) ___________ make our beds each morning and wash (**7**) ___________ after dinner every night.

I grew up (**8**) ___________ the town. I often go out to a café (**9**) ___________ my two best friends. My favourite café has the best ice cream. It (**10**) ___________ made with fresh fruit and tastes amazing!

__/10

Total score __/50

EXAM SKILLS

Tick the statements that are true for you. Review the skills in the unit if you need more help.

I can ...	**Unit/page**
☐ identify incorrect answer options in multiple-choice activities	Unit 11 p114
☐ take notes when I listen	Unit 11 p118
☐ talk about jobs people do	Unit 11 p120
☐ use indefinite and relative pronouns	Unit 11 p121
☐ plan my article before I start writing	Unit 11 p122
☐ understand words with opposite meanings	Unit 12 p124
☐ check my answers	Unit 12 p128
☐ agree and disagree in a discussion	Unit 12 p130
☐ identify words that show the order of events	Unit 12 p131
☐ write a story with different paragraphs	Unit 12 p132

OPTIMISE YOUR EXAMS | Reading and Writing

OPTIMISE

In **Part 1** of the exam, you will read the short texts (e.g. short emails, text messages, web messages, signs and notices) and decide what type of text they are and where you might see them. This will help you understand the meaning. Read the texts, and the three multiple-choice answers (A, B or C) next to each one. Underline the important words or phrases in the texts that are similar to the ideas in the answers. Then compare the option with the text before choosing an answer.

1 **Read the texts and the questions. For each question, choose the correct answer.**

1

From: Jamie
To: Tom

Do you have Mike's phone number? I've lost it. I'm coming to his birthday picnic tomorrow but I don't know what to bring!

Why has Jamie sent this email?

A Jamie wants Tom to tell him what to bring.
B Tom should give Jamie a phone number.
C Jamie is asking Tom to come to a picnic with him.

2

If you're coming on the museum trip, you must pay Emma £10 before Friday.

A You can pay Emma the money on Friday.
B You have to go on the school trip to the museum.
C You need to pay Emma the money before the end of the week.

3

Katie,
If you go shopping this morning, could you pick me up some milk? Let me know the cost – I'll pay you back later today.
Dan

Dan would like Katie to

A collect something for him.
B return the money he lent her.
C decide when they will go shopping.

4

Hi Becky,
I'm going shopping with Tanya tomorrow. We're meeting at the station at 2 o'clock. Do you want to come?
Anna

A Becky should tell Anna if she can go to the shops.
B Becky has to tell Anna if she can meet her at the station.
C Becky needs to tell Anna what time she can meet her.

5

Latest books for teenagers
50% off children's toys
Clothes for 0–5 year olds

What is the notice telling customers?

A A wide variety of books for all ages are now on sale.
B There is a discount on the types of things children play with.
C Some things cost less in the teenager clothes department.

6

CLOSE DOOR.
ADD WASHING POWDER.
PUSH BUTTON.
(DON'T PUSH IT BEFORE CLOSING THE DOOR.)

A You need to wait until the door is closed before pushing the button.
B You should push the button before closing the door.
C You should add washing powder, then close the door.

OPTIMISE

In **Part 2** you will read the seven questions and underline any key words or phrases. Then read the three texts quickly to understand the general meaning and main topic. Next, scan the texts to find the words that are similar in meaning to the underlined words in the questions. You may not understand every word, but to help you work out the meaning of a word or phrase, it's a good idea to look at the words before and after it.

Remember to think logically when the answer isn't immediately clear. For example, if the question says *Which person prefers working outdoors?*, the text might contain the sentence *'I don't like working in an office or shop because I like being near nature.'* It can often be helpful to look for words with the opposite meaning in the text as sometimes these will give you the correct answer. For example, *It was light outside …*, may be written as *It wasn't dark outside*.

2 **Read the article. For each question, choose the correct answer.**

		Izzy	Kate	Amira
1	Who knows what job she wants to do when she's an adult?	A	B	C
2	Who says she does less housework than one of her parents did?	A	B	C
3	Whose family has help from someone who's not in the family?	A	B	C
4	Who likes the plan her family has?	A	B	C
5	Who likes to know where her things are?	A	B	C
6	Who thinks she should do more housework?	A	B	C
7	Who doesn't like helping in the kitchen?	A	B	C

Helping in the house

Izzy

I help with jobs at home, but I think I could do more. When my mum was my age, she had to wash the dishes, tidy her room and look after her sister every day. I think I wash the dishes once a week and sometimes I help cook dinner, which I enjoy. I work hard at school so in the evenings I try to rest. Maybe in the summer holidays, when I'm not so busy, I will have time to tidy!

Kate

I have four brothers so there's lots to do. My dad writes a list of jobs and a different person does each job every week. It's a good idea because it doesn't get boring. This week, I'm tidying the living room, so I need to clean the table, the bookcase and the TV every day. My favourite job is helping to cook dinner. It's good because I want to be a chef when I'm older.

Amira

I make my bed and tidy my room every day, but a cleaner does a lot of the other jobs in the house. My parents pay her to clean the house. I'm tidy so my room doesn't get messy. I enjoy putting the books on my bookcase and my clothes in the wardrobe because then I know where everything is. My least favourite job is helping with the cooking because I'm not good at it. I ask my brother to help because he's much better at it.

OPTIMISE

In **Part 3** of the exam, you will read a longer text such as a magazine or newspaper article. Under the article are five multiple-choice questions with three options (A, B or C). The order of the questions follows the order of the text, unless there is a final global question. First, skim the text to get a general idea of the topic. Read the five questions carefully and underline any key words or phrases without reading the options (A, B or C). Next, read the text in detail to try and answer the questions in your own words before checking which option is similar to your idea. You should also read the other two options and decide why they are wrong. If there are two options that you think might be correct, think about how they are different and if one of them doesn't answer the question fully.

3 **Quickly read the magazine article. What is the main idea of the article?**

World champion snowboarder

Chloe Kim is an 18-year-old snowboarder who lives in California, USA. She has already won three gold medals at the X-Games and she became the youngest person to win gold in the women's competition at the Winter Olympics in Pyeongchang in 2018. She was too young to take part in the 2014 games in Sochi, but she was as good as some Olympic gold winners. Her parents Jong and Boran came from Korea, but Chloe is American. Her dad first took her snowboarding when she was four. At first, she wasn't keen on doing it, but she soon became very good at it. She can now do the most difficult jumps and has taken part in competitions since she was six years old. She speaks French as well as English because she lived with her aunt in Switzerland for two years when she was at primary school. Her parents visited her in the school breaks and took her snowboarding in France. Chloe is well known in the USA, both for her snowboarding talent and also for her hair. She often changes her hair colour and she likes to colour it pink for competitions.

By Aimee Hughes, age 11

4 **Read the article again and the questions. For each question, choose the correct answer.**

1 Why does Aimee say that it was special that Chloe Kim won the Winter Olympics?
- **A** It was her third gold medal.
- **B** It was the first time she won a gold medal.
- **C** She was the youngest girl to win a gold medal.

2 In the third sentence, Aimee says
- **A** Chloe was better than the Olympic gold winner.
- **B** Chloe was the same level as other Olympic gold winners.
- **C** Chloe was not as good as other Olympic gold winners.

3 How did Chloe feel about snowboarding?
- **A** She had wanted her dad to take her when she was four.
- **B** She didn't like it until she was six years old.
- **C** She started to like it when it became easier.

4 Why can Chloe speak more than one language?
- **A** Because she lived in a different country.
- **B** Because her parents taught her.
- **C** Because her parents took her to France in the holidays.

5 What does Aimee say that Chloe is famous for in the USA?
- **A** Just for winning snowboarding competitions.
- **B** For being good at snowboarding and for her interesting hair.
- **C** Just for having unusual hair.

OPTIMISE

In **Part 4** of the exam, you will read a short text with six gaps. You choose the correct word from three options (A, B or C). The main focus is vocabulary and not grammar. First, read the text quickly to get the general idea. Then, read the sentences with gaps and all the answers. Choose the best answer for each gap and think why the others are wrong. When you have completed all the gaps, read the text again to check it makes sense.

5 **Read the article. Six words have been removed from the text. For each question, choose the correct answer.**

A famous stone circle

Stonehenge is an ancient stone circle in the south of England and the most famous stone circle in Europe. Many people from around the world are **(1)** _______ in visiting Stonehenge and over a million people visit it each year.

No one really **(2)** _______ why Stone Age people built Stonehenge over four thousand years ago. It may have been a **(3)** _______ of clock which people used to tell the longest and shortest days of the year.

Many historians agree that Stone Age people probably used machines to **(4)** _______ the stones to Stonehenge. This is because some of the stones **(5)** _______ from Wales, which is about 225 km away! Historians think that it took about 31 million man hours to build the stone circle we can **(6)** _______ today!

	A	B	C
1	interested	pleased	excited
2	thinks	knows	believes
3	type	set	group
4	arrive	travel	move
5	came	entered	went
6	watch	look	see

6 **Read the article. For each question, write the correct answer. Write ONE word for each gap.**

OPTIMISE

In **Part 5** of the exam, you will read a short text with six gaps. You need to write one word in each gap. This part of the exam focuses on grammar and spelling. First, read the text quickly for general meaning. Then, read it again and think of a word for each gap. Pay attention to words surrounding the gap to help you decide which word fits the gap. When you have completed all the gaps, read the text again to check it makes sense.

When I was younger, I was _in_ Junior Masterchef. It is a TV cooking competition **(1)** _______ nine to twelve-year-olds. When I was on the show, **(2)** _______ were 2,000 children who wanted to be in the competition, but only 30 children **(3)** _______ successful. I was one of the lucky children and I was able to be on the programme. When there were only eight children left in the competition, we all had **(4)** _______ cook food for a famous boy band. In the final of the competition, four of us took **(5)** _______ and in the end they told everyone the name of the winner. This time I was **(6)** _______ lucky. The winner was Georgia Brown.

OPTIMISE

In **Part 6**, you will read a situation and write either a note or an email of 25 words or more. You will be told to give three pieces of information in your message. Remember to think about what type of text you are writing, who you are writing it for and if you need to use a formal or informal style. It's a good idea to write notes before writing your final answer. You should also check that you have written at least 25 words. Try not to write a lot more than 25 words because you might make more mistakes.

After you have written your text, check that you have included all the necessary information and that your spelling, punctuation and grammar are correct. You may lose marks for any incorrect spelling, so if you aren't sure how to spell a word, think of a different word or phrase that means the same.

7 **Read the exam task and write notes. Then write your email. Remember to check your email carefully.**

You are meeting your English friend, Alex, for dinner tomorrow.

Write an email to Alex.

In your email:

- say where you want to meet
- ask what time you should meet
- tell Alex what type of food you want to eat.

Write **25 words** or more.

OPTIMISE

In **Part 7** of the exam, you will look at three pictures and then write a short story about what's shown in the pictures. It is important to look carefully at what's happening in each picture. There will be one event in each picture and you need to include each one in your story. It is important to plan what you are going to write first. You can write a rough draft before writing your final answer. You will need to write 35 words or more. You should try and include different tenses in your story and make the order of events clear with linking words. After you have written your story, check that you have written the right number of words and for any spelling, punctuation or grammar mistakes.

8 **Look at the pictures and read the exam task. Write notes and then write your story. Remember to check your work when you have finished.**

Look at the three pictures.

Write the story shown in the pictures.

Write **35 words** or more.

A

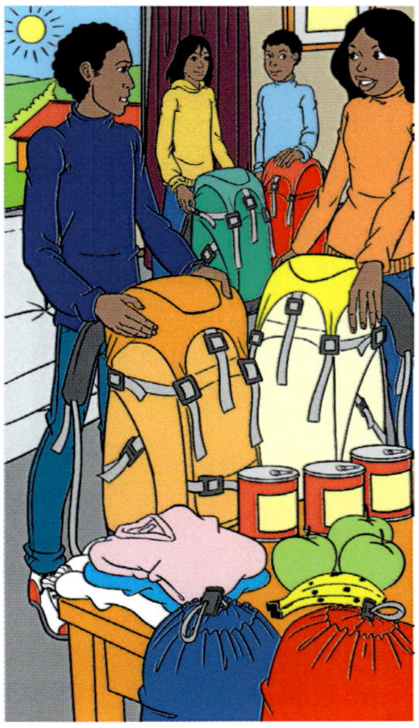

B

C

OPTIMISE YOUR EXAMS | Listening

OPTIMISE

In **Part 1** of the exam, you should look carefully at what the pictures are showing and think about what words you might hear. Think about what is different in the pictures and what words or phrases you might hear about each one. For example, you might hear words to describe different places, things or activities. Then read the questions and underline the important words. Use the first listening to listen for the specific information, and then the second time to check your answers.

1 3.33 **For each question, choose the correct picture.**

1 Where is Kara's bag?

A

B

C

2 What time does the film start?

A

B

C

3 Where are Kevin and his sister going at the weekend?

A

B

C

4 What is Dad going to buy Mum for her birthday?

A

B

C

5 What's the weather going to be like tomorrow?

A

B

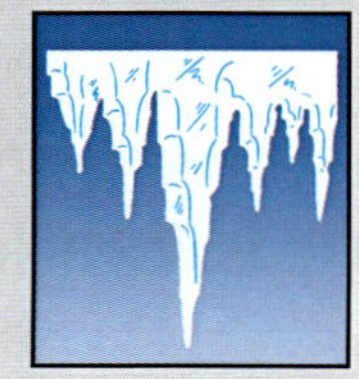
C

OPTIMISE

In **Part 2** of the exam, you will need to complete a note with specific information from a monologue, such as prices, times, dates or telephone numbers. First, read the note to see what type of information you need to listen for. Then, listen for specific information and finally listen again to check your answer or to complete the gaps you have missed. Spell words correctly when they are spelt out by the speaker. It's important to write only one word in each gap.

2 3.34 **Listen to a teacher telling his students about a trip to the theatre. For each question, write the correct answer in the gaps. Write one word or a number or a date or a time.**

SCHOOL TRIP TO THEATRE	
City:	*London*
Day of trip:	(1) ....
Play starts:	(2) .... *pm*
Name of the play:	(3) ....
Name of the theatre:	(4) .... *Theatre*
Cost of ticket:	(5) £ ....

OPTIMISE

In **Part 3** of the exam, you will listen to an informal conversation between two speakers and then choose the correct answer from three options (A, B or C). Read the questions and options and think about the context of the conversation. This part of the test includes questions about specific details, opinions and feelings of the speakers. First, listen to try and understand the gist of the conversation and think about the best option for each question. Then, listen again for specific information and then check all your answers carefully.

3 3.35 **You will hear Matt talking to his friend Joanna about going to a concert. For each question, choose the correct answer.**

1 Joanna is going to the concert with
- **A** Tim and Matt.
- **B** Peter and Matt.
- **C** Jill and Peter.

2 The Birds play
- **A** dance music.
- **B** classical music with rock guitars.
- **C** rock music with some classical instruments.

3 Joanna
- **A** often spends time listening to this kind of music.
- **B** thinks she'll like the concert.
- **C** thinks it sounds like the usual kind of music she listens to.

4 Matt and Joanna are going to the concert by
- **A** bus.
- **B** train.
- **C** car.

5 Matt thinks
- **A** the last band they saw was awful.
- **B** the last band they saw was much better than *The Birds*.
- **C** the last band they saw is always thinking of new ways to play music.

OPTIMISE

In **Part 4** of the exam, you will hear five short monologues or dialogues, each with a 'context setter' telling you what the conversation is about, a question and three options (A, B or C). Look at each option and underline the key words. First, listen and focus on the words you have underlined before carefully choosing your answer. Remember that sometimes an answer may contain some of the right information, but you should only choose it if it has exactly the same meaning as what you hear. In this part of the exam, you are listening for the main idea, so it's a good idea to listen to the whole monologue or dialogue before choosing your answer.

4 3.36 **Listen to the question and then choose the correct answer.**

1 You will hear two friends talking about their day. What did they do first?
- **A** They went shopping.
- **B** They played sport.
- **C** They went for a meal.

2 You will hear a teacher talking to a student. What does she want him to do?
- **A** Complete his homework again.
- **B** Listen in class.
- **C** Talk to his friends.

3 You will hear a man talking about feeling ill. What should he do?
- **A** drink more water
- **B** stay in bed
- **C** wear warm clothes

4 You will hear a boy talking to his friend about shopping. Why did he buy the T-shirt?
- **A** He had to buy a present for a friend.
- **B** He wanted the same T-shirt as his friend.
- **C** He needed it for his sports team.

5 You will hear a father talking to his daughter. Why is he unhappy?
- **A** She made the floor dirty.
- **B** She was late returning home.
- **C** She forgot to buy something.

OPTIMISE

In **Part 5** of the exam, you will listen to a longer conversation between two people who know each other and then match two lists. There is an example to help you.

First, listen to try and understand the gist of the conversation and choose the best option for each question. Listen again for specific information and then check your answers. There are three options you don't need, so check that these aren't correct. Remember that just hearing one of the options in the second column doesn't mean it is a correct answer.

5 3.37 **Listen to Fiona talking about what she did on her holiday last week. Which place did she go to on each day?**

0 Monday	G	**A**	the beach
1 Tuesday	☐	**B**	the park
2 Thursday	☐	**C**	a farm
3 Friday	☐	**D**	the mountains
4 Saturday	☐	**E**	home
5 Sunday	☐	**F**	a waterfall
		G	the forest
		H	the cinema

OPTIMISE YOUR EXAMS | Speaking

OPTIMISE

To prepare for **Part 1**, Phase 1 of the exam, practise asking and answering questions about yourself. Try to avoid answering with only *Yes/No* or single word answers. In Phase 2 of the exam, when the examiner asks, *Tell me about …* give reasons for your opinions or give examples. The focus in this part of the exam is on typical everyday questions. Remember that it's okay to ask the examiner to repeat the question.

1 **Watch Part 1 of the video and tick the questions you hear. Then watch the video again and make notes on Eva and Marie's answers. Compare your answers with a partner.**

What's your name?	☐	What's your favourite type of food?	☐
Where do you live?	☐	Do you like pizza?	☐
Where do you go at the weekend?	☐	What did you have for breakfast this morning?	☐
What time do you start school?	☐	What do you usually eat for lunch?	☐
What time do you get up on a Sunday morning?	☐	What do you usually eat for dinner?	☐
Who do you spend time with at the weekend?	☐	When do you go out to eat in restaurants?	☐
What do you do on Saturday evening?	☐	Do you like fast food?	☐
What do you do on Friday night?	☐	Tell me something about what you like to eat at the weekend.	☐
Tell me something about what you did last weekend.	☐	Do you like to eat in restaurants?	☐

2 **Work in pairs and ask and answer the questions.**

Tell me something about the food you eat on special occasions.

Tell me what you like doing with your friends.

Tell me something about the homework you have to do.

Tell me something about your favourite hobby.

OPTIMISE

In **Part 2**, Phase 1 of the exam, discuss five pictures with your partner for up to 2 minutes. The pictures could show topics about daily life, school, free time activities, transport, towns and cities, or holidays. Talk about each picture with your partner and say why you like or dislike it. Remember to respond to what your partner says and to ask him/her questions. In Phase 2 of the exam, the examiner will ask you two more questions about the topic you discussed with your partner. Sometimes you will be asked about your preferences, so it's a good idea to practise phrases for comparing two things and to give reasons for your preferences.

3 **Look at the pictures showing different places to visit. Do you like these different places? Why/Why not? Complete the first column of the table with notes of your ideas.**

	You	Marie	Eva
cinema			
park			
museum			
library			
mountains			

4 **Watch the first part of Part 2 of the video and complete the table for Marie and Eva.**

5 **Read the text below and complete the gaps with words or phrases from the box.**

because | me too | agree with | but | think

Eva: I like going to the cinema (**1**) ______ I like watching films with my family or friends …

Marie: … (**2**) ______. I (**3**) ______ it's funny and I like watching comedy.

Eva: … Museums are also interesting for me (**4**) _____ not all of them. Some of them are very boring.

Marie: Yeah. I (**5**) ______ you … I like fashion museums. I think they're cool.

6 **Read your answers in Exercise 5 and then say if the words or phrases are agreeing (A), giving reasons (R), giving opinions (O) or giving contrasting information (C).**

7 **In pairs, discuss the pictures from Exercise 3. Use your notes from the first column of the table to help you. Remember to use words and phrases to:**

- give reasons.
- give contrasting information.
- give opinions.
- show whether you agree or disagree with your partner.

8 **Watch the second part of Part 2 of the video. Complete the examiner's questions with a place from the first box and an adjective from the second box.**

mountains | park | cinema | museum

expensive | interesting | exciting | fun

1 Do you think going to the ___________ is ___________?
2 Do you think climbing ___________ is ___________?
3 Do you think visiting a ___________ is ___________?
4 Do you think going to the ___________ is ___________?

9 **In pairs, ask and answer the questions from Exercise 8.**

10 **Read the sentences below describing preferences and choose the correct options.**

1 I prefer football **than / to** tennis because it's more exciting.
2 He prefers **go / going** shopping **than / to play / playing** chess.
3 They like swimming **the / a** best because it's so relaxing.

11 **Watch the second part of Part 2 of the video again and complete the statements below.**

city | countryside | interesting | fun | prefers

1 Eva likes places in the city because it's more ___________ for her.
2 Marie prefers the ___________ to the ___________ because there are more activities.
3 Eva thinks a concert is more ___________ if it's music she likes.
4 Marie ___________ going to a concert if it's pop music.

12 **In pairs, ask and answer the questions. Try to use phrases from Exercise 10 and give reasons for your preferences.**

1 Is it better to visit places in the city or places in the countryside?
2 Which is more fun, visiting a museum or going to the park?
3 Do you prefer doing activities inside or outside?
4 Which is more exciting, climbing a mountain or going to an outdoor concert?

GRAMMAR REFERENCE

GRAMMAR REFERENCE | Unit 1 | Present simple, adverbs of frequency, imperatives

Present simple

FORM:

Positive
I/You/We/They ***live*** *here.*
He/She/It ***lives*** *here.*
Negative
I/You/We/They ***do not live*** */* ***don't live*** *here.*
He/She/It ***does not live*** */* ***doesn't live*** *here.*
Questions
Do *I/you/we/they* ***live*** *here?*
Does *he/she/it* ***live*** *here?*
Short answers
Yes, I/you/we/they ***do****.* *No, I/you/we/they* ***don't****.*
Yes, he/she/it ***does****.* *No, he/she/it* ***doesn't****.*

Spelling patterns for the present simple after *he*, *she* or *it*

- We add *-s* to most verbs: ***I wear*** → ***he wears***
- We add *-es* to verbs that end with *o*: ***they go*** → ***she goes, I do*** → ***he does***
- If the verb ends in *-s, -sh,-ch, -x* or *-z* we add *-es*: ***you finish*** → ***it finishes***
- If the verb ends in a consonant + *-y*, the *-y* changes to *-ies*: ***we study*** → ***he studies***
- If the verb ends in a vowel + *-y*, the *-y* does not change: ***I play*** → ***she plays***

Common irregular verbs

- *Have* is irregular: *I/you/we/they* ***have*** → *he/she/it* ***has***
- *Be* is irregular: *I* ***am*** → *you/we/they* ***are*** → *he/she/it* ***is***

USE: to talk about: **1** habits or things we do often, and **2** things that are usually or always true:

1	*I* ***walk*** *to school.*
2	*She* ***lives*** *in Spain. It* ***rains*** *in winter.*

Adverbs of frequency

We use adverbs of frequency to say how often something happens:

never *sometimes* *often* *usually* *always*

0% ________________________________ 100%

FORM: Adverbs of frequency usually come before the main verb:

I ***usually play*** *tennis on Saturday.*

I ***don't often eat*** *pizza.*

She ***never listens*** *to the radio.*

! Adverbs of frequency come after *be* when it is used as a main verb:

It ***is usually*** *very hot in August.*

I ***am never*** *late for school.*

Sometimes can also come at the beginning or end of a sentence:

Sometimes *I make dinner. / I make dinner* ***sometimes****.*

Time expressions

every day
every week
twice a week
three times a week

We use time expressions to show when we do things:

He rides his bike ***every day****.*
She plays tennis ***twice a week****.*

Imperatives

FORM: Imperatives use the bare infinitive of a verb. The verb doesn't change when you are talking to one person or more than one person:

Find *a club to join.* ***Wait*** *there children!*

For negative imperatives, we use *don't*:

Don't do *that!* ***Don't worry****.*

USE: to give instructions or orders, or to make a strong suggestion:

Open *your book.* ***Write*** *your name.*

Try *a new sport …*

! We don't have to use the subject (e.g. *you*) with imperatives:

Come *here!* ***Look*** *at that!*

! We can use *please* with imperatives to be more polite:

Please be *quiet. /* ***Be*** *quiet,* ***please****.*

! We can also use *never* and *always* with imperatives for general instructions or orders:

Never eat *or* ***drink*** *in class.*
Always listen *to your teacher.*

GRAMMAR REFERENCE | Unit 1 | Possessive *'s*, prepositions of time and place

Possessive *'s*

FORM: Add *'s* to a singular noun:

*I like to play games on **Paul's** computer.*

*I sometimes ride my **friend's** bike.*

Add *'s* to irregular plural nouns:

***Children's** toys are expensive here.*

*Are these **men's** shoes?*

Add *'* to plural nouns ending in *-s*:

*This is my **parents'** car.*

*Those are **girls'** clothes.*

USE: to show possession (who something belongs to / who owns something):

*Jack has a football. It's **Jack's** football.*
*The book belongs to **Ellie**. It's **Ellie's** book.*

! If we use possessive *'s* in an answer, we don't have to repeat the noun:

Whose bike is this?	*It's Jan's bike. / It's **Jan's**.*
Whose phone is this?	*It's my brother's phone. / It's my **brother's**.*

Prepositions of time and place

FORM: Prepositions of time or place go before nouns or pronouns:

***at** 7 pm / **in** summer / **on** the floor/ **in** her garden*

USE: to tell us when something happens, or where something or someone is:

*When do you ride your bike? I ride it **at** the weekend.*

*Where's Kim? She's **in** the house.*

GRAMMAR REFERENCE | Unit 2 | Present simple and present continuous

Present simple

See Grammar reference, Unit 1, page 150 for information about the form and use of the present simple.

Present continuous

FORM:

am/is/are + verb + *-ing*

Positive
*I **am/'m playing**.*
*He/She/It **is/'s playing**.*
*You/We/They **are/'re playing**.*
Negative
*I **am/'m not playing**.*
*He/She/It **is not / isn't playing**.*
*You/We/They **are not / aren't playing**.*
Questions
***Am** I **playing**?*
***Is** he/she/it **playing**?*
***Are** you/we/ they **playing**?*
Short answers
*Yes, I **am**.* *No, I**'m not**.*
*Yes, he/she/it **is**.* *No, he/she/it **isn't**.*
*Yes, you/we/they **are**.* *No, you/we/they **aren't**.*

USE: to talk about: **1** things that are happening at the moment, **2** actions happening around now, **3** temporary or changing situations, and **4** descriptions of pictures:

1	*I**'m enjoying** this food.*
2	*Where **are** you **living** these days?*
3	*I**'m staying** at my aunt's house this week.*
4	*All the people in the picture **are looking** at their phones.*

Spelling patterns for the present continuous

- We add *-ing* to the bare infinitive of most verbs: ***start*** → ***starting***
- If the verb ends in *-e*, we take away the *-e* before adding *-ing*: ***make*** → ***making***
- If the verb ends in *-ie*, we change the *-ie* to *-y* before adding *-ing*: ***lie*** → ***lying***
- If the verb has one or two syllables and ends in a vowel + a consonant, we double the consonant before adding *-ing*: ***stop*** → ***stopping, begin*** → ***beginning, travel*** → ***travelling***

! There are some verbs, called stative verbs, which we usually only use in the present simple form. These include:

- verbs about thinking, e.g. *know, believe, understand*

✔ *I **understand** this book.*

✘ *I**'m understanding** this book.*

- verbs connected with likes/dislikes, e.g. *like, love, hate*

✔ *I **love** that film.*

✘ *I**'m loving** that film.*

- verbs connected with possession, e.g. *belong to, have, own, possess*

✔ *I **have** shoes like that.*

✘ *I**'m having** shoes like that.*

! We don't use contracted forms (*I'm, they're, she's*, etc.) in positive short answers:

Are you reading a book?

✔ *Yes, I am.*

✘ *Yes, I'm.*

Present simple and present continuous

- It is possible to have verbs in both the present simple and the present continuous in the same sentence. The present simple talks about a habit or something we do often, and the present continuous talks about an action happening now or around now, or a temporary situation:

*I usually **walk** to school but this week **I'm going** by bus.*

GRAMMAR REFERENCE | Unit 2 | Present continuous for future use

USE: to talk about future plans and arrangements:

*We**'re watching** a new film later.*

***I'm meeting** Jess at the library tomorrow morning.*

! We usually use the present continuous to talk about future plans and arrangements that are already agreed/planned. We usually give a time, day, etc. in present continuous sentences that talk about the future:

*They**'re travelling** to London tomorrow.*

*Mum **isn't working** next weekend.*

! We can also use the present simple to talk about the future, when we're talking about timetables or programmed events:

*The exam **starts** at 10:30 am.*

GRAMMAR REFERENCE | Unit 3 | Past simple: regular verbs, *Wh-* words

Past simple, regular verbs (positive)

FORM: verb + *-ed*

Positive
I/You/He/She/It/We/They **worked** yesterday.

See Grammar reference, Unit 3, page 153, for information about the negative, question and short answer forms of the past simple.

USE: to talk about: **1** something that happened once in the past, **2** something that happened again and again in the past, and **3** something that was true for some time in the past:

1	*I **played** basketball at the weekend.*
2	*She always **visited** her grandmother in the summer holidays.*
3	*Katy **helped** her mum prepare all the family meals.*

Spelling patterns for the past simple of regular verbs

- We add *-ed* to the bare infinitive of most verbs: ***work** → **worked**, **start** → **started***
- If the verb ends in *-e*, we add *-d*: ***live** → **lived**, **love** → **loved***
- If the verb has one syllable and ends in a vowel and a consonant, we double the consonant: ***stop** → **stopped**, **plan** → **planned**, **travel** → **travelled***
- With verbs that end in a consonant + *-y*, we change the *-y* to *-ied*: ***try** → **tried**, **study** → **studied***

! We often use time expressions with the past simple:

***in**: in 2027, in the 1990s, in winter/summer, in the morning/afternoon/evening, in October*

***last**: last week/month/year, last December, last night*

***this**: this morning, this week*

***on**: on Saturday, on Monday night, on 29th March*

***at**: at eight o'clock, at weekends, at night*

Wh- words

FORM:
*Wh-*question word + verb + subject
***What** is your name?*

USE: to start many questions. *Wh-* words are used to get more information than *yes/no* questions, e.g. ***Did** you live abroad? Yes, I did.*

***Where** did you live? I lived in Oxford, a city in England.*

! *What, which*, and *whose* can be followed by a noun:

***What music** do you like? **Which bag** is yours? **Whose phone** is this?*

What can be used if there are many possible answers:

***What** do you want to eat?*

Which can be used if there are a few possible answers:

***Which** do you prefer, apples or pears?*

How can be followed by an adjective or adverb:

***How old** is your brother? **How fast** is the internet connection?*

How can also be followed by *much* and *many*:

***How many** times have you played this game?*
***How much** cheese do you want?*

GRAMMAR REFERENCE | Unit 3 | Past simple: irregular verbs

FORM:

Negative
I/You/He/She/It/We/They ***did not / didn't come*** *yesterday.*
Questions
Did *I/you/he/she/it/we/they* ***come*** *yesterday?*
Short answers
Yes, I/you/he/she/it/we/they ***did****.* *No, I/you/he/she/it/we/they* ***didn't****.*

! Both regular and irregular verbs follow the same pattern in the past simple for negatives, questions and answers. However, irregular verbs do not follow a pattern for the positive form in the past simple. You need to learn the past simple positive form of irregular verbs.

Some common irregular verbs

be → ***was/were***
buy → ***bought***
choose → ***chose***
come → ***came***
do → ***did***
drink → ***drank***
eat → ***ate***
get → ***got***
go → ***went***
have → ***had***
meet → ***met***
see → ***saw***
teach → ***taught***
think → ***thought***

See the *Irregular verbs reference,* page 175, for a full list of irregular verbs used in the A2 Student's Book.

GRAMMAR REFERENCE | Unit 4 | Past continuous, linking words

Past continuous

FORM:

was/were + verb + *-ing*

Positive
I/He/She/It **was eating**. You/We/They **were eating**.
Negative
I/He/She/It **was not / wasn't eating**. You/We/They **were not / weren't eating**.
Questions
Was I/he/she/it **eating**? **Were** you/we/they **eating**?
Short answers
Yes, I/he/she/it **was**. No, I/he/she/it **wasn't**.
Yes, you/we/they **were**. No, you/we/they **weren't**.

USE: to talk about: **1** something that was happening over a period of time at a specific time in the past, **2** background information or description in a story, **3** an action in progress in the past when another thing happened (possibly interrupting it or stopping it), **4** two actions in progress at the same time, and **5** a temporary situation in the past:

1	*At four o'clock yesterday afternoon, I* ***was playing*** *online games.*
2	*I looked out of the window. Rain* ***was falling*** *heavily.*
3	*He* ***was watching*** *TV when his phone rang.*
4	*When I arrived, Katy* ***was reading*** *and Ellie* ***was sleeping****.*
5	*I* ***was using*** *his phone because I couldn't find mine.*

! The past continuous is not used to talk about repeated actions in the past:

✔ *I* ***checked*** *my emails ten times yesterday.*

✘ *I* ***was checking*** *my emails ten times yesterday.*

Linking words

USE: we use linking words (*and, because, but, or, when*) to link phrases, clauses and sentences.

We use *and* to link phrases and clauses:
She swims in the mornings ***and*** *she goes jogging in the evenings.*

We use *because* for a reason:
We walked ***because*** *it was a sunny day.*

We use *but* to link two different ideas:
I like apples ***but*** *I hate oranges.*

We use *or* to link alternatives:
Would you like a hot ***or*** *cold drink?*

We use *when* to link clauses with time:
I liked school ***when*** *I was eight.*

! We can use *because* and *when* at the beginning and in the middle of a sentence:

I went to bed ***because*** *I was feeling tired.*

Because *I was feeling tired, I went to bed.*

GRAMMAR REFERENCE | Unit 4 | Past simple and past continuous

Past simple

See Grammar reference, Unit 3, pages 152 and 153 for information about the form and use of the past simple.

Past continuous

See Grammar reference, Unit 4, page 153, for information about the form and use of the past continuous.

! It is possible to have verbs in both the past simple and the past continuous in the same sentence. The past continuous talks about what was happening when another shorter action happened. We use the past simple for the shorter action that happened:

*I **was listening** to music in my room when Mum **walked** in.*

! In stories or descriptions, we use the past continuous to describe the situation or to give background information, and we use the past simple to talk about events and actions:

*It **was raining** outside so we **stayed** in and **played** a game.*

! In questions, we can use the past continuous to ask about what was happening before an action or event, and we can use the past simple to ask about what happened after an action or event:

*What **were** you **doing** when it **started** to snow? We **were walking** in the woods.*

*What **did** you **do** when it started to snow? We **went** home.*

GRAMMAR REFERENCE | Unit 5 | Quantifiers with countable and uncountable nouns

Countable and uncountable nouns

Countable nouns can be counted and have a singular and plural form, e.g. *one book, three books, one child, five children*.

Uncountable nouns are often ideas (e.g. *information*), materials (e.g. *water, wood*) or groups of similar things (*furniture, luggage, money,* etc.). After uncountable nouns, we use a verb in the singular, even if we are talking about more than one object:

*All the furniture **was** old.*

*Their luggage **is** heavy.*

! To talk about one part of something that we usually refer to as a group of things, we can use words like *piece, slice, glass*, etc. We usually use *of* after these words, and we can use plural verbs with these words, where appropriate:

***Are** two **pieces of** cake enough?*

*There **are** two **slices of** meat left on the plate.*

! Some nouns are both countable and uncountable, e.g.

Uncountable: *The **glass** in the window is broken.*

Countable: *Put the **glasses** of juice on the table.* (**glasses** = things to drink from)

Uncountable: *I need more **paper** to write on.*

Countable: *Dad reads the **papers** every morning.* (**papers** = newspapers)

Uncountable: *I love **chocolate**!*

Countable: *Let's buy Mum some **chocolates**.* (**chocolates** = small sweets in a box/bag)

Quantifiers

USE:

much/many

We use *much* with uncountable nouns in questions and negatives:

***How much water** do you drink every day?*

*He doesn't want **much cake**.*

We use *many* with countable nouns in questions and negatives:

***How many books** have you got?*

*There weren't **many people** at the party.*

! *Too much* and *Too many* have a negative meaning. We use them to mean *more than the right amount*:

*There are **too many** people here. Let's go somewhere quieter.*

some/any

We use *some* when we don't know, or don't want to say, the exact number of something:

*I think **some** people are coming.* (I don't know how many.)

We use *some* in positive sentences and in questions when we think the answer will be yes:

*Do you want **some** milk to drink?*

We use *any* before countable and uncountable nouns in negative sentences to mean a zero amount:

*There isn't **any** time to call her now.*
*There aren't **any** free apps that I like.*

We use *any* in questions when we don't know if the answer will be *yes* or *no*:

*Do you need **any** help?*

! *No* means the same as *not any*:

*There **isn't any** money in my bag. /*
*There's **no** money in my bag.*

a few / a lot of

A few means *a small number of*. We use it in positive sentences with countable nouns:

*I bought **a few** T-shirts.*

We use *few* in sentences with a negative meaning:

*There are **few** shops open today.*

Both *a lot of* and *lots of* mean *a large number or quantity*. We use both phrases with countable and uncountable nouns:

Lots of* / *A lot of *people play computer games every day.*

A little means *a small number or quantity*. We use it in positive sentences with uncountable nouns:

I ate ***a little*** *soup and felt better.*

We use *little* in sentences with a negative meaning:

There's ***little*** *point in phoning him. He never answers.*

GRAMMAR REFERENCE | Unit 5 | Comparatives and superlatives

FORM:

Type of adjective	Adjective	Comparative	Superlative
Adjective (one syllable)	*old*	+ *-er* ***older***	+ *-est* ***oldest***
Adjective (one/ two syllables) ending in *-e*	*wide*	+ *-r* ***wider***	+ *-st* ***widest***
Adjective (one syllable) ending in a vowel + consonant	*big*	double the final letter + *-er* ***bigger***	double the final letter + *-est* ***biggest***
Adjective (two syllables) ending in *-y*	*happy*	replace *-y* with *-ier* ***happier***	replace *-y* with *-iest* ***happiest***
Other adjective (two or more syllables)	*beautiful*	*more* + adjective ***more beautiful***	*most* + adjective ***most beautiful***
Irregular adjectives	***good*** ***bad*** ***far*** ***little*** ***many/much***	***better*** ***worse*** ***farther/ further*** ***less*** ***more***	***best*** ***worst*** ***farthest/ furthest*** ***least*** ***most***

USE: we use the comparative form of adjectives + *than* to compare two people, things, etc:

This game is ***newer than*** *the others.*

we use *the* + the superlative form of adjectives to compare more than two people, things, etc.:

This is ***the most interesting*** *website ever!*

! We don't always use *than* with comparatives when we are comparing something which is obvious:

This is my ***older*** *sister. (= older than me)*

In the winter, the weather is usually ***worse***. *(= worse than at other times)*

! We don't always use *the* with superlatives. We replace *the* with a possessive adjective:

This is ***my*** *best score so far.*

! We can use *even* and *much* with comparatives to make them stronger:

My design is good, but Sasha's design is ***even/much*** *better!*

GRAMMAR REFERENCE | Unit 6 | Present perfect simple with *ever* and *never*

FORM:

have/has + the past participle of the main verb

Positive
I/You/We/They ***have/'ve played*** *football.*
He/She/It ***has/'s played*** *football.*
Negative
I/You/We/They ***have not / haven't played*** *football.*
He/She/It ***has not / hasn't played*** *football.*
Questions
Have *I/you/we/they (ever)* ***played*** *football?*
Has *he/she/it (ever)* ***played*** *football?*
Short answers
Yes, I/you/we/they ***have***. *No, I/you/we/they* ***haven't***.
Yes, he/she/it ***has***. *No, he/she/it* ***hasn't***.

! The past participles of regular verbs end in *-ed*.

See the *Irregular verbs reference*, page 175, for the past participle of irregular verbs.

! We don't use contracted forms (*I've, they've, she's*, etc.) in positive short answers:

Have you lived here long?

✔ *Yes, I have.*

✘ *Yes, I've.*

USE: to talk about: **1** past actions when the time they happened isn't important or isn't known, **2** to talk about experiences, **3** with *ever*, in questions asking about experiences up to now, and **4** with *never*, in sentences to talk about experiences that have not happened up to now:

1	***I've bought*** *lots of pairs of shoes.*
2	*They****'ve lived*** *all over the world.*
3	***Have*** *you* ***ever seen*** *one of these?*
4	***I've never eaten*** *food like this before.*

GRAMMAR REFERENCE | Unit 6 | Present perfect simple and past simple

Present perfect simple and past simple

USE: we use the present perfect simple: **1** to talk about a finished action in the past that is still linked to the present, **2** to report information or news, and **3** for a situation which has gone on up to the present:

1	*Anna **has bought** her train ticket.*
2	*I'**ve bought** a new phone.*
3	*We'**ve lived** here for four years.*

We use the past simple: **1** to talk about finished actions in the past; we usually know when the action happened, **2** to give details or explanations, and **3** for a situation in the past which has now finished:

1	*Anna **bought** her train ticket last week.*
2	*I **bought** a new phone at the shopping centre last week.*
3	*We **studied** there for four years.*

GRAMMAR REFERENCE | Unit 7 | *going to*

FORM:

be + *going to* + bare infinitive

Positive
*I **am/'m going to** play.*
*You/We/They **are/'re going to** play.*
*He/She/It **is/'s going to** play.*
Negative
*I **am/'m not going to** play.* *You/ We/They **are/'re not going to** play.* *He/She/It **is not / isn't going to** play.*
Questions
***Am** I **going to** play?*
***Are** you/we/they **going to** play?*
***Is** he/she/it **going to** play?*

Short answers
*Yes, I **am**.* *No, I'**m not**.*
*Yes, you/we/they **are**.* *No, you/we/they **aren't**.*
*Yes, he/she/it **is**.* *No, he/she/it **isn't**.*

USE: we use *going to* to: **1** talk about future plans, and **2** to predict something because of what see or know now:

1	*We'**re going to visit** my grandparents next month.* *What **are** you **going to do** at the weekend?*
2	*He's very near the goal. I think he'**s going to score**.* *Who **is going to win** the race?*

! When we have already made an arrangement with someone else, we can also use the present continuous:

*I'm **playing** tennis with Nina this evening.*

GRAMMAR REFERENCE | Unit 7 | *will* and *going to*

See Grammar reference, Unit 7, above, for information about the form and use of *going to*.

FORM:

will + bare infinitive

Positive
*I/You/ He/She/It/We/They **will play**.*
Negative
*I/You/He/She/It/We/They **will not / won't play**.*
Questions
***Will** I/you/he/she/it/we/they **play**?*
Short answers
*Yes, I/you/he/she/it/we/they **will**.* *No, I/you/he/she/it/we/they **won't**.*

USE: we use *will*: **1** when we decide to do something at that moment, **2** to say what we think or guess what will happen, and **3** to make offers or requests:

1	*I'm cold. I'**ll close** the window.*
2	*I don't think the test **will be** difficult.* *Do you think everyone in the class **will pass**? Yes, I think they **will**.*
3	***Will** you **help** me with my homework?* *I'**ll get** you a drink if you're thirsty.*

! Sometimes *will* and *going to* are both correct. We usually use *going to* when we speak:

*Do you think the teacher **will** give us any homework?*
*'Do you think the teacher **is going to** give us any homework?'*

GRAMMAR REFERENCE | Unit 8 | Modals (1): ability, necessity, obligation, possibility

FORM:

Modals have only one form and are usually followed by the bare infinitive of the main verb.

Positive
I/You/He/She/It/We/They ***may/can/must***, etc. ***go***.
Negative
I/You/He/She/It/We/They ***may not / can't/mustn't***, etc. ***go***.
Questions
May/Can/Must, etc. *I/you/he/she/it/we/they* ***go***?
Short answers
Yes, I/you/he/she/it/we/they ***may/can/must***, etc. *No, I/you/he/she/it/we/they* ***may not / can't/mustn't***, etc.

! *Need* and *have to* change form like a regular verb:

✔ *She* ***needs*** *to go.*

✘ *She* ***need*** *to go.*

✔ *It* ***has to*** *go.*

✘ *It* ***have to*** *go.*

! We use *don't need to* or *needn't* with the bare infinitive.

We ***don't need to*** *finish our homework tonight.*

We ***needn't*** *finish our homework tonight.*

! We don't use *can* as an infinitive. We use *be able to*:

✔ *I'd like to* ***be able to*** *run a marathon.*

✘ *I'd like to* ***can*** *run a marathon.*

USE: to talk about ability, possibility, and obligation.

Ability – *can/could*

To talk about ability in the present, we use *can*:

Tom ***can*** *speak three languages.*

Linda ***can't*** *swim.*

! We don't use *can* to talk about ability in the future. We use *will be able to*.

✔ ***I'll be able to*** *speak Spanish well in a few years' time.*

✘ ***I can*** *speak Spanish well in a few years' time.*

To talk about general ability in the past, we use could:

Andrea ***could*** *play the piano when she was six.*

Sam ***couldn't*** *read when he was four.*

! We don't use *could* for specific ability in the past. We use *was/were able to*:

✔ ***I was able to*** *finish my homework in one hour last night.*

✘ ***I could*** *finish my homework in one hour last night.*

Necessity – *need/needn't*

To say that something is necessary in order to achieve something else, we use *need*:

I ***need to*** *pass the exam to go to university.*

You ***need to*** *go to bed early because you've got an exam tomorrow.*

To say that something isn't necessary, we use *needn't*:

You ***needn't*** *shout. I can hear you!*

You ***needn't*** *answer both questions. You can just choose one.*

Obligation – *have to / must*

When something is necessary, we use *have to*:

I ***have to*** *arrive at school before 9:00 every morning.*

My dad ***has to*** *go to work on Saturdays.*

When something isn't necessary, we use *don't have to*:

We ***don't have to*** *go to school on Sundays.*

My sister ***doesn't have to*** *wear a uniform to school.*

! We often use *have to* to talk about something that someone else says is necessary:

We ***have to*** *stand up when our teacher comes in the classroom.*

! To talk about obligation in the past, we usually use *had to*:

✔ ***I had to*** *go to school yesterday.*

✘ ***I must*** *go to school yesterday.*

To talk about things that are essential or necessary to do, because other people say so or because the person doing the action believes so, we use *must/mustn't*:

You ***must*** *go to school.*

We ***mustn't*** *be late.*

! *Must* is not common in the question form. We usually use *have to*:

Do you have to *wear a school uniform?*

Possibility – *may/might*

To say that something is possibly true or not true, or will possibly happen or not happen, we use *may/might*:

I ***may*** *need some help to finish my homework.*

It ***might not*** *be the correct answer. I'm not sure.*

GRAMMAR REFERENCE | Unit 8 | Modals (2): advice, permission, polite requests, prohibition

FORM: *modal verb* + bare infinitive

Positive
*I/You/He/She/It/We/They (**should**) leave.*
Negative
*I/You/He/She/It/We/They (**should not / shouldn't**) leave.*
Questions
*(**Should**) I/you/he/she/it/we/they leave?*
Short answers
*Yes, I/you/he/she/it/we/they (**should**).* *No, I/you/he/she/it/we/they (**shouldn't**).*

USE: to talk about advice, permission, polite requests, prohibition.

Advice – *should*

We also use *should* when we want to ask for and give advice:

***Should** I buy this shirt?*

*You **should** eat a lot of fruit and vegetables.*

When we want to say something is a good or bad idea but not necessary, we use *should* or *shouldn't*:

*Everyone **should** learn how to swim.*

*You **shouldn't** play video games late at night.*

Permission – *can*

To ask for, give and refuse permission now, in the future, or generally, we use *can*:

***Can** I watch TV?*

*I **can** go out with my friends at the weekend.* (Mum has already given me permission.)

*We **can't** eat or drink in class.* (The teacher never gives us permission to do this.)

! To talk about permission in the past, we don't use *could*. We often use *be allowed to*:

✔ *I **wasn't allowed to** play video games when I was young.*

✘ *I **couldn't** watch video games when I was young.*

Polite requests – *could*

To make a polite request, we use *could*:

***Could** you open the window, please?*

***Could** I ask a question?*

Prohibition – *mustn't*

To talk about something that is not allowed, we use *mustn't*:

*You **mustn't** copy your friend's homework.*

*You **mustn't** use your phone in class.*

GRAMMAR REFERENCE | Unit 9 | Zero conditional, first conditional

Zero conditional

FORM:

If + present simple, present simple

*If you **push** the button, the door **opens**.*

! The *if* clause can be at the beginning or the end of the sentence. If it is at the beginning, it has a comma after it:

***If** the weather is good, we play in the park.*

*We play in the park **if** the weather is good.*

***If** you have a headache, what do you do?*

*What do you do **if** you have a headache?*

USE: to talk about things that are always or usually true, and facts:

*If it's sunny, our cat usually **spends** the day in the garden.*

*Water **turns** to ice if the temperature **falls** to zero degrees.*

! We can use *when* or *if*. The meaning is the same:

***If** I don't feel well, I usually stay at home.*

***When** I don't feel well, I usually stay at home.*

First conditional

FORM:

If + present simple, *will/won't* + bare infinitive

*If it's cold this evening, **I'll turn on** the heating.*

*If it **rains** this afternoon, I **won't go** outside.*

USE: to talk about possible events/actions now or in the future, and the results of those events/actions:

*If the internet **doesn't work**, **we'll play** some board games.*

*If it **doesn't snow** this winter, we **won't go** skiing.*

*You**'ll get wet** if you **don't take** an umbrella.*

GRAMMAR REFERENCE | Unit 9 | Second conditional

Second conditional

FORM:

If + past simple, *would/wouldn't* + bare infinitive

*If I **had** a helicopter, I **would fly** to school every day.*

! The contracted form of *would* is *'d*:

*If I **had** a helicopter, **I'd fly** to school every day.*

USE: to talk about events/actions that are impossible or unlikely now or in the future, and what the results of the events/actions would be if they did happen:

*If you **were** much taller, you**'d be** the best basketball player at school.*

*You **wouldn't speak** Spanish if you **lived** in France.*

! We can also use other modal verbs.

*If my sister **spoke** English, she **could help** me with my homework.*

! We can use both *was* and *were* with *I, he, she* and *it*, in second conditional sentences.

*If **I was** a scientist, I'd help to protect plants and animals.*

*If **I were** a scientist, I'd help to protect plants and animals.*

GRAMMAR REFERENCE | Unit 10 | Present perfect simple: *for, since, already, just, yet*

See Grammar reference, Unit 6, pages 155 and 156, for information about the form and use of the present perfect simple.

USE:

There are some words we can use with the present perfect simple tense which help to tell us more about when something happened.

for and *since*

When we use the present perfect simple tense to talk about something that began in the past and is still true, we can use *for* and *since* to give more information.

We use *for* to talk about a period of time and *since* to talk about the time something started:

*I've been a waiter **for** eight years.*

*I've been a waiter **since** 2010.*

already, just and *yet*

When we use the present perfect simple tense to talk about a finished action in the past that is still linked to the present, we can use *already, just* or *yet* to give more information.

We use *already* when something happened before now:

*I've **already** brushed my teeth.* (I did it earlier.)

We use *just* when we want to say something happened a very short time ago:

*The match has **just** finished.* (The players are still on the field.)

We use *yet* with negative sentences and questions:

*The doctor hasn't arrived **yet**.* (We are waiting for him/her.)

*Has the doctor arrived **yet**?* (Is the doctor here now?)

GRAMMAR REFERENCE | Unit 10 | Verb patterns: verb + infinitive / *-ing*

Verb + infinitive / *-ing*

FORM:

Sometimes we use one verb followed by another verb. The second verb can be in the infinitive or the *-ing* form:

verb + infinitive form of the second verb

verb + *-ing* form of the second verb

*She **wants to give** me a present.*

*He **enjoys reading** about animals.*

Verbs or phrases usually followed by the full infinitive (+ *to*)
be able, agree, ask, choose, decide, forget, hope, learn, need, offer, plan, prepare, promise, tell, wait, want, would like *Gemma **decided to go** skateboarding.* *We **didn't wait to see** the end of the film.*

Verb or phrases usually followed by the *–ing* form of a verb
dislike, enjoy, finish, hate, keep, like, love, (don't) mind, miss, practise, understand *He **enjoyed playing** the new video game.* *They **practised speaking** in English.*
Verb followed by the full infinitive or *-ing* form of the verb, with no change in meaning
begin, continue, hate, love, start *They **began to watch** a film. / They **began watching** a film.* *Ethan **loves to go** climbing. / Ethan **loves going** climbing.*
Verb followed by the full infinitive or *-ing* form of the verb, with a change in meaning
forget, go on, like, mean, remember, stop, try ***I remember buying** this book for Mum.* (I remember when I bought it.) ***I remembered to buy** a book for Mum.* (I didn't forget to buy the book I wanted to get for Mum.)

GRAMMAR REFERENCE | Unit 11 | Indefinite pronouns

FORM:

	People	Places	Things
every-	*everyone*	*everywhere*	*everything*
some-	*someone*	*somewhere*	*something*
any-	*anyone*	*anywhere*	*anything*

USE: to talk about people, places or things without saying exactly who or what they are.

We use pronouns ending in *-body* or *-one* for people, pronouns ending in *-thing* for things and pronouns ending in *-where* for places:

I think there is ***someone*** *in the garden.*
(We don't know who it is.)

I like ***everything*** *about this house.*
(the bedrooms, the kitchen, the garden, the view, etc.)

Is there ***anywhere*** *you'd like to go?*
(This could be any place.)

! We use the *he/she/it* form of a verb after indefinite pronouns:

Everyone ***wants*** *to go to the party.*

Tell me when something ***happens****.*

When we want to talk about all of the people, places or things without saying exactly what they are, we use *everyone, everywhere* or *everything*:

Everyone *I know likes this TV programme.*

I've looked ***everywhere*** *for my keys, but I can't find them.*

Everything *he said to me is true.*

When we want to talk about a person, place or thing that we don't know or that isn't important, we use *someone, somewhere* or *something*:

Someone *phoned earlier but they didn't leave a message.*

I left my bicycle ***somewhere*** *near here.*

I'm sure I have forgotten ***something*** *important.*

! We don't usually use *someone, somewhere* or *something* in negative sentences:

✔ *I haven't got* ***anything*** *in my bag.*

✘ *I haven't got* ***something*** *in my bag.*

In questions and negative sentences, we use *anyone, anything* and *anywhere*:

Did ***anyone*** *visit while I was at the shops?*

Is there ***anything*** *we need to do before we go on holiday?*
We didn't go ***anywhere*** *at the weekend.*

! We can also use *anyone, anything* and *anywhere* in positive sentences:

You can have ***anything*** *you'd like in the shop.*

We can go ***anywhere*** *you want on holiday.*

! We can add possessive *'s* to indefinite pronouns:

We found ***somebody's*** *phone in the park.*

Is this ***anybody's*** *bag?*

GRAMMAR REFERENCE | Unit 11 | Relative clauses: *who, which, that*

FORM:

Pronoun	Use	Example
who or *that*	for people	*He's the man* ***who*** *lives next door.*
that or *which*	for things	*I work for a company* ***that*** *sells computers.* *Dad works in a factory* ***which*** *makes cars.*

USE: we use **relative clauses** to say exactly who or what we are talking about:

Mr Ackmann is the man ***who checks the money****.*
(It tells us exactly who Mr Ackmann is.)

This is the card ***that opens the office door****.*
(It tells us what the card does.)

We use *who* to talk about people (and sometimes animals):

I think he's the boy ***who*** *broke my phone!*

We use *which* to talk about things (and sometimes animals):

Is this the book ***which*** *the teacher was talking about yesterday?*

We use *that* for people or animals and things:

Is she the girl ***that*** *you were telling me about?*

! We can use *that* instead of *who* or *which*.

I think he's the boy ***that*** *broke my phone!*

Is this the book ***that*** *the teacher was talking about yesterday?*

GRAMMAR REFERENCE | Unit 12 | Present simple passive

FORM: *be* + past participle

Positive
*I **am/'m taught** English every day.*
*You/We/They **are/'re taught** English every day.*
*He/She/It **is/'s taught** English every day.*
Negative
*I **am/'m not taught** English every day.*
*You/We/They **are not / aren't taught** English every day.*
*He/She/It **is not / isn't taught** English every day.*
Questions
***Am** I **taught** English every day?*
***Are** you/we/they **taught** English every day?*
***Is** he/she/it **taught** English every day?*
Short answers
*Yes, I **am**.* *No, I **am/'m not**.*
*Yes, you/we/they **are**.* *No, you/we/they **are not / aren't**.*
*Yes, he/she/it **is**.* *No, he/she/it **is not / isn't**.*

USE: we use the present simple passive when: **1** we don't know who does the action, **2** it isn't important who does the action, and **3** when everyone knows who does the action:

1	*The window **is broken**.* (We don't know who broke the window.) *Bicycles **are** often **stolen** outside the railway station.* (We don't know who steals them.)
2	*The best tomatoes **are grown** in Romania.* (We aren't interested in the person who grows them.) *The building **is painted** once a year.* (It isn't important who paints the building.)
3	*We **are given** homework every day.* (Everyone knows the teacher gives us homework.) *Lunch **is served** every day from 12–2 pm in the restaurant.* (We know that the waiters serve lunch.)

GRAMMAR REFERENCE | Unit 12 | Past simple passive and *by*

FORM: *was/were* + past participle

Positive
*I/He/She/It **was hurt** during the game.*
*You/We/They **were hurt** during the game.*
Negative
*I/He/She/It **was not / wasn't hurt** during the game.*
*You/We/They **were not / weren't hurt** during the game.*
Questions
***Was** I/he/she/it **hurt** during the game?*
***Were** you/we/they **hurt** during the game?*
Short answers
*Yes, I/he/she/it **was**.* *No, I/he/she/it **was not / wasn't**.*
*Yes, you/we/they **were**.* *No, you/we/they **were not / weren't**.*

USE: we use the past simple passive when: **1** we don't know who did the action, **2** it isn't important who did the action, and **3** when everyone knows who did the action:

1	*This car **was made** in Spain.* (We don't know which people made the car.)
2	*The dogs **weren't taken** for a walk last night.* (The person who didn't take the dog for a walk is not important.)
3	***Were** the students **given** a test yesterday.* (We know tests are given by teachers.)

! When we want to say who or what does the action, we can use *by*:

*The garden is looked after **by** my father.*

*Dinner is usually cooked **by** my grandmother.*

We use *by* when it is important to say who or what did the action:

*We were given this picture **by** a local artist.*

*This book was written **by** Roald Dahl.*

! We always put *by* before the person or thing that did the action:

✔ *They were sent this postcard **by** their friends in Brazil.*

✘ *They were sent **by** this postcard their friends in Brazil.*

! We don't use *by* when we don't know who did the action or it isn't important:

This fridge was made ~~by people in a factory~~ in Germany.

The lights were turned on ~~by someone~~ before we arrived.

VOCABULARY REFERENCE

Introduction

This *Vocabulary reference* contains all the target vocabulary from *Optimise A2* Student's Book. The words and phrases are grouped in unit order, so you can look at them as you work on the vocabulary lessons throughout the book. You can also use these pages for revision when you're preparing for a test or an exam.

The target vocabulary has been divided into five groups:

Topic vocabulary

The **Topic vocabulary** sections focus on words connected to the unit topic. Learning these words and being able to use them correctly will help you in your exams. Having a wide vocabulary is important for Reading and Writing and Speaking exams.

Word formation

The **Word formation** sections give you all the different parts of speech – verbs, adjectives, nouns and adverbs – that come from root words that appear in *Optimise A2* Student's Book. Exams often test you on word formation, so learning all the forms of a word is a good way to make sure you are prepared for your exam.

Collocations

Collocations are phrases with two or more words which go together in English. Learning collocations will help you in some exam tasks. It will also improve your English in Speaking and Writing exams.

Word patterns

Word patterns are phrases which use a range of grammatical structures, for example, phrases with prepositions (*good at, interested in*) or nouns that go together (*car park, petrol station*).

Phrasal verbs

Phrasal verbs are made of a verb (*take, come, look,* etc.) plus a word called a particle. The particle can be an adverb (*up, down,* etc.) or a preposition (*in, on,* etc.). Remember that some phrasal verbs have more than one meaning; in the tables, the meaning given for the phrasal verb always matches the one used in the unit.

These are the main types of phrasal verbs:

Type 1: the verb is transitive (has an object).

When the object is a noun, we can put the particle before or after the noun:

*I'll **pick** Jo **up** at six. / I'll **pick up** Joe at six.*

When the object is a pronoun, the pronoun must separate the two parts of the phrasal verb:

✔ *I'll **pick** her **up**.*

✘ *I'll **pick up** her.*

Type 2: the verb is intransitive (does not have an object) and you cannot separate the two parts of the verb:

✔ *Please **come in** and get warm.*

✘ *Please **come** and get warm **in**.*

! Some phrasal verbs may have different meanings when they are used transitively or intransitively:

*The plane **took off** at ten thirty. (= leave the ground and go into the sky) I'll **take** my jacket **off** when I feel warmer. (= remove clothing)*

Type 3: the verb is transitive (has an object) but you cannot separate the two parts of the verb:

✔ *Can you **look after** the cat while I'm away?*

✘ *Can you **look** my cat **after** while I'm away?*

Throughout the *Vocabulary reference*, you will see different abbreviations. This key explains what they all mean.

KEY: adj = adjective; adv = adverb; n = noun; sth = something; v = verb

UNIT 1

TOPIC VOCABULARY | Words connected with *hobbies*

Word	Example sentence
cycling (n)	My history teacher goes cycling every summer.
horse-riding (n)	Elly sometimes goes horse-riding in Wales with her school.
painting (n)	I don't enjoy drawing with a pencil, but I like painting.
playing computer games (n)	Mark loves playing his favourite computer games at the weekend.
reading (n)	Liam loves reading, so he buys lots of books.
rock climbing (n)	Helen often hurts her knee when she goes rock climbing.
skateboarding (n)	I never go skateboarding! It looks dangerous.
swimming (n)	She says that swimming is her favourite sport.
barbecue (n)	We sometimes have a barbecue in our garden during the summer.
beach (n)	Do you ever play volleyball on the beach?
collect (v)	Jamie collects old comics – he's got more than two hundred!
magazine (n)	His picture looks great in the magazine.
photograph (n)	Lizzie has about 200 photographs for her school project.
tent (n)	I don't like sleeping in a tent because I get cold.

WORD FORMATION | Nouns/verbs

Core word	Derivatives
guitar (n)	guitarist (n), play the guitar (v)
music (n)	musician (n), musical (adj), make/play music (v)
paint (n)	painting (n), painter (n), paint (v)
photograph (n)	photographer (n), photography (n), photograph / take photographs (v)
video (n)	video (v), video gamer (n), play video games (v)

PHRASAL VERBS

Phrasal verb	Meaning	Example sentence
come in (type 2)	enter	It's cold outside! Come in and get warm.
come round (type 2)	visit	Rebecca comes round for dinner on Fridays.
get back (type 2)	return after going somewhere	When did you get back from Ireland?
get off (type 2)	leave a bus or train	We get off the train at Hallwood station then walk home.
look after (type 3)	take care of something	Tom always looks after our dog when we go on holiday.
turn off (type 1)	stop a machine	Turn off the alarm clock! It's Sunday!
turn on (type 1)	start a machine	Turn on the TV please, the news is on.

UNIT 2

TOPIC VOCABULARY | Words connected with *entertainment*

Word	Example sentence
art gallery (n)	Mary loves the paintings of famous people in the art gallery.
concert hall (n)	My aunt plays the piano in a concert hall once a month.
gaming café (n)	I enjoy going to the gaming café to meet my friends.
museum (n)	Bridget's looking at the old cars in the museum.
opera house (n)	I sometimes go to the opera house with my class and listen to famous singers.
theatre (n)	Do you like going to see plays at the theatre?

WORD PATTERNS | Words + prepositions

Core word	Example sentence
act in	Matt sometimes acts in school plays.
dance with	Amber danced with her sister at the concert in the park.
go out	Do you usually go out with your friends on Saturdays?
listen to	Please listen to me when I'm talking to you.
look at (sth)	What are you looking at?
play with	Do you play with your classmates after school?
stay in	We usually stay in when there is a bad storm.
try (sth) **on**	I always try shoes on before I buy them.

COLLOCATIONS | Collocations with nouns

Collocation	Example sentence
board game	This board game is boring – can we play *Cluedo* instead?
cinema screen	Dan doesn't wear his glasses when he watches films on a cinema screen.
DVD player	We watch films on the computer, so we don't use our DVD player now.
newspaper article	She reads newspaper articles about sport every morning.
TV programme	What is your favourite TV programme? I think *Friends* is great!

UNIT 3

TOPIC VOCABULARY | Words connected with *food*

Word	Example sentence
apple (n), **banana** (n)	Apples and bananas are my favourite fruits.
beans (n)	Dad grows beans in the garden, so we often eat them with our meals.
beef (n)	We're having beef for dinner.
bread (n)	My mum bakes very nice bread. I love it with honey on it.
carrots (n), **cereal** (n)	My favourite food is carrots, but Ellie's is cereal.
cheese (n)	I am having a cheese sandwich for lunch.
chicken (n)	We often have chicken salad for dinner.
honey (n)	Do you like honey with yoghurt?
lettuce (n)	Ryan doesn't like salad, so he never eats lettuce!
milk (n)	My dad buys milk every week from the supermarket.
oil (n)	Mum usually cooks the potatoes in the oven – she puts oil on them.
onions (n)	Do you usually eat onions with your steak?
oranges (n)	We always have oranges in the house. Mum likes us to eat an apple or an orange every day.
pasta (n)	You can make a nice meal with pasta and tomatoes.
potatoes (n), **rice** (n)	Do you prefer potatoes or rice with your beef?
salt (n)	Tim never puts salt on his food, but I do.
steak (n)	I never eat meat, but my brother's favourite meat is steak.
strawberries (n)	We love eating strawberries and ice cream in the summer.
tomatoes (n)	Mum prepared a tomato salad for us to have with the chicken.
vinegar (n)	Do you put vinegar on fish and chips?
yoghurt (n)	Adam eats yoghurt on his cereal for breakfast.

WORD FORMATION | Verbs/adjectives

Core word	Derivatives
bake (v)	baked (adj), baker (n)
boil (v)	boiled (adj), boiler (n)
fry (v)	fried (adj), fryer (n)
grill (v)	grilled (adj), grill (n)
roast (v)	roasted (adj), roast (n)

COLLOCATIONS | Collocations with verbs

Collocation	Example sentence
bake bread	Colin learnt to bake bread because he wants to be a baker one day.
do homework	Do you prefer doing homework at home or in the library?
have lunch	Can we have lunch in a restaurant on my birthday?
make breakfast	Who makes breakfast in your house?
take an exam	All the students are taking an exam at the moment.

UNIT 4

TOPIC VOCABULARY | Words connected with *travel*

Word	Example sentence
bridge (n)	The Golden Gate Bridge in San Francisco is very big!
bus stop (n)	Matt is waiting for you at the bus stop.
delayed (adj)	Flights are often delayed at Christmas time.
miss (v)	Be quick! I don't want to miss the bus.
railway station (n)	The railway station is near my house.
roundabout (n)	You need to stop at the roundabout!
traffic (n)	There's always a lot of traffic in the city centre.
traffic lights (n)	Cars stop when the traffic lights are red.

WORD PATTERNS | Compound nouns

Core word	Example sentence
car park	He is trying to find a space in the car park.
driving licence	You can get a driving licence in England when you're 17.
helicopter ride	She is going on a helicopter ride and she's very excited about it.
petrol station	There is a petrol station at the end of my road.
sailing boat	Dad is planning a holiday on a sailing boat next summer.
ticket machine	The ticket machine isn't working so we can't buy our train tickets here.
tour guide	Ed wants to be a tour guide when he's older.
traffic news	My grandpa always checks the traffic news before he leaves the house.

PHRASAL VERBS

Phrasal verb	Meaning	Example sentence
come in (type 2)	what somebody says to invite you into a place	Come in and have a drink of juice.
go in (type 3)	to enter a place	Let's go in the house – it's snowing!
pick up (type 1)	to collect something or somebody, often in a car	Rachel is picking me up at three o'clock.
set off (type 2)	to start a journey	Henry is setting off now to go to the skateboarding competition.
take off (type 2)	to leave the ground and go into the sky	How do you feel when the plane takes off?
turn off (type 1)	to leave a main road	Turn off at the next exit. That's the road to Edinburgh.

UNIT 5

TOPIC VOCABULARY | Words connected with *communication and technology*

Word	Example sentence
camera (n)	Harry often uses his dad's new camera to take pictures at the weekend.
keyboard (n)	My grandma can use a keyboard, but she's a bit slow.
laptop (n)	Danielle sometimes takes her laptop to school.
mouse (n)	My computer works well, but the mouse isn't very good, so I want a new one.
printer (n)	This printer only prints in black and white!
screen (n)	That screen is broken, so I can't see the picture.
blogging (v)	Vespa's new hobby is blogging about school. She often posts photos as well.
download (v)	I want to download Rihanna's song onto my phone.
graphics (n)	The graphics in his last film are amazing!
online (adj)	Did you find all the information for your project online?
software (n)	It's important to have good computer software because it means you can do more things.
stream (v)	I am thinking of streaming the *Harry Potter* films on my computer.

WORD PATTERNS | Compound nouns

Core word	Example sentence
CD player	Not many people use CD players these days.
cell phone	In America, they call mobile phones cell phones.
computer software	Some people spend a lot of money on new computer software.
laptop computer	Do the pupils in your school use laptop computers in class?
web page	Our school has its own web page.

COLLOCATIONS | Collocations with verbs

Collocation	Example sentence
download a piece of software	Do you want me to download that piece of software for you?
make a phone call	I need to make a phone call to my grandma now.
open a file	Did you open the correct file?
send a text message	Jed sent me a text message to say what time he wanted to meet.
start a conversation	He started a conversation with me about blogs and blogging.
take a photograph	Lisa says she wants to take a photograph of our school from a helicopter!
watch a DVD	Darren wanted to watch a DVD, but he decided to read a book instead.

UNIT 6

TOPIC VOCABULARY | Words connected with *fashion, clothes and shopping*

Word	Example sentence
bill (n)	Don't forget to ask the waiter for the bill.
buy (v)	Are you buying those shoes?
cash (n)	Robert lost his backpack, but luckily he keeps his cash in his pocket.
change (n)	Here's your £2 change.
cheque (n)	I never pay for anything by cheque.
cost (v)	How much does that jacket cost?
credit card (n)	I'm going to use my credit card to pay to join the gym.
customer (n)	It's my job to ask customers what they want.
department store (n)	They sell lots of different things in that department store.
market (n)	All the fruit in the market looks lovely.
receipt (n)	Liz got a receipt for the clothes she bought.
shop assistant (n)	Let's ask the shop assistant if he has these shoes in a bigger size.
shopper (n)	There aren't many shoppers here today because the weather is so bad.
shopping centre (n)	There are always a lot of people in the shopping centre on Saturdays.
spend (v)	Do you spend a lot of money going horse-riding every month?
supermarket (n)	Grant, will you go to the supermarket and get some bread, please?

WORD PATTERNS | Verbs + prepositions

Core word	Example sentence
pay for	I will pay for your new tennis racket.
pay in	Is Sam paying in cash for the cinema tickets?
put on	Put your coat on – it's cold outside.
take back	Seth didn't like the jeans so he took them back to the shop and changed them.
take off	Please take your dirty trainers off before you come in.
write down	Mum always writes down what she wants before she goes shopping for food.

COLLOCATIONS | Collocations with verbs

Collocation	Example sentence
catch a/the bus	Do you catch the bus to school or do you walk?
do the shopping	Mum does the shopping every Saturday.
for sale	There are some trainers for sale in *Sporty Shoes* today.
go shopping	My friend and I go shopping together.
keep the change	That's nine pounds, fifty, please. Here's ten pounds – keep the change.
save money	Bez is saving money because he wants to buy a new laptop.

UNIT 7

TOPIC VOCABULARY | Words connected with *school and studying*

Word	Example sentence
biology (n)	I'm not going to study biology at university. I'm not interested in plants and animals.
board (n)	My English teacher writes new words on the board.
bookshelf (n)	Did you have a bookshelf in your old room?
desk (n)	Elinor has got a lot of books on her desk.
dictionary (n)	We can use our dictionaries in English lessons.
eraser (n)	Can I borrow your eraser, please?
geography (n)	I enjoy geography because I like learning about different countries.
history (n)	We learnt about Henry VIII in history today.
learn (v)	Nadine thought she would learn a lot during her acting course.
maths (n)	I heard that Albert Einstein wasn't good at maths when he was at school.
music (n)	Do you sing in your music lessons, or do you just play the piano?
physics (n)	We did an experiment in physics today.
practise (v)	It's good to practise speaking English every day.
remember (v)	Did you remember to do your homework?
study (v)	Hugo is studying very hard because he wants to become a doctor.
teach (v)	Can you teach me how to play the violin?

WORD PATTERNS | Words + prepositions

Core word	Example sentence
arrive at	We need to arrive at the airport by 12:00 a.m.
at work	What did you do at work today?
borrow (sth) **from**	Can I borrow a pencil from you, Harriet?
help with	She said she needed help with preparing dinner.
learn about	We learn about pronunciation in English lessons.
learn from	I learnt a lot from the teachers in my old school.

COLLOCATIONS | Collocations with verbs

Collocation	Example sentence
do homework	I need to do homework before we go out.
draw a picture	Can you draw a picture of me with my cat?
go to university	My brother is going to go to university in September.
learn a foreign language	My mum wants to learn a foreign language – French.
leave school	He left school early because he didn't feel well.
take a course	I'm going to take a photography course.

UNIT 8

TOPIC VOCABULARY | Words connected with *sport*

Word	Example sentence
badminton (n)	Badminton is the best sport I have ever played!
cricket (n)	My grandpa is very good at cricket and plays every weekend in the summer.
kit (n)	Mum, where's my kit? I'm going to play football.
pool (n)	The pool near my school is busy on Saturdays because lots of children go swimming at the weekend.
skiing (n)	She loves skiing, but it doesn't snow very often where she lives.
stadium (n)	We enjoyed going to the stadium to watch the rugby match.
table tennis (n)	Will you teach me to play table tennis?
winner (n)	And Will is the winner of the competition!

WORD FORMATION | Verbs/nouns

Core word	Derivatives
play (v)	player (n)
run (v)	running (n), runner (n)
surf (v)	surfing (n), surfer (n)
swim (v)	swimming (n), swimmer (n)
win (v)	winning (n), winner (n)

COLLOCATIONS | Collocations with verbs

Collocation	Example sentence
climb a mountain	She is going to climb a mountain in March.
enter a competition	He entered the competition, but he hasn't started training yet.
go swimming	I am going to go swimming every week next term.
play cricket	Playing cricket looks easy, but it's not.
throw a ball	Are you going to throw the ball to me or not?
win a race	And Bolt wins the race again!

UNIT 9

TOPIC VOCABULARY | Words connected with *weather and nature*

Word	Example sentence
cloudy (adj)	It's cloudy, but the planes are still taking off.
fog (n)	We couldn't see the lake because of all the fog.
foggy (adj)	It is dangerous to drive when it's foggy.
ice (n)	There was ice on the road so we decided to go back to the hotel.
rainy (adj)	We don't go camping when it's very rainy.
snow (n)	When I woke up and looked outside, the garden was covered in snow.
sun (n)	Let's go out and play – the sun's shining now.
sunny (adj)	It's so sunny today! I am going to stay inside.
thunderstorm (n)	We aren't taking the dog for a walk in this thunderstorm!
windy (adj)	Don't wear a hat – it's too windy!
beach (n)	He could go to the beach if he is bored.
forest (n)	Can we take the dog for a walk in the forest?
hill (n)	You can see our house from the top of that hill.
mountain (n)	Look! There's snow on the top of the mountain.
river (n)	Can we go for a boat trip on the river?
sky (n)	It isn't cloudy so we can see a lot of stars in the sky tonight!

WORD PATTERNS | Words + prepositions

Core word	Example sentence
do experiments	It's interesting to do experiments and learn about why things happen.
good at	Suzi is good at singing and playing the guitar.
important to	It's important to study hard for your exams.
learn about (sth) **by**	I learnt about cooking by watching a video on YouTube!
the best time for/to	What is the best time of the year to visit your country?
want to	We all want to do well in the English test.

WORD FORMATION | Nouns/adjectives

Core word	Derivatives
cloud (n)	cloudy (adj)
fog (n)	foggy (adj)
ice (n)	icy (adj)
rain (n)	rainy (adj), rain (v)
snow (n)	snowy (adj), snow (v)
sun (n)	sunny (adj)

UNIT 10

TOPIC VOCABULARY | Words connected with *health*

Word	Example sentence
ankle (n)	When did you hurt your ankle? Were you running at the time?
arm (n)	I broke my arm so I can't write at the moment.
back (n)	You can get back problems if you sit at the computer for too long.
brain (n)	Is it true that your brain remembers everything you've ever done?
ear (n)	My grandma had her ears checked last month because she can't hear well.
eye (n)	Some people have one blue eye and one green eye.
face (n)	He looked at his face in the mirror and then brushed his hair.
finger (n)	My finger hurts because my brother shut the door on it!
foot (n)	These trainers don't fit well – I think I've got one foot bigger than the other.
hand (n)	Luke held his mum's hand while they walked across the busy road.
heart (n)	Running makes your heart go faster.
knee (n)	Lots of people hurt their ankles or their knees when they try skateboarding for the first time.
leg (n)	Jack had never been in an ambulance before he broke his leg.
neck (n)	She had a beautiful scarf round her neck.
nose (n)	The football hit Fred on the nose and broke it!
stomach (n)	Cows have four stomachs!
throat (n)	Your throat's going to hurt if you keep singing!

WORD PATTERNS | Words + prepositions

Core word	Example sentence
appointment with	I need to make an appointment with Doctor Jones, please.
course in	I took that course in English last year.
danger to	If you eat too much fast food, it could be a danger to your health.
hospital for	This is a hospital for people with back problems.
matter with	What is the matter with Dan? He looks worried.
medicine for	Keri has to take medicine for her sore throat.
pain in	I've got a pain in my leg. I hurt it climbing.
problem with	Sophie's got a problem with her ear, so she's seeing the doctor later.

COLLOCATIONS | Collocations with verbs

Collocation	Example sentence
break your leg	Amy broke her leg when she went skiing last year.
brush your teeth	Do you brush your teeth twice a day?
catch a cold	I think I've caught a cold. I feel hot and my throat hurts.
feel ill/better	Fed is feeling much better since he took his medicine.
make an appointment	Millie is feeling ill so we need to make an appointment with the doctor.
take your temperature	Does your mum take your temperature when you're not feeling well?

UNIT 11

TOPIC VOCABULARY | Words connected with *work and jobs*

Word	Example sentence
actor (n)	She's wanted to be an actor since she was five years old.
cleaner (n)	Have you seen the cleaner who looks after our offices?
engineer (n)	You have to go to study if you want to be an engineer.
firefighter (n)	The firefighters helped everyone to leave the building before the fire got too big.
journalist (n)	Ned is a journalist and he writes for a car magazine.
pilot (n)	The pilot managed to land the plane safely on a river!
police officer (n)	The police officer asked us questions about the robbery.
shop assistant (n)	The shop assistant helped me to find the right shoes.
career (n)	Mari has a good career as an actress in a new TV programme.
company (n)	Some young people have started their own companies.
customer (n)	All the customers love the new pizza restaurant.
earn (v)	Vicky is saving the money she earns to buy a new car.
manager (n)	If there's a problem, we speak to the manager.
meeting (n)	I have meetings all day today; I hope I have time for lunch.
social media officer (n)	Why do you want to work as a social media officer?
staff (n)	The manager is meeting the new staff today.
worker (n)	All the workers enjoy working for this company.

WORD FORMATION | Words with *–ian / -ress / -ist / -er / -r*

Core word	Derivatives
art (n)	artist (n), artistic (adj)
chemist (n)	chemistry (n)
clean (n/v)	cleaner (n)
dentist (n)	dentistry (n)
drive (v)	driving (n), driver (n)
engine (n)	engineer (n), engineering (n)
explore (v)	explorer (n)
farm (n)	farmer (n)
football (n)	footballer (n)
journal (n)	journalist (n)
manage (v)	manager (n)
music (n)	musical (adj), musician (n)
photograph (n)	photographer (n), photography (n)
reception (n)	receptionist (n)
wait (v)	waiter/waitress (n)
write (v)	writing (n), written (adj), writer (n)

WORD PATTERNS | Words + prepositions

Core word	Example sentence
diploma in	She just got a diploma in engineering.
manager of	He is the manager of a famous football team.
meeting with	I have an important meeting with my manager later today.
singer in	Sanjay is a singer in a local rock band.
works for	Beth works for a big company.
writer of	She is famous as a writer of children's stories.

UNIT 12

TOPIC VOCABULARY | Words connected with *houses and homes*

Word	Example sentence
armchair (n)	My grandma loves sitting in her comfortable armchair.
bath (n)	I usually have a shower in the mornings, but sometimes I lie in the bath and listen to music.
bed (n)	The bed in the hotel wasn't comfortable.
blanket (n)	Can you give me a blanket please? I'm a bit cold.
bookcase (n)	Seb's bought a new bookcase for all his books.
chair (n)	Let's take the chairs outside and sit in the sun.
cooker (n)	Mum's standing by the cooker, preparing dinner.
fridge (n)	Can you get the cheese out of the fridge, please?
lamp (n)	I have a lamp so I can read in bed.
pillow (n)	I put my head on the pillow and fell asleep immediately.
shower (n)	It takes me five minutes to have a shower.
sink (n)	Please wash those dishes in the sink before you leave.
sofa (n)	Let's sit together on the sofa and watch TV.
table (n)	Put the food on the table please while I bring the water.
toilet (n)	Please may I go to the toilet?
towel (n)	You're wet! Here's a towel for you.

PHRASAL VERBS

Phrasal verb	Meaning	Example sentence
find out (type 3)	to discover	She finally found out who the present was from.
get up (type 2)	to get out of bed after sleeping	Please get up! You'll be late for school.
go out (type 2)	leave home and go somewhere else	Can we go out somewhere tomorrow, Dad?
grow up (type 2)	to become older	Where did you grow up?
lie down (type 2)	to place your body in a flat position, e.g. on a bed	I need to lie down for a minute because I'm so tired!
wash up (type 1)	to wash plates, spoons, etc. after a meal	Can you start washing up for me, please?

COLLOCATIONS | Collocations with verbs

Collocation	Example sentence
do the washing-up	She does the washing-up to help her mum.
have a shower	I want to have a shower before we go out.
make my bed	I make my bed every morning, as soon as I get up.
move house	Have you and your family ever moved house or have you always lived here?
tidy your room	I tidy my room every Saturday morning before I go out to meet my friends.
wash the floor	Harry walked in with dirty trainers on so Mum had to wash the floor.

WRITING REFERENCE

AN INFORMAL EMAIL | Example task

Read the email from your English friend, Ethan.

Hi Jake!

Thanks for your email. I went to the cinema at the weekend with my friends and played tennis with my brother. Do you play tennis?

What are your hobbies? Do you have the same hobbies as your friends and family?

Email soon!

Ethan

Write an email to Ethan and answer his questions.

Write 100 words.

To: Ethan Wallace <ewallace@fastmail.com>
Subject: My Hobbies

Use Hi *or* Hello *and your friend's first name.*

Hi Ethan!

Thank your friend for their email.

Respond to what your friend said in their email. Ask some questions about what they said.

Thanks for your email. I like hearing about your weekend. Did you and your friends enjoy the film? I like films, too, but I don't like tennis!

Answer your friend's first question.

Answer your friend's second question.

You asked about my hobbies. Well, I don't have a lot of free time, but I like playing computer games. I play with friends online. I have friends all over the world and we enjoy playing together.

Answer your friend's third question.

Use short forms.

I also really like collecting coins. My uncle gave me a coin from China last year. I've got ten coins from different countries!

Use exclamation marks to show excitement or surprise.

At the end of the email say Write soon, Write back, Email back. *You can also use* Take care, Love *or* I look forward to hearing from you *to end an informal email.*

Write soon, and send me some photos of your family.

Jake

Write your first name at the end.

Read the email from your English friend, Ella.

Hi!

Thanks for your email. I went out with my friends for dinner at the weekend. We ate Chinese food.

What food do you like eating? What was the last meal you cooked? Do you have any interesting food in your country?

Write back soon!

Ella

Write an email to Ella and answer her questions.

Write 100 words.

A STORY | Example task

Your English teacher wants you to write a story with the title *'A cat – and my cousin – in a tree!'*.

Write your story in 100 words.

Give your story an interesting title.

In the first paragraph, answer the questions When?/Where?/Who?/What were you/they *(doing/playing/eating, etc.)?*

A CAT – AND MY COUSIN – IN A TREE!

Last summer, my cousin Ed came to stay. One Saturday morning, we were playing in the garden when we heard someone shout 'Help!' in the street.

Use the past continuous to show a situation in progress when something else happened.

Use the past simple for main events in a story.

We ran into the street and saw Mrs Taylor, our neighbour. She was pointing at the top of a big tree. 'What's the problem, Mrs Taylor?' I asked.

In paragraph 2, say what happened next.

Use quote marks to show the exact words people say.

'My cat, Fluffy, is in the tree and she can't get down.'

'Don't worry, Mrs Taylor,' said Ed. 'I'm good at climbing trees. I'll get her.'

If different people speak, start each person's speech on a new line.

Ed climbed the tree. It was difficult but after twenty minutes, he shouted, 'I'm at the top! And I can see Fluffy! She's fine!'

Then, a minute later, he shouted loudly, 'Oh, no! I can't move! Help!'

Adverbs such as loudly *and adjectives such as* difficult *make the story more interesting.*

I went to find Dad.

Say what happened next. Use words/ phrases such as then, after that *and* next.

In the end, Fluffy climbed down the tree. She was fine and Mrs Taylor was very happy. My dad climbed the tree and helped Ed. He finally came down with a red face. We thought it was really funny!

In the last paragraph, say what happened at the end of the story. Use phrases such as in the end, finally *or* at last.

Your English teacher wants you to write a story.

The story must begin with the sentence *'I was surprised when I heard a knock at the door …'*.

Write 100 words.

A LETTER GIVING ADVICE | Example task

Read the letter from your friend, Rupert. Write a letter to him giving advice.

> Hi Joanne,
>
> How are you? I passed my cycling test last week. I'm so happy!
>
> But now I have to do a project and it's really difficult. I have to write about an English king or queen from history. I don't know who to write about! Can you help me with some ideas?
>
> Write back soon,
>
> Rupert

Write 100 words.

Write Dear *or* Hi, *+ first name only. Remember to put a comma or exclamation mark after the name.*

Thank your friend for their letter. Talk about something in their letter (but not the project yet).

Hi Rupert,

Thanks for your letter. I'm glad you passed your cycling test.

So, you've got to do a history project? Maybe you should choose a king in a Shakespeare play, like Richard III or Henry VIII (he had six wives!). Or, why not choose a famous queen? The other students will probably choose men. What about Queen Victoria or Elizabeth I?

I've got one more idea! How about choosing someone who was only a king or queen for a very short time? For example, Lady Jane Grey. She was queen for only nine days!

I hope you like my ideas. Write back and let me know who you choose!

Bye for now!

Joanne

Some short forms are acceptable in an informal letter.

We can use should, why don't you, how about, why not *and* what about *to make suggestions.*

Talk about the project. Make your first suggestion.

Make another suggestion.

Make another suggestion.

You don't need to write complete sentences in an informal letter.

Use exclamation marks to show excitement or surprise.

Say goodbye (and express your love if you want to). You can use other phrases such as Cheers, Thanks a lot, Write back soon *to end an informal letter.*

Write your first name.

This is a part of a letter you receive from an English friend.

> I'm visiting your city in the summer! Can you give me some advice on things to do? What places should I visit? What things should I bring with me?

Write a letter answering your friend's questions.

Write 100 words.

A MAGAZINE ARTICLE | Example task

Write an article for a magazine about how school life is different now from in the past.

Write 100 words.

Give your article an interesting title.

Introduce the topic and say a few general things.

Ask questions to attract your readers' attention.

Make your first main point, e.g. describe what things were like in the past.

Use we, us *and* our *to get close to your reader.*

Make your next main point, e.g. describe what things are like now.

Summarise your opinion and conclude. Use words and phrases such as In summary …, So …, So you can see …

Use however *and* but *to make contrasting points.*

School life then and now

Everyone goes to school when they are young. But have you ever thought about how schools have changed? In the past, school life was very different from today.

When our parents were at school, they didn't have so much technology. There was no internet, no mobile phones and very few computers. They did all their work on paper.

Today, we have computers and the internet to find things out. We still have books, but they often have a link to download more material.

So in summary, school life today is very different from our parents' school life. However, education is just as important today as it was then.

You have been asked by the editor of your school magazine to write an article on the following topic.

Today's television programmes are worse than programmes ten years ago.

Write 100 words.

IRREGULAR VERBS REFERENCE

Bare infinitive	Past simple	Past participle
be	was/were	been
become	became	become
begin	began	begun
break	broke	broken
bring	brought	brought
build	built	built
buy	bought	bought
catch	caught	caught
choose	chose	chosen
come	came	come
cost	cost	cost
cut	cut	cut
draw	drew	drawn
do	did	done
drink	drank	drunk
drive	drove	driven
eat	ate	eaten
fall	fell	fallen
feel	felt	felt
find	found	found
fly	flew	flown
forget	forgot	forgotten
get	got	got
give	gave	given
go	went	been/gone
grow	grew	grown
have	had	had
hear	heard	heard
hit	hit	hit
hold	held	held
hurt	hurt	hurt
keep	kept	kept
know	knew	known
leave	left	left
let	let	let
lie	lay	lain

Bare infinitive	Past simple	Past participle
lose	lost	lost
make	made	made
mean	meant	meant
meet	met	met
pay	paid	paid
put	put	put
read	read	read
ride	rode	ridden
ring	rang	rung
run	ran	run
say	said	said
see	saw	seen
sell	sold	sold
send	sent	sent
set	set	set
shine	shone	shone
show	showed	shown
sing	sang	sung
sit	sat	sat
sleep	slept	slept
speak	spoke	spoken
spend	spent	spent
stand	stood	stood
steal	stole	stolen
swim	swam	swum
take	took	taken
teach	taught	taught
tell	told	told
think	thought	thought
throw	threw	thrown
try	tried	tried
understand	understood	understood
wake	woke	woken
wear	wore	worn
win	won	won
write	wrote	written

Macmillan Education Limited
4 Crinan Street
London N1 9XW

Companies and representatives throughout the world

Optimise A2 Student's Book ISBN 978-1-380-03189-1

Written by Jeremy Bowell and Richard Storton
Additional material by Angela Bandis, Elaine Boyd and Ursula Mallows

The authors have asserted their right to be identified as the authors of this work in accordance with the Copyright, Designs and Patents Act 1988.

This edition published 2019
First edition entitled "Optimise A2 Student's Book" published 2017 by Macmillan Education Limited.

Concept and text design by Designers Collective
Illustrated by David Belmonte, Dani Geremia, Andrew Painter and Red Gira e.
Cover design by Designers Collective
Cover photograph by **Getty Images**/Echo; **Shutterstock**/ProStockStudio and Shutterstock/phototy (background)
Picture research by Penelope Bowden, Proudfoot Pictures

Authors' acknowledgements
Jeremy and Richard would like to thank the team at Macmillan and all the many teachers and students around the world who helped make this wonderful project possible.

The authors and publishers would like to thank the following for permission to reproduce their photographs:
123RF/Dmitriy Shironosov p14(inset cr), 123RF/Olha Shtepa p19(a); **Alamy**/America p126(b), Alamy/Cultura RM p12(t), Alamy/Tim Gainey p92, Alamy/Mandy Godbehear p14(inset tr), Alamy/Hero Images Inc p53, Alamy/Juice Images p100, Alamy/Lumi Images p11, Alamy/Mint Images Limited p58(cl), Alamy/Andrey Moisseyev p103(bl), Alamy/Nagelestock.com p44, Alamy/Shotshop GmbH p7(4), Alamy/Slik Pictures Ltd p84(inset tl), Alamy/Travelstock44.de/Juergen Held p60, Alamy/Friedrich von Hörsten p126(t); **Blend Images**/John Fedele p54(b); **BrandX** pp93(background, t), 114(lm); Children's Railway/By kind permission of **Children's Railway** p115(tr, cl); **Classcraft** p77; **Comstock Images** p29; **FANCY** p125(lamb); **Getty Images** pp5(tr), 27(main), 63(background), 114(tc), 114(c/background), 114(bm), 125(berries), 129(building), 137(tl) Getty Images/Atlantide Phototravel p125(house), Getty Images/Brian Bailey p121, Getty Images/Barcroft Media p75, Getty Images/Ben Pipe Photography p14(inset cm), Getty Images/Torsten Blackwood p103(tl), Getty Images/Blend Images/Jose Luis Pelaez p98, Getty Images/Caiaimage/Paul Bradbury p20(r), Getty Images/Caiaimage/Robert Daly p50, Getty Images/Caiaimage/Tom Merton p7(7), Getty Images/Caiaimage/Chris Ryan p81(tl), Getty Images/David Clapp p93(cl), Getty Images/CommerceandCultureAgency p71(tr), Getty Images/DGLimages p85, Getty Images/DrAfter123 p70, Getty Images/EyeEm p26, Getty Images/EyeEm/Tom Chambers p19(background concert), Getty Images/EyeEm/Brigita Rafanelli p58(l), Getty Images/Flashpop p124, Getty Images/Peter M. Fisher p63, Getty Images/fstop123 p52, Getty Images/gbh007 p7(2), Getty Images/GoodLifeStudio p14(inset l), Getty Images/Priscilla Gragg p55(3), Getty Images/Eric Hanson p41, Getty Images/David Henderson p99, Getty Images/Chris Hepburn p37(background), Getty Images/Hero Images pp5(tl), 137(tm), Getty Images/Hill Street Studios p7(8), Getty Images/Zsolt Hlinka p81(tr), Getty Images/Imageegaml p110, Getty Images/ImageSource p55(2), Getty Images/imagestock p19(background t-shirts), Getty Images/iStockphoto pp93(Background, cm), 125(owl), Getty Images/iStockPhoto/seb_ra p40, Getty Images/iStockphoto /Thinkstock pp49(background right), 115(background), 125(background, carrots), Getty Images/Jessicaphoto p138, Getty Images/Jose Luis Pelaez Inc p137(tr), Getty Images/Michael Jung p76, Getty Images/Jupiterimages p58(r), Getty Images/kali9 p88, Getty Images/Kevinruss p38, Getty Images/kasto80 p37(a), Getty Images/Keystone/Stringer p82, Getty Images/Andreas Kuehn p58(cr), Getty Images/Loop Images/Alan Novelli p132(2), Getty Images/Lucia Lambriex p84(inset bl), Getty Images/Justin Lewis p4(l), Getty Images/Rob Lewine p55(1), Getty Images/Mattricphoto p66, Getty Images/Tom Merton p80, Getty Images/Daniel Milchev p7(1), Getty Images/Monkey Business Images Ltd p23(tr), Getty Images/Moxie Productions p34, Getty Images/Robert Niedring p4(tr), Getty Images/Nycshooter p83(tennis player), Getty Images/PeopleImages p83(rugby), Getty Images/Photodisc p114(c, bl), Getty Images/Marc Romanelli p7(3), Getty Images/RTimages p83(cricketer), Shutterstock/Gino Santa Maria p83(female footballer), Getty Images/Scisettialfio p59(bottles), Getty Images/Ariel Skelley pp4(rc), 118, Getty Images/Martin Siepman p93(cr), Getty Images/Stevecoleimages p119, Getty Images/STRDEL/Stringer p72, Getty Images/Syldavia p7(5), Getty Images/Topalov p74, Getty Images/Betsie Van Der Meer p49(iphone selfie), Getty Images/Vertigo3d p18, Getty Images/Westend61 pp4(tc), 27(chef), Getty Images/WIN-Initiative p7(6), Getty Images/Yalana p62, Getty Images/Yellow Dog Productions p122(tr); **Glow Images**/Sam Edwards p73; **Paul Grecaud** p114(bm/background); **ImageSource** pp94(inset), 97(background) 129(brush), ImageSource/Bill Miles p129(r), ImageSource/Craig Wetherby p129(ruler), ImageSource/Jasper White p19(background cinema); **iStockPhoto** p87;
Johnny Cupcakes p59(boxes, store); **George Kaponay/Réka Kaponay** - Dreamtime Traveler p43; **MTJ Media** pp142, 143; **PhotoDisc** p32, Photodisc/Getty Images p115(t), PhotoDisc/Getty Images/Siede Preis p94(background), PhotoDisc/Getty Images/Lisa Zador p19(background dice)
Dean Ryan p114(tr); **Shutterstock** p114(cmr), Shutterstock/1000 words p128, Shutterstock/Aaron Amat p114(br), Shutterstock/Valentin Ayupov p93(cm), Shutterstock/Ruth Black p28, Shutterstock/Chris Brignell p114(tl), Shutterstock/Marie Charouzova p97(cow), Shutterstock/Chirapbogdan p33, Shutterstock/Dimedrol68 p114(mr), Shutterstock/EFKS p83(background), Shutterstock/ESB Professional p19(background boys), Shutterstock/Leszek Glasner p59(background), Shutterstock/Peter Hermes Furian p71(cl), Shutterstock/ImageFlow p106, Shutterstock/Brian A Jackson p102(tr), Shutterstock/JeniFoto p132(1), Shutterstock/John Kasawa p114(bcr), Shutterstock/A Katz p122(tl), Shutterstock/Kikovic p30, Shutterstock/Kues p114(tcr), Shutterstock/Amy Laughinghouse p37(b), Shutterstock/Lolo1960 p109(a), Shutterstock/LTim p4(cm), Shutterstock/Cristi Lucaci p102(l), Shutterstock/Macknimal p81(tennis green), Shutterstock/Maradon 333 p36, Shutterstock/matthi p37(c), Shutterstock/Minerva Studio p120, Shutterstock/Sergey Mironov p17, Shutterstock/Monkey Business Images p14(inset cl), Shutterstock/Morrowlight p19(b), Shutterstock/Sergey Novikov p84(main), Shutterstock/Oneinchpunch p61, Shutterstock/Pikselstock p59(boy), Shutterstock/Pinkomelet p114(girl), Shutterstock/PKpix p12(b), Shutterstock/Rawpixel.com pp54(a), 117, Shutterstock/Roman Rvachov p16, Shutterstock/Sdecoret p48, Shutterstock/Syda Productions p109(b), Shutterstock/Charles Taylor p21, Shutterstock/TonyNg p22, Shutterstock/TravnikovStudio p102(br), Shutterstock/Varuna p104, Shutterstock/Wavebreakmedia p5(cl), Shutterstock/YanLev p14(main), Shutterstock/Zonda p114(tcl); **Springer Nature Ltd** pp27(chillis), 125(cow); **SWNS** p15(t, cr); Thinkstock p114(br/background); **Lisa Payne** p23(tl); **Photodisc** p125(bird).

Printed and bound in Argentina

2022
23